MORNING IN SOUTH AFRICA

John Campbell

A Council on Foreign Relations Book

ROWMAN & LITTLEFIELD
Lanham • Boulder • New York • London

Published by Rowman & Littlefield
A wholly owned subsidiary of The Rowman & Littlefield Publishing Group, Inc.
4501 Forbes Boulevard, Suite 200, Lanham, Maryland 20706
www.rowman.com

Unit A, Whitacre Mews, 26-34 Stannary Street, London SE11 4AB, United Kingdom

British Library Cataloguing in Publication Information Available

Library of Congress Cataloging-in-Publication Data
Names: Campbell, John, 1944– author.
Title: Morning in South Africa / John Campbell.
Description: Lanham : Rowman & Littlefield, 2016. | "A Council on Foreign Relations book".
Identifiers: LCCN 2015046908 (print) | LCCN 2015047657 (ebook) | ISBN 9781442265899 (cloth : alk. paper) | ISBN 9781442265905 (electronic)
Subjects: LCSH: South Africa—Politics and government—21st century—Congresses. | South Africa—Economic conditions—21st century—Congresses. | South Africa—Social conditions—21st century—Congresses. | South Africa—Foreign relations—United States. | United States—Foreign relations—South Africa.
Classification: LCC DT1971 .C36 2016 (print) | LCC DT1971 (ebook) | DDC 968.06—dc23
LC record available at http://lccn.loc.gov/2015046908

∞ ™ The paper used in this publication meets the minimum requirements of American National Standard for Information Sciences Permanence of Paper for Printed Library Materials, ANSI/NISO Z39.48-1992.

Printed in the United States of America

CONTENTS

ACKNOWLEDGMENTS

I had the privilege of serving as head of the political section at the American embassy in Pretoria from 1993 to 1996, the years of South Africa's final transition to "nonracial" democracy. Nelson Mandela's inauguration as South Africa's president in 1994 was a mountaintop experience. With perhaps the most sweeping guarantees of human rights in the world, South Africa was "the city upon the hill."

Mountaintop experiences do not last forever, and I am grateful to the Council on Foreign Relations (CFR) for the opportunity to assess where South Africa is today. I am indebted to President Richard N. Haass and Senior Vice President and Director of Studies James M. Lindsay for their support, encouragement, and criticism of *Morning in South Africa*. The book also benefited from the help of the CFR David Rockefeller Studies Program staff, particularly Director for Fellowship Affairs Janine Hill, Director for Administration Amy Baker, and Editorial Director Patricia Dorff. I would like to thank the Global Communications and Media Relations team, especially Vice President Lisa Shields, and Media Coordinator Samantha Tartas. I am also appreciative of CFR's National Program and Outreach team for their book-promotion efforts, namely Vice President Irina Faskianos and Associate Director Alyssa Eisenfeldt. I greatly benefited from conversations with Council colleagues Laurie Garrett, Shannon O'Neil, Micah Zenko, CFR National Intelligence Fellow Deborah Macdonald, CFR International Affairs Fellow Matthew Page, and former CFR colleague, now ambassador, Isobel Coleman.

I wish to dedicate *Morning in South Africa* to the three research associates with whom I have been fortunate to work at the Council on Foreign Relations: Asch Harwood, Emily Mellgard, and Allen Grane. All three combine brilliance, energy, patience, and a critical eye. Cheerful and positive, they were good company on the pilgrimage that is writing any book. Without them, the journey would never have started, let alone ended.

While writing *Morning in South Africa* I was ably supported by CFR interns who helped to research, edit, and improve the book. I am indebted to Fily Ba Camara, Melissa Bukuru, Tyler Falish, Nathaniel Glidden, Charlotte Renfield-Miller, Amanda Roth, Kyle Schneps, Diptesh Soni, Charles Warren, Claire Wilmot, and Thomas Zuber. In addition, I am grateful to Aala Abdelgadir for her editorial and other assistance.

I am grateful to Susan McEachern, Janice Braunstein, and Audra Figgins at Rowman & Littlefield for their crucial role in bringing this book to publication.

Morning in South Africa is an interpretation based on what I have seen and heard from South Africans. Since 2011, I have interviewed many opinion leaders and others during four separate trips to South Africa with the understanding that they would remain anonymous. Hence they are not listed here. But, I owe them much. I am grateful to the Council on Foreign Relations, the Stanley Foundation, ABSA Bank, and the U.S. Naval Post Graduate School for facilitating travel to South Africa during that period for research, often in conjunction with workshops.

But, what does it all mean, especially for an American audience? Talking with those who know South Africa well helped shape my understanding of what I was hearing. Hence my gratitude to my 1993–1996 embassy colleagues who have remained in touch on South Africa: Ambassador Princeton Lyman, Priscilla Clapp, Terry Pflaumer, Robyn Hinson-Jones, and Daniel Whitman. Others from the diplomatic and policy communities who taught me much were Pauline Baker, Ambassador Herman J. Cohen, former Assistant Secretary for Africa Chester Crocker, Ambassador Michelle Gavin, Ambassador Don Gips and his team at the U.S. embassy in Pretoria and the consulates general in Johannesburg and Cape Town, Bill Lucas, and James Sanders. Academics—American, British, and South African—who broadened my understanding were Chris Alden, Bernadette Atuahene, Jeff Herbst, Ambassador John Hirsch, Morten Jerven, Richard Joseph, J. P. Landman, Peter Lewis, Merle Lipton, Greg Mills, and Nic Wolpe. From the business community, I am grateful for conversations with Anthony Carroll, John Causey, Simon Fremantle, and Errol de Montille. Ebrahim Rasool, South Africa's former ambassador to the United States, and his staff were unfailingly helpful. Finally, I am deeply indebted to the two anonymous reviewers of an early draft of *Morning in South Africa*.

Among South Africans, and the Rainbow Nation's foreign friends and observers, there are differing perspectives on the country's history and current situation. Those who have so patiently provided me with help and advice do not necessarily share my point of view or agree with my conclusions. The responsibility for the interpretations and judgments in this book is entirely my own.

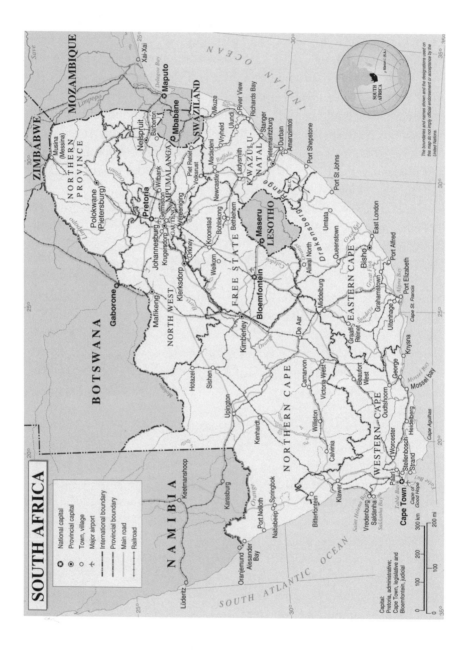

INTRODUCTION

The final act of South Africa's structured transition from the apartheid regime based on white supremacy and segregation to "nonracial" democracy began with Nelson Mandela's release from prison on February 11, 1990, and nominally closed with his inauguration as president on May 10, 1994. During that dramatic period Americans and others in the West paid more attention to South Africa than to any other African country. With their own history of unresolved racial issues, American friends of Africa were especially fascinated by the possibilities of a democratic transition in a black-majority but multiracial country, and some even tried rhetorically to take credit for it.[1]

However, unlike that of the European former colonial powers, American engagement with Africa is usually episodic and short-lived, reflecting the constricted universe of shared political and economic interests. True to form, once the liberation movements and the ruling National Party government negotiated the demise of the legal and political dimensions of apartheid and Nelson Mandela was inaugurated as president of the "new" South Africa, American attention moved on. By contrast, for example, the United Kingdom, with its deeper historical ties, restored links through the Commonwealth and familial connections, and an important trade and investment relationship continued a greater degree of engagement long after inauguration day.

Post-1994 South Africa has not been subject to the periodic humanitarian crises seen in places such as Darfur, Somalia, South Sudan, or the West African venues of the Ebola epidemic that might generate renewed American popular interest and security or humanitarian concern. South Africa has not been a locale of international terrorism, either as an incubator or as a victim. South Africa is sorely tested by HIV/AIDS and by violent crime. But, as the disease is a worldwide pandemic, its specific presence in South Africa receives only episodic American attention. An often lurid focus on crime, not least by the country's own media, has discouraged broader interest in the continent's only true "nonracial democracy" and its most modern economy. Even Nelson Mandela's December 15, 2013, state funeral, the celebration of a hero that riveted the American media for several days, did not translate into a revival of serious interest in South Africa.

Yet, it is in our own practical interest that we pay more attention to South Africa, as the United Kingdom, the European Union, and BRICS do.[2] The country is a trade and investment entry point for a continent undergoing accelerated economic development. Pretoria, the administrative capital of South Africa, also has the potential to lead Africa as it faces challenges ranging from the easily recognizable, such as jihadi militancy, to the less obvious, such as the incubation of new diseases, including HIV/AIDS and Ebola. These challenges cannot be quarantined only in Africa but will affect all of us, perhaps in unpredictable ways. Pretoria is deeply involved in multilateral diplomacy and is active within the United Nations system, often at cross-purposes with, say, American or European Union (EU) interests and perceptions. In addition, beyond immediate economic, security, and health issues, there are valuable insights to be had from considering the historical parallels between South Africa and the United States with respect to white supremacy and overcoming its consequences.

This book intends to introduce or reintroduce the "rainbow nation" to those who lost contact after apartheid left the stage or who came of age since the transition to democracy in 1994.[3] Now, more than twenty years after Nelson Mandela's inauguration, it is no longer the dawn of racially inclusive democracy in South Africa. But it is still "morning," in that democratic institutions and practices are still evolving, consolidating, and sometimes challenged.

Under the Jacob Zuma presidential administration, the country is treading water with respect to poverty, corruption, and addressing the lasting consequences of apartheid. The style of governance has become more "African" and less "Western" in the years since Nelson Mandela left the political stage. Nevertheless, the argument here is that the country's democratic institutions and culture remain strong enough to weather its current round of lackluster governance and to incorporate a governing style that reflects the overwhelming majority of the population. President Ronald Reagan's campaign theme for reelection in 1984 was "It's morning in America." That slogan reflected his, and America's, optimism about the future at a time when there was seemingly little progress on poverty and race. The title of this book suggests there are grounds for parallel optimism about South Africa, notwithstanding the troubling slow pace of economic and social change since the end of apartheid, the disappointing behavior of many of its political figures, and the growing saliency of corruption. With its current dysfunctional leadership at the top, it is easy to lose sight of the positive side of the ledger: freedom of speech is absolute, the rule of law is established, the judiciary is independent, the political system is providing new options for the electorate, and the economy is largely market driven. Hence, on balance, the assessment here of South Africa's prospects is positive.

The title of this book also deliberately recalls the mixed legacy of the Reagan presidency with regard to the bilateral relationship between the United States and South Africa. On the one hand, President Reagan vetoed the Comprehensive Anti-Apartheid Bill, though the veto was subsequently overturned by Congress. Memories and resentment of the veto remain among the current political leadership of South Africa. Later, however, and long before apartheid's end, President Reagan appointed the first African American ambassador to South Africa, a step largely forgotten today by that same leadership.

A word about terminology: ethnic or racial classification, using criteria and labels of apartheid origin, still plays a central role in the post-apartheid South African conversation. Black South Africans usually call themselves "black." Whites are usually "white." Within a black or white identity, many differentiate themselves further by spoken language, between "English" and "Afrikaner" among whites or "Zulu," "Xhosa," "Tswana," and numerous others among blacks. (Nine of South Africa's eleven official languages are African.) "Coloureds" usually regard themselves as a separate ethnicity rather than of mixed race, though some coloured politicians insist that they are "black" because of the shared history of apartheid oppression. (Unlike in the United States, "coloured" is not pejorative in South Africa.) Persons of Asian heritage number about one million of South Africa's total population of about fifty million. The majority is of South Asian descent, and they often call themselves "indians." They have full access to affirmative-action programs. South Africans of Chinese heritage who arrived before the 1994 end of apartheid, but not after, are considered to be "black" for purposes of access to affirmative-action programs.[4] However, South Africans of Japanese descent, considered to be "honorary whites" under apartheid, do not have access. The reasoning is that the former were victims of apartheid, but the latter were not and therefore they do not merit affirmative action. In this book, South Africans of Asian descent are called "asians," with a lowercase *a*, while persons from Asia are called "Asians," with an uppercase *A*. Similarly, South Africans of Indian descent are called "indians," while persons from the Union of India are called "Indians," with an uppercase *I*.

In addition to these formal categories inherited from apartheid, there are persons who are regarded to be of mixed race. Perhaps the best-known contemporary South African entertainer in the United States is the comedian Trevor Noah, the television anchor of Comedy Central's *The Daily Show*. His mother had one parent who was Xhosa, and the other was Jewish. His father was a Swiss German. South Africans do not regard him as coloured. Though three of his four grandparents were white, he self-identifies as "black" on his U.S. television show. A theme of his comedy is the artificiality and absurdity of racial classifications in South Africa and the United States.

"Civil society" has played an outsized role in the fight against apartheid and in the development and preservation of human rights based on the constitution and the rule of law. More recently, civil society has also been an effective advocate on behalf of HIV/AIDS patients, and its agencies deliver a wide range of health services.[5] It is at the forefront of the contemporary fight against corruption, including the organization of mass protests that recall those against apartheid. Here, civil society is understood to be communities of citizens sharing common interests and collective activity, usually separate from, and often parallel to, the state. In the South African context, civil society usually refers to nongovernmental organizations that come together to pressure the government, initially to end apartheid and promote human rights but now increasingly to improve the quality of governance, the delivery of health services, the suppression of corruption, and the protection of the environment. Perhaps because of their role in the struggle against apartheid and, later, their opposition to the Mbeki administration's official denial of the HIV/AIDS crisis, civil society in South Africa is stronger than in other, more mature democracies, such as France and Spain.[6]

We outsiders are often puzzled by South Africa's description of itself since 1994 as a "nonracial democracy" when racial distinctions have been an overwhelming reality, now as well as in the past. The term is strictly technical. In the last decade of apartheid, electoral lists were organized according to race. There was a separate one for whites, coloureds, and asians. Blacks, the overwhelming majority of the population, could not vote in national elections and had no national list.[7] In the 1994 elections, for the first time there was a single, nationwide electoral list with no racial designations. Hence, elections since 1994 have been "nonracial" in that every South African has the right to vote, and electoral lists make no reference to race. Accordingly, South Africans call themselves a "nonracial" democracy.

This book is intended for a Western, especially American, audience. South Africans may find little that is new, and many will likely disagree with its conclusions. Yet how South Africa appears to a sympathetic American commentator may be of interest, falling under the rubric of "seeing ourselves as others see us."

I served at the American embassy in Pretoria/Cape Town from 1993 to 1996, those exhilarating years when the transition from apartheid was taking place.[8] Like everybody else, I was probably too optimistic on Nelson Mandela's inauguration day. Nevertheless, more than twenty years into the new South Africa and following many subsequent visits, I am hopeful still while acknowledging the challenges to be overcome.

I

THE ARGUMENT

More than two decades after Nelson Mandela's 1994 inauguration as post-apartheid South Africa's first democratically elected president, many South Africans and their foreign friends in the developed world are disappointed by the way the country has seemingly squandered its promise.[1] The present levels of corruption, crime, poverty, and sky-high unemployment are far from the popular expectations for the "rainbow nation" on Nelson Mandela's inauguration day. More immediately, for everybody, rich and poor, personal pessimism is also fed by demoralizing electric power cuts, euphemistically called "load shedding."

The 2014 trial of the celebrated Paralympian Oscar Pistorius for the murder of his live-in girlfriend was an occasion for national soul-searching about ubiquitous gender-based violence and a pervasive sense of the lack of accountability by those "in charge" over the entire range of public and private entities, including sport. (Convicted of manslaughter, Pistorius was sentenced to a five-year term in prison; after serving one year on good behavior, he was paroled to house arrest. Subsequently, on the prosecution's appeal, a higher court found him guilty of murder; he will be resentenced.)

In the Western democracies, the country's "brand" has declined in value. If "Madiba" Mandela was the face of democracy and racial reconciliation, President Jacob Zuma is the image of a different and less attractive South Africa.[2] He has been indicted for rape (he was acquitted). He faces charges of corruption involving foreign contracts for weapons procurement for the South African military. He has been deferential to obscurantist tribal politics, especially those of his fellow Zulu, King Goodwill Zwelithini. He is accused of misappropriation of public funds for Nkandla, his private residential compound. The Zuma administration even illegally (under South African law) thwarted both the International Criminal Court (ICC) and the South African high court by failing to arrest Sudanese president Omar al-Bashir, indicted for crimes against humanity, when he was in South Africa for a 2015 African Union heads of state summit.

The slow pace of economic and social change since the end of apartheid has also disappointed 1994 expectations. While wages and salaries have become more equal across racial lines, especially in the skilled trades, the professions, and corporate management, most blacks remain mired in poverty. The gulf between individual white wealth (beyond wages and salaries) and that of persons in other racial groups is commonly accepted to be larger now than it was in 1994.[3] Moreover, a few wealthy blacks, often connected to the ruling African National Congress (ANC), have joined the hitherto all-white elite. There is a small, non-white middle class mostly based in the public sector of the economy and, especially among asians, small-scale retail enterprises. However, township and rural dwellers demonstrate little connection with the privileged of any race.

In 1998, then–deputy president Thabo Mbeki observed that South Africa is "two nations . . . one of these nations is white, relatively prosperous, regardless of gender or geographic dispersal. It has ready access to a developed economic, physical, educational, communication, and other infrastructure. The second and larger nation is black and poor, with the worst affected being women in rural areas. This nation lives under conditions of a grossly underdeveloped economic, physical, education, communication, and other infrastructure. It has virtually no possibility to exercise what in reality amounts to a theoretical right to equal opportunity."[4] Mbeki's observation requires little updating.

Improving health and education for the majority of the population remains challenging. Thabo Mbeki, Mandela's successor as chief of state, approached the HIV/AIDS epidemic from an antiscientific perspective and with a depleted treasury inherited from apartheid days. The consequences of both for public health were devastating. However, under the Zuma administration there has been a reversal of policy, with a significant reduction of AIDS-related deaths. While there have been laudable attempts at educational reform, a large percentage of black children are schooled under poor conditions similar to "Bantu education" during apartheid. Abroad, Mandela, Mbeki, and Zuma did little or nothing effectively to rein in Robert Mugabe as he ran roughshod over the rule of law in Zimbabwe and generated destabilizing migrant flows into South Africa.

In the aftermath of the 2014 national elections, Jacob Zuma and the people around him have acted on occasion as though they are not subject to constitutional limitations. They stonewalled the judiciary with respect to al-Bashir. The Zuma administration was unresponsive to the opposition parties in parliament on the spending of public funds on Nkandla. Personalities in the ANC and the government have on occasion attacked the provisions in the constitution that limit executive power as "antidemocratic" because they "thwart the will of the people." Moreover, some party members complained that the ANC has been moving away from its democratic roots toward authoritarianism since the 1999–2008 Mbeki administration. In the last years of his administration, there were accusations that President Zuma's primary goal was to protect itself from investigation and prosecution for official corruption, rather than the welfare of the South African people.

Of late, the economy's performance has also been disappointing. South Africa has been slow to recover from the Great Recession that began in 2008 in the United States and then spread around the world and was exacerbated by falling commodity prices. From 1995 to 2008, the economy grew at a nominal rate of 3.3 percent per year; more recently it has been 2 percent.[5] (In 2015, according to the World Bank, gross domestic product increased by only 1.5 percent; it remained less than 2 percent in 2015.)[6] By the end of 2014, the national currency, the rand (ZAR), was continuing to fall against the U.S. dollar. Of particular concern has been the decline in investment in South Africa's economy by South Africans themselves because it may indicate a decline in domestic confidence about the country's future.

Widespread power shortages and even blackouts reduce the competitiveness of the South African economy. They are the result of chronic public underinvestment in the power sector, stalled privatization strategies, and rapid urbanization. More positively, the power shortages also reflect a new, post-apartheid demand for electricity by township and rural dwellers who had minimal or no access to it under apartheid.

Poverty, inequality, and anger are fueled by poor educational opportunities for most nonwhites, a heavy disease burden, uneven delivery of government services in the townships and rural areas, and a capital-intensive economy that does not address high unemployment with jobs for the unskilled, who make up a large percentage of the black and coloured populations. There is a near universal perception that corruption is escalating and is a drag on economic growth. Many South Africans express concern that corruption is becoming "structural," that it shapes and deforms the way economic and political life is conducted, as it does in other African states such as Nigeria, Kenya, and the Democratic Republic of the Congo. But corruption is not accepted as inevitable, as it is elsewhere in Africa. For example, in September 2015, civil organizations organized mass marches against corruption in South Africa's largest cities that recalled demonstrations against apartheid. Corruption is also a constant theme of the South African media that is not afraid to name names.

Critics also charge that ANC-led efforts to increase the black majority's participation in the modern economy, grouped under an umbrella of affirmative-action measures commonly called Broad-Based Black Economic Empowerment (BBBEE), has not worked. In the October 2015 Nelson Mandela Lecture, celebrity French economist Thomas Piketty said, "I think it's fair to say that black economic empowerment strategies, which were mostly based on voluntary market transactions . . . were not that successful in spreading wealth."[7] Numerous critics say that BBBEE and antecedent strategies have promoted clientelism, fed corruption, and done little for the poor. In the black townships, some of which have emerged even after apartheid's end in 1994, demonstrations and riots over the failure of the municipal authorities to deliver promised services such as water and sanitation were by 2016 a common occurrence. Instances of police brutality, as at the Marikana platinum mine in 2011, recall apartheid-era behavior.

Radical rhetoric calling for the seizure of white economic assets without compensation has become louder and was part of the platform of the new Economic Freedom Fighters (EFF) party, which emerged from the 2014 elections. Under South Africa's system of proportional representation, it is the third-largest party in the National Assembly, though with only 6.35 percent of the vote.[8] A credible survey released in 2010 shows that a third of black South Africans favor the state seizure of all white-owned land without compensation.[9] They would seem to be a natural EFF constituency. However, as we shall see, most South Africans favor seizure without compensation only if it were done according to the law. A law authorizing seizures without compensation would be challenged in the courts as contrary to the constitution, which recognizes the right to private property. As a practical matter, achievement of the EFF platform would require a dismantling of the constitution and the 1994 settlement, for which there appears to be little appetite.

Some blacks, especially those newly middle class and competing with whites and asians to climb the corporate ladder, complain that "real liberation" has not been achieved because the government has not moved forcefully enough against the white establishment. Others in this cohort see their personal success as a just reward for their support for the struggle against apartheid in the past and their present links to the ANC rather than any contribution they may make to the economy.[10]

JACOB ZUMA

Jacob Zuma, born in 1942 in KwaZulu-Natal, has no formal education. His father, a policeman, died when Jacob was a child; his mother was a domestic worker. An early member of the ANC's armed wing, Zuma was imprisoned on Robben Island from 1963 to 1973 with Nelson Mandela. He was a member of the South African Communist Party for about thirty years until he resigned in 1990. After his release from Robben Island, he went into exile. Abroad, he rose to become the chief of intelligence structures (including counterintelligence) for the ANC from 1987 to 1990. Following the transition to nonracial democracy, Zuma reenergized and reorganized the ANC as a political party in KwaZulu-Natal, and that province has remained his electoral base ever since. (His fellow Zulus are almost a quarter of South Africa's population.) He served as deputy president under Thabo Mbeki and subsequently helped orchestrate Mbeki's removal as party leader; Mbeki later resigned as chief of state because he no longer had the confidence of the ANC majority in parliament. After a short interregnum under acting president Kgalema Motlanthe, Zuma became chief of state in 2009 following regularly scheduled national elections.

South African critics accuse him and his allies of undermining the liberal, democratic institutions enshrined in the constitution. More specifically, they charge that Zuma and allied elements within the governing ANC seek to reduce the political independence of the judiciary, restrict the freedom of the media, rein in whistle-blowers, and call into question property rights that are recognized by the constitution.[11] Such an agenda, Zuma's critics say, fits a former security operative mired in corruption and its cover-up rather than a democratic chief of state committed to the rule of law.

Corruption at high levels does appear to have grown under Jacob Zuma, contributing to the national mood of disillusionment. Transparency International's 2013 Global Perceptions Index showed that almost three-quarters of South Africans believed that corruption had increased between 2007 and 2010.[12] The corruption trajectory is also disappointing. In 2014, Transparency International ranked South Africa sixty-seventh (out of 175 countries) for corruption, downgrading the country by five places from the previous year. The 2014 index cites Zuma's unwillingness or inability to take responsibility for the extravagant expenditure on Nkandla.[13]

At home, critics claim that the ANC government is increasingly unable and uninterested in addressing the needs of many of South Africa's citizens, despite dramatic improvements in housing and the delivery of such essential services as water and sanitation since apartheid ended. They do acknowledge that the ANC government has improved access for the poor to permanent housing during its more than two decades in power. Since 1994, the ANC government has provided more than 2.5 million houses and another 1.2 million serviced sites (plots with water and electricity where occupants build their own houses). However, during the same period, the estimated housing backlog increased from 1.5 million to 2.1 million units, while the number of "informal settlements" (often shantytowns) has grown from 300 to 2,225. The government housing subsidy per household has increased from ZAR 12,500 in 1994 to ZAR 160,500 in 2015, only in part because the currency has steadily declined in value.[14] Perhaps a more meaningful statistic is that state spending on housing and "community amenities" has increased from 1 to 3 percent of gross domestic product (GDP).[15] The beneficiaries are mostly black and coloured.

Ongoing housing shortages and the increase in informal settlements in large part reflect the country's rapid urbanization. Popular expectations about housing remain high, perhaps unrealistically so in a developing country, with complaints that the quality of the new construction is poor. Critics suggest that ANC housing construction in apartheid-era townships has been far from employment opportunities and without the provision of necessary services, especially electricity. For such critics, South Africa's housing realities, like so much else, continue to be shaped by apartheid.

Julius Malema, a young hothead who has allegedly been financially subsidized by Zimbabwe's Robert Mugabe and is the object of extensive media coverage, exploits racial inequality as a political issue. He was born in 1981 in Limpopo, one of South Africa's poorest provinces. He was enrolled for two years in the University of South Africa, an "open" university. (Courses are given by correspondence or online.) Once the head of the ANC youth league, Malema was expelled from the party for disobedience. He is the founder of a new political party, the Economic Freedom Fighters (EFF). He has been convicted of the use of hate speech. Whites and "haves" across the racial spectrum fear that Malema is articulating the views of the poor and dispossessed, a reason why the media pay him so much attention. The privileged often see Malema as driving Zuma and the ANC in an authoritarian direction to avoid being outflanked on the left.

CHALLENGES

Despite current pessimism, there is little that is new about South Africa's root challenges. They include the economic and social consequences of apartheid, post-apartheid exposure to new competition from the international economy, and pandemic disease, especially HIV/AIDS and tuberculosis. Corruption, too, was a characteristic of the apartheid state. The gloom, the extent of which *is* new, owes much to the slow economic recovery from the worldwide slump of 2008 and to discontent with Jacob Zuma's style of governance. In 2015, parts of the Zuma administration, under siege from accelerating accusations of corruption, cronyism, and criminal behavior, did seem to be trying to control or eviscerate constitutionally mandated institutions. There were rhetorical attacks on the national prosecuting authority, the police, the revenue service, the national broadcasting authority, the public protector, and the human rights commission. Thus far, these assaults have been unsuccessful. Even so, economic recovery and a change in presidential leadership would certainly lighten the mood.

Nevertheless, treading water during an administration is not a sign of impending governance failure. In fact, South African democracy and its institutions based on the rule of law are growing in strength, not least because they are acquiring the benefits of longevity. The highly respected Ibrahim Index of African Governance for 2015 places South Africa at the top of its five analytical categories: safety, rule of law, human rights, economic opportunity, and human development. The only states the index rates higher are small and wealthy, such as Mauritius, Botswana, and Cape Verde.[16] The ANC government has not been a dictatorship, either by the party or the chief of state. After all, in 2007, orchestrated by Jacob Zuma and Julius Malema among others, the ANC removed Thabo Mbeki from his leadership and, in effect, the presidency while more or less adhering to party procedures.[17]

ACCOMPLISHMENTS

There is certainly more to celebrate about post-apartheid South Africa than the current disillusionment suggests. In an era of persistent economic recession and, at best, mediocre governance, it is easy to lose sight of how much South African government and society have accomplished since 1994. The institutional and ideological props of white supremacy are gone. In education, the ANC government has rationalized and deracialized the nineteen different systems inherited from apartheid. In public health, under Zuma, there has been a turn for the better, perhaps his signature accomplishment as president.[18] South Africa's public health system is meeting the challenge of HIV/AIDS, and death rates have plummeted, even while the rate of new infections remains disappointingly high. The ANC government has established a safety net of allowances that have mitigated the lot of the very poor. Despite complaints of state profligacy, beneficiaries are mostly children, the elderly, the sick, and the disabled. A National Development Plan provides a blueprint for advancing a broad range of sectors to improve economic growth, including further reform of education and public health. Adopted by the Zuma administration, it faces some opposition from the ANC's "Africanist" wing and their Communist Party allies. But the Plan shapes the current national conversation.[19] Solidifying democratic institutions and a political culture increasingly "African" in style provides a future way to address its deep-seated social and economic problems. The reality is that South African governance and politics are more than merely internal ANC politics and Jacob Zuma. If the glass is half empty, it is also half full.

Since the 1910 formation of the Union of South Africa, the country has been characterized by the rule of law, even if it was sorely tested under apartheid, was compromised by official security service violence, and benefited only one racial group. Nevertheless, at present, on the contentious question of land redistribution, at least 80 percent of the population across all racial lines believes that it should be done strictly according to the law. Blacks much more than other racial groups believe that whites are due no compensation for their property that the state redistributes. But they, too, affirm that any such distribution must be governed by the law.[20] The country conducted credible national elections in 1994, 1999, 2004, 2009, and 2014; in addition, there have been four, also credible, local government elections nationwide. The Economist Democracy Index in 2012 rated the quality of South African elections as only slightly below those of Japan and the United States.[21] Nobody has credibly questioned the integrity of the 2014 national elections.

South Africa has even produced a democratic hero. President Nelson Mandela towered over other world leaders in his integrity, magnanimity, and political skill. Under his presidential leadership, democratic South Africa shed its former pariah status as the apartheid state and moved to the center of international affairs. Post-apartheid South Africa was widely seen as the moral leader of the African continent south of the Sahara, though President Zuma's personal reputation may have tarnished that image.

President Mandela voluntarily left office at the end of one term, though an additional term would have been his for the asking. Mandela proved to be a democratic alternative to the African "big man," such as

Zimbabwe's Robert Mugabe or the Congo's Sese Mobutu. The model Mandela established has persisted. Few observers see future "presidents for life" as a realistic South African option. A 2015 boomlet for Zuma to run for a third time as ANC party leader, opening the door to the possibility of an unconstitutional third presidential term, is likely to come to nothing. But it contributed to the 2015 disquiet.

Black poverty, a direct consequence of centuries of racism culminating in apartheid, is an unmet challenge, though not for want of trying. There are new possibilities, however. As J. P. Landman points out, South Africa's economy is still growing faster than its population, despite the slow recovery from the international financial crisis of 2008. He cites a population growth rate of 1.34 percent per year. Even now with an anemic, probably temporarily low, growth rate of 1.5 percent, the economy is still growing faster than the population. His argument is that if the economy grows faster than the population, over time, poverty is likely to fall as structural racial income disparities are addressed, especially through improved educational and health services.[22]

Democracy in South Africa remains a popular cause twenty-two years after Mandela's inauguration. An Afrobarometer poll in 2011 showed that 72 percent of the respondents were committed to democracy, 11 percent were indifferent, and 15 percent held that nondemocratic methods are sometimes preferable.[23] Since 1994, South Africa has been a functioning democracy conducted according to the rule of law, largely without legal reference to race even if social and economic change has been slow and incomplete.

Democratic, nonracial governance under the rule of law is certainly challenged. EFF demonstrations on the floor have disrupted parliament from time to time. The Zuma administration has tried to thwart the judiciary and parliament, especially with respect to foreign policy issues, including withholding visas for the Dalai Lama or by ignoring the legal requirement to hand over Sudan's al-Bashir to the International Criminal Court. Broad-Based Black Economic Empowerment (BBBEE), a bundle of affirmative-action programs designed to increase the black presence in the modern economy, is a big exception to the usual nonracialism of government policy. Critics maintain that BBBEE has introduced race unduly into relations between the government and big business and has promoted cronyism and corruption.[24]

Challenges to the judiciary, parliament, and the rule of law raise concerns that South Africa may be moving toward the authoritarian, corrupt, and inefficient African "big man" style of governance. It must remain an open question whether the democratic aspirations of the South African people will be strong enough to preserve the institutions conducted according to the rule of law that emerged from the 1994 settlement. Grounds for optimism are their success thus far in blocking efforts to restrict freedom of speech, the continued independence of the judiciary, the decline in the electoral predominance of the ANC, a stronger official opposition, and the likely emergence of a new, left-wing political party broadly modeled after the left wing of the United Kingdom's Labour Party. Governance is opening up within a framework of the rule of law.

POST-APARTHEID BEGINNINGS

Post-apartheid South Africa began well. With the coming of "nonracial democracy" in May 1994, many South Africans believed that their country would pave a new way toward a just, inclusive, democratic, "nonracial" society—Archbishop Desmond Tutu's "rainbow people of God." It would be a model for the rest of Africa and even the world. Post-apartheid South Africa's constitution swept away the remaining legal vestiges of apartheid that court rulings and the governing National Party's leadership had not already eroded during the previous decade under pressure from civil society, labor, the judiciary, and international opinion. It adopted an electoral system based on proportional representation. The country's new federalism, if tepid in comparison with the United States or Germany, contrasted favorably with the overcentralized apartheid state and with most other postindependence African nations.

The Truth and Reconciliation Commission (TRC) chaired by Archbishop Tutu was a means by which the nation confronted its bloody and racist past, even if the upper reaches of both the apartheid former administration and the liberation movements did not subject themselves to it.[25] (In fact, only a handful of those who did not seek amnesty were ever prosecuted.) An independent and professional judiciary buttressed the rule of law, and its bench slowly but steadily moved from being nearly all white to reflecting the demographic makeup of the country. The trial of Oscar Pistorius, the celebrated white athlete, before a black female judge with little or no negative public comment would have been unimaginable twenty years previously.

Nevertheless, even with its firmly "nonracial" structure of governance, racial identities continue to shape political life. South Africans are often uncomfortable acknowledging that the "nonracial rainbow nation" remains a distant aspiration, and race continues to drive many dimensions of life, private as well as public.

The 1994 settlement was not the result of a straightforward triumph of the ANC and the liberation movements over those who had benefited from apartheid. Nor was it a social or economic revolution. It was a political compromise negotiated between the liberation movements and civil society assisted by the international community on the one hand and the apartheid state that controlled the security services and was led by the National Party on the other. The compromise largely left in place white economic privilege inherited from the apartheid state and centuries of racial oppression. As the constitutional legal expert Pierre de Vos puts it, "all the big companies and big business and the ANC basically agreed that 'Well, if you leave us alone we will leave you alone.' So, in that context, it was not thought possible politically and economically to actually include those things in the constitution that would fundamentally threaten the vested interests of big business."[26]

Moreover, the Mandela and Mbeki governments reintegrated South Africa's economy with the world's markets after a generation of antiapartheid sanctions of varying efficacy, subjecting it to market forces that they could not control as much as they probably had thought they could. The economic policy of the Mandela, Mbeki, and Zuma governments has broadly followed the Washington Consensus of liberal economics reflected by the international financial institutions. Hence, there is a focus on property rights, free markets, and sound fiscal policies.[27] Post-apartheid government policies had the unintended consequences of solidifying the power of capital and of the traditional elites that already had it and new elites with access to it through their connections with the former liberation movements, especially the ANC. Moreover, the goal was to grow the economy, not to redistribute already existing wealth. It should be no surprise that the economic slowdown since 2008 has led to a resurgence of those who question the Washington Consensus.

The economy continued its slow evolution from one based primarily on the extraction, production, and trading of commodities, especially gold, diamonds, platinum, and coal, and agricultural production (including wine), to one that is information based. By 2014, mining and quarrying were only 8 percent of the economy.[28] South Africa's traditional, large manufacturing sector experienced a relative decline, while high-tech enterprises and financial services boomed. However, contrary to some Washington Consensus policy prescriptions, social safety nets have been established or expanded, and privatization of state-owned enterprises has been largely forgone. The economy grew, but not fast enough for a substantial reduction of poverty. The South African perception is that unemployment actually increased over the past decade. Joblessness is a major driver of the persistent township and rural poverty that is a backdrop to service-delivery riots.[29]

Successive post-apartheid governments have tried to address poverty and racial inequality of opportunity. The most important government initiatives were ongoing land reform on a modest scale; an Employment Equity Act (1998) that established "affirmative action" in employment for the victims of apartheid; the 2000 Preferential Procurement Finance Act, which mandated "minority" (asian, black, and coloured) shareholding in various enterprises; and a 2007 Code of Good Practice that tried to consolidate and improve previous legislation. But all such efforts were underfunded, slow to be implemented, and did little for most people, though they did facilitate the growth of a small black elite. The National Development Plan, rolled out in 2013 with a seventeen-year implementation schedule, looks more promising.[30] The plan's focus is on economic growth, job creation, and educational reform. But, it remains to be seen how the national leadership will implement the plan when it is opposed by some of the ANC's traditional core constituencies that still favor a state-directed, rather than market, economy.

A brake to genuine transformation of South Africa's apartheid economy was that the ANC government inherited an empty treasury in 1994 and soon faced the distraction of one of the highest HIV/AIDS prevalence rates in the world. The constitution's bill of rights discouraged, even if it did not outlaw, expropriation of private property. Accordingly, every acre of land the government redistributed was paid for at full market value. If the Department of Labour and the Department of Trade and Industry would borrow to advance social goals, the treasury and the central bank successfully ensured fiscal probity and moderate rates of taxation designed to promote economic growth along the lines of the Washington Consensus. Indeed, South Africa's fiscal management gets high marks. No major financial institutions collapsed due to the Great Recession that started in 2008, and in 2015 the country's ratio of debt to gross domestic product was 32 percent, compared to 100 percent in the United States.[31] Nevertheless, this prudent fiscal policy slowed the pace of social and economic transformation.

Economic activity, while more diversified in its ownership in part because of BBBEE, continues to be dominated by large, often multinational corporations with white leadership at their pinnacle. Mining companies sought the much higher profit margins available outside the country, both elsewhere in Africa and also farther afield in South America and Central Asia.

Highly entrepreneurial, often information-based small startups, which were usually white owned, grew as a proportion of the economy. Financial services and the information technology (IT) sector generated wealth for white owners and well-connected blacks. And there has been a cycle of real estate boom and bust, especially in the Western Cape, an international tourist destination, and in the province of Gauteng, where Johannesburg, the commercial capital of the country, is located.

The Congress of South African Trade Unions (COSATU), the Department of Labor, and the Department of Trade and Industry pursued high-wage employment policies that promoted a highly skilled, well-paid labor aristocracy but did little for the unskilled and poorly educated masses. Success in overcoming COSATU and others' lack of interest in creating the low-wage jobs necessary to move the unskilled into the workforce remains to be seen.

With slow growth, increased income inequality, and the persistence of strong racial identities, it is no surprise that more than twenty years after apartheid there are renewed calls for radical change, even at the expense of the constitutional protections that seem to entrench property rights and thereby, it is argued, white privilege. The Zuma government, like those of Mandela and Mbeki, has thus far largely resisted such calls, and where it has not, it has been blocked by civil society, spurred by a free press and opposition parties in parliament. Nevertheless, authoritarian, left-wing, even radical political rhetoric is reappearing for the first time since the end of the "liberation" struggle, notably within Julius Malema's new party, the EFF.

THE QUESTION

In the aftermath of Mandela's death, the persistent question is whether South Africa's democratic culture and institutions can continue to flourish in a context in which race remains a powerful element of personal identity and where economic development for its largest racial community continues to lag.

This book looks at some potential "Achilles' heels" inhibiting poverty alleviation, fueling discontent among the racial majority, and threatening to erode the institutional progress made thus far. Specifically, they are the failure to address township and rural aspirations for better educational opportunities, the shortcomings of the health system for the majority, the majority's alleged aspirations for land reform, and the potential reordering of South Africa's current liberal political dispensation into more authoritarian channels. There are other negative trends such as the erosion of the professional standards of the civil service, the growth of violent labor unrest, the growing saliency and politicization of a variety of Christianity that is often fundamentalist in outlook, and what is widely believed to be a tsunami of official corruption. Nevertheless, education, health, land, and governance provide a point of entry into the central question of the resilience of South African democracy, maintenance of the rule of law, and institutional creativity and flexibility. Improved delivery of education and medical services is crucial to reduction of unemployment and poverty. These are issues currently much debated by South Africans, and they feature prominently in the Zuma administration's National Development Plan.

To introduce or reintroduce this fascinating country to an audience of Americans and others, the following chapters look at South Africa's transition to a "nonracial" democracy and the expectations that surrounded it. Without being rigidly determinist, South Africa's history has framed the options open to it post-apartheid. Therefore, there is a brief overview intended to orient the nonspecialist reader to this historical inheritance with reference to some of its similarities to the American

South. A look at the presidential inaugurations of Nelson Mandela and Jacob Zuma and Mandela's funeral illustrates some of the ways South African public life has become more "African" in style since 1994. Because South Africans still strongly identify themselves and others by race, there is a review of the current demography using those categories. The remainder of the book considers education, health, and the direction of political developments, including land reform, with an eye to how South Africa's democratic institutions are responding to those challenges. The final chapter considers the prospects for a closer U.S.–South Africa bilateral relationship.

I conclude that South Africa's messy and incomplete democratic governance has shown flexibility and adaptability. Ownership of the economy continues to be dominated by whites, now joined by well-connected blacks, but the "face" of South Africa, ranging from television presenters to post office clerks, reflects the country's racial demographics. Blacks are present in elite institutions ranging from formerly all-white universities to hospitals and country clubs, though by no means in proportion to their share of the population. Nevertheless, black Africans are no longer strangers in their own country.

Political and social institutions remain strong, perhaps the strongest on the African continent. Rare in Africa, nobody in South Africa is above the law, though President Zuma at the time of this writing is challenging that proposition with respect to allegations of his personal corruption, and he appears prepared to flout the judiciary and break the law where foreign policy is involved.

Nevertheless, South Africa is all but unique in sub-Saharan Africa in the strength of its democratic institutions based on the acknowledgment and definition of fundamental rights and the rule of law. Lawful, democratic governance is generations old. But, in the past, only whites participated in it and benefited from it. With the collapse of apartheid, participation in governance has spread from a privileged minority to encompass the entire population. Unlike in other parts of Africa, a political culture based on the rule of law did not have to be created out of whole cloth. It is this strength, protected and supported by civil society groups and a slowly growing multiracial middle class that cares about good government, that is grounds for optimism about South Africa's future, despite the economic and political challenges of the present.

South African politics are also opening up. The ANC's party membership and elective support is in decline; the official opposition, the Democratic Alliance (DA), is shedding its identity as a mostly white and coloured party; and the National Union of Metal Workers is likely to form a new, left-wing party before the 2019 national elections. Should it do so, it could marginalize the EFF and deepen the nation's pool of potential leaders, with positive consequences.

It remains to be seen whether South Africans will demand inclusive leadership in the model of Nelson Mandela that would address the needs of the majority population without compromising the country's democratic institutions. Cyril Ramaphosa, the current deputy president and an architect of the 1994 settlement, has demonstrated political skill, engenders confidence among the business community inside and outside the country, and has become rich enough not to be tempted by Zuma-style corruption. He may have the potential to be the leader South Africa needs, though he is probably more popular outside South Africa than within the ANC.

However, the charismatic but irresponsible Julius Malema exploits the politics of grievance and envy. His policies could lead to domestic and foreign divestment, erosion of the economy, and a compromise of rights guaranteed by the constitution. The result likely would be the wholesale decline of democratic institutions, the economy, and the potential for any South African leadership role on the African continent.

In 2016, with slow economic growth, rounds of xenophobic violence in the townships sparked by the 2015 comments of Zulu king Goodwill Zwelithini, and a chief of state mired in scandal, South Africa is treading water. Nevertheless, thanks to the strength of its democratic culture and institutions, I believe that South Africa will meet successfully its current challenges.

2

THE HISTORICAL TRAJECTORY

History shapes and limits the possibilities for change. In the particular case of South Africa, the state based on white supremacy is gone. But the economic and social structures both reflected and developed by apartheid endure and are evolving only slowly. If racial categories no longer define political institutions, they and their history still frame the opportunities open to most of the population. Voting behavior largely reflects racial identification. In the 2014 elections, of those who voted, most cast their ballots along racial lines: blacks for the African National Congress (ANC) and whites, coloureds, and asians for the opposition Democratic Alliance (DA). (Small numbers from all races also voted for numerous minor parties.) Nevertheless, in a development that is hopeful for the development of "nonracial" democracy, the DA is now attracting a significant number of black votes, especially in the Johannesburg metropolitan area.[1]

South Africa is a democracy whose governing party, the ANC, has a largely black constituency and a large parliamentary majority that was, however, diminished in the 2014 elections. The ANC won 62 percent of the vote with a turnout of 73 percent of registered voters. However, not only has voter registration declined since 1994, but the ANC's share of *eligible* voters (not just registered voters) has also declined. It was 53 percent in 1994, falling to 36 percent in 2014.[2] Hence, the ANC's domination of the electoral landscape is no longer as overwhelming as it was in the immediate post-apartheid years.[3]

South Africa's political culture limits what any majority party can do. The ANC and its government are constrained by the rule of law manifested in a constitution with a bill of rights and supported by an independent judiciary and a free press. Public opinion strongly supports the constitution and the rule of law. The official opposition in parliament, the DA, is well organized and skilled in legislative tactics.

South Africa has perhaps the most sweeping protections of human rights in the world. Among those is a recognition of the right to property. While the state may take private property for public purposes, the process is defined by law. As a practical matter, whites are secure in their property accumulated under the apartheid economy.

As we will see, not only is the gulf between white individual net worth and that of blacks and coloureds larger than that found almost anywhere else in the world, but it is also growing.[4] (The difference between white and black net worth is also growing in the United States.)[5] Post-apartheid South Africa therefore is a predominately black democracy based on the rule of law in which the principal economic beneficiaries remain mostly if not exclusively white, especially those who are English speaking, and most of the poor and disadvantaged are black and coloured. This is the South African paradox.

The resolution of this paradox could be achieved by the revolutionary redistribution of wealth from the rich, mostly whites but now including a small number of blacks, to everybody else, or by very high rates of economic growth, a tide that would lift all boats, including the poor. The first option was foreclosed by the terms of the political bargain that determined the 1994 transition to nonracial democracy. Were it to be overturned now, revolutionary redistribution would almost certainly ruin South Africa's economy. Few South Africans want to go down the Zimbabwe road, where revolutionary redistribution led to famine. The second option remains open, with the potential creation of many low-skill jobs that could lift the black majority out of poverty, as South Africans generally expected in 1994. This has not yet happened, in large part because of the consequences of apartheid—the limits imposed by history—especially with respect to poor education and bad health facilities for the black majority and their limited opportunity to accumulate capital in a capitalist, largely free-market economy. Whites often build on capital inherited from previous generations; under apartheid, nonwhites had little opportunity to accumulate capital for the current generation to inherit. This is now changing, with the current generation of nonwhites having the opportunity to amass capital and many doing so. But the process is slow.

South Africa's population today consists of four major racial groups—asians (often identified as "indians"), blacks, coloureds, and whites. By no means internally cohesive, their relationships—or, more commonly, their internal divisions and their struggles within themselves and against one another—have driven the history of South Africa.

Since the beginning of European settlement in the mid-seventeenth century, racial distinctions have dominated South African society and politics.[6] They are the building blocks of the history of modern South Africa.

UN PEU D'HISTOIRE

The Guide Michelin, the celebrated series of French travel guides, often includes for its readers a note called *un peu d'histoire* ("a little history") for a place to be visited. It provides just enough historical background to enhance the visitor's experience. That is the inspiration for this brief review of South African history, from the first European settlement in 1652 to 2016.[7]

THE PRECOLONIAL PERIOD

Histories of South Africa published in the early twentieth century often provided maps that showed waves of African migration into what is now South Africa starting at about the same time the Dutch first settled in 1652. These alleged African migrants were identified as Bantu speakers, part of a large linguistic family. The implicit point of such maps was that Bantu speakers had no rights based on prior occupancy of the land before the Dutch arrived.[8] But, contrary to such maps, Bantu speakers and other indigenous peoples in reality were already present in South Africa in 1652.

South Africa was far from empty. The Khoisan family of ethnic groups was probably the largest of the indigenous peoples living in the areas of early Dutch settlement around what is known as the Cape of

Good Hope. They were highly skilled pastoralists but did little agriculture. Their way of life was characteristic of the Stone Age, and they had no metal-working technology.[9] Over time, they were pushed aside both by the European settlers and the Bantu-speaking peoples.

The core location of the Bantu-speaking peoples, at present the largest part of the black South African population, was five hundred miles east and north of present-day Cape Town.[10] They slowly spread south and west, and they divided into numerous groups that engaged in frequent internecine warfare. These groups spoke many different languages. While Xhosa and Zulu, both part of the Nguni branch of the Bantu languages, were mutually intelligible, they were very different from Sotho, Tswana, and Pedi.[11]

Bantu material culture was more developed than that of the Khoisan ethnic groups. Eighteenth-century speakers of the Bantu family of languages were similar to Bronze Age Celts in material culture, and only after the British Empire absorbed the Cape in the nineteenth century did whites have an incontestable war-fighting advantage over them. Even that late, the European advantage was not absolute. In 1879, the Zulus, who were the most militarily advanced of the African groups, inflicted on the British a stunning military defeat at the Battle of Isandhlwana.[12]

Most of the principal black groups were politically fragmented, certainly in comparison with the Dutch and later the British, which was a disadvantage during the almost continuous frontier wars. However, during the nineteenth century, there was some black consolidation into larger political entities, such as that of the Zulu Kingdom.

Differences among Bantu groups were based primarily on language. Otherwise, broadly speaking, their ways of life were similar—based on cattle ownership, with the household headed by a patriarch, and broader government provided by a chief. Shamans were also integral to the governing system and played an important role in warding off witchcraft, which was the source of evil and the explanation for why bad things happened to good people. In principle, Bantu-speaking societies were more equal than European ones, and there was a greater emphasis on the collective rather than the individual good.

THE COMING OF THE EUROPEANS

Whites came to what is now South Africa as part of Europe's colonial expansion during the seventeenth century. While the Portuguese and other navigators had visited earlier numerous times, there was no permanent European settlement before the Dutch established Kaapstad in 1652. That settlement became the center of their Cape of Good Hope colony. The distance from Europe, the paucity of harbors along the southern African coastline, and the lack of easily exploitable wealth such as gold or spices discouraged earlier settlement. Kaapstad was initially only a way station for ships plying between Europe and the Indies, hardly a colony. The Dutch East India Company founded it as a place of rest and recuperation for sailors and other travelers. It also served as a food and water replenishment station. The company established its own farms, the location now of the "Company Gardens," a large park in central Cape Town. At first, the Dutch were company employees. Only gradually did the company cede to them the right to private farms, a development that transformed them from sojourners into settlers.

Like other colonial enterprises and governments, the Dutch East India Company did not encourage the geographic expansion of the colony in its early days. There was no provision for self-government, and the Dutch Reformed Church was established by law and enjoyed a religious monopoly. Unlike New Amsterdam (later New York), there was no significant European population of religious dissenters; indeed, according to travelers, there was little "religion" of any sort. But, after French king Louis XIV's 1685 revocation of the Edict of Nantes ended France's toleration of Protestants, there was an influx of French Huguenot refugees to Kaapstad, though they were far smaller in number than those who fled to the British Isles, the British colonies in North America, and Prussia. Later, some Germans, also victims of Louis XIV's depredations in the Rhineland, fled to South Africa.

Early European immigration to South Africa did not last long. Some British immigrants did go to the Cape after it was incorporated into the British Empire. But there was little large-scale immigration until the diamond and gold rushes three generations later. In that sense, Kaapstad resembled Quebec in New France, where European immigration peaked in the seventeenth century, and whites remained a tiny minority compared to the indigenous population, the First Nations. The British colonies in North America were very different, where the "swarming of the English" and other Europeans accelerated throughout the colonial period. Nevertheless, such was the burden of disease of European origin on the indigenous peoples that the total population of British North America, including all races, was less in 1776 than it had been in 1607. By the eighteenth century, the population of European origin in the thirteen colonies was 2.4 million (1775),[13] 70,000 in New France (1760),[14] and 62,000 in Dutch South Africa (1797).[15]

The Boers

The descendants of seventeenth-century European settlers amalgamated into the Afrikaner people, often called "Boers" ("farmers" in Dutch). Over three centuries they developed their own language, Afrikaans, out of Dutch. One eighteenth-century European visitor commented on the arrogance of whites, who regarded themselves as "gentlemen." Hard labor was for blacks, not them. They were not "farmers," but "plantation owners." "What evolved was a semi-literate peasantry with the social status of a landed gentry."[16] (Seventeenth-century visitors to America made similar comments about the English settlers in Virginia.) Dutch governance in South Africa relied on violence, though probably no more so than in seventeenth-century Europe and Virginia.

As contact with indigenous peoples evolved, the Boers became increasingly self-consciously "white," "European," and "Christian" of a Calvinist persuasion. Yet, as the years passed, there were fewer personal ties to the Netherlands. Insulated by distance from the universalism of the Enlightenment, the French Revolution, or the Romantic movement, eighteenth- and nineteenth-century Boers became progressively more insular than their forebears. They saw their presence at the southern tip of Africa as the result of a divine "calling" and their plantations as an act of God. Their religious identification with the land of South Africa did much to shape the country's history, and it still influences the thinking of some Afrikaners. They saw parallels between their arrival in South Africa and God's gift of the Promised Land to the Hebrews. It did not occur to them that indigenous peoples had rights, any more than the Children of Israel recognized the rights of the Jebusites and other peoples that already occupied the Promised Land. Increasingly,

Boer religion was racially exclusive, and they made little attempt to convert persons of other races to Christianity before the nineteenth century. Nevertheless, by the twenty-first century, most of South Africa's blacks were Christian, the result of nineteenth-century missionary efforts, especially by evangelicals and later Pentecostals and the emergence of "African" churches, independent of European-origin denominations.[17] By the twentieth century, most South Africans of all races were Christian, with only very small Muslim, Hindu, and Jewish minorities.

The British

During the Napoleonic Wars (1803–1815), the British captured the Cape from the Netherlands, which at the time was allied with France. Kaapstad became Cape Town, a position between their British home ports and their Indian empire. There followed periodic small waves of British immigration into the Cape. English, Irish, and Scots, always few in number, were slow to intermarry outside their specific group or with the Boers.[18] While the British valued Cape Town as a rest stop and a food-provisioning and coaling station, London, as Amsterdam had been, was reluctant to oversee an expansion of European settlement from the coast into the interior.

Larger English-speaking immigration took place only after the discovery of gold and diamonds during the second half of the nineteenth century. Many of those later, ostensibly "English" immigrants came from continental Europe. There was an important wave of Jewish settlers from the Russian Empire around the turn of the twentieth century driven by pogroms associated with the Cossacks. At its height in the mid-twentieth century, that community may have numbered 118,200.[19] After World I and continuing to the present, other European communities have established themselves in South Africa, including Italian, Greek, and Portuguese speakers. Arrivals from Europe usually adopted English as their language rather than Afrikaans.

THE FORMATION OF THE COLOUREDS

Kaapstad was a society built on slaves, as was the American antebellum South. But chattel slaves in the Cape who were comparable to those in Virginia were often not of African origin. Instead, the Dutch imported an estimated total of sixty thousand slaves from various parts of Africa and Asia, especially the Straits of Malacca, to their Cape Colony.[20] By comparison, according to the Trans-Atlantic Slave Trade Database, the territories included in what is now the United States directly imported approximately 305,000 slaves from Africa over more than two centuries.[21] South Asian slaves were often skilled craftsmen; the highly prized "Cape Dutch" furniture they made is but one example of their artistry. They intermarried with both whites and indigenous peoples, with their offspring evolving over time into the racial group known as "coloureds." The Khoisan peoples around Kaapstad sometimes reached an accommodation with the Boers, exchanging their labor for a victual allowance, housing, and a few animals in an arrangement that recalls peonage. Some became Dutch speaking and Dutch Reformed in religion. Following frequent intermarriage with other ethnic groups, they, too, contributed to the formation of the coloureds. There was also a small Muslim community introduced by South Asian slaves, often called "Cape Malays," that regarded itself as separate from the coloureds, a distinction usually not recognized by South African law during the apartheid period; they were subsumed under the "coloured" label.

The Boers sometimes referred to coloureds as "little brothers." The coloureds provided a buffer between whites and blacks; no such equivalent existed in the United States outside of New Orleans, which also had a highly developed, racially mixed community that formed an intermediate group between whites and blacks. But, under apartheid, coloureds increasingly faced the same restrictions as blacks. The Boers, maintaining strict racial boundaries, refused to accord coloureds legal or social equality of any sort. The British had allowed them to vote in the Cape if they met property qualifications, a privilege that was taken away by the Boer-dominated government under apartheid. Eventually, the coloureds established their own, separate Dutch Reformed denominations. Until late in the twentieth century, they were predominately rural, and many remained mired in poverty, though it was not as severe as among blacks. They still provide much of the labor for the Cape's famous vineyards.

If the Boers strictly separated themselves from the coloureds and blacks, many coloureds did the same with respect to Bantu-speaking Africans. Even as late as the twentieth century, many coloureds insisted that, in comparison with black Africans, they were "Europeans."[22] In the context of twentieth-century racial politics, some coloureds were open to forming an alliance with the Afrikaners. The latter, however, blinded by racist ideology that ignored cultural similarities, refused. In the 1980s, National Party and Boer leader P. W. Botha consigned coloureds to a separate house of parliament rather than allowing them to sit in the "white" parliament and vote in "white" elections. Rebuffed by the Nationalists, many coloureds turned to the ANC as apartheid collapsed, if only temporarily.

Today, coloureds are the largest ethnic group in the Western Cape and in the Northern Cape, together comprising more than half of the country's land area. Post-apartheid, and as the ANC has become more "African" under President Zuma, they have tended to vote for the historically "white" Democratic Alliance (DA), joining a voter base that is also growing from the support of other minority groups. However, the irony is that the DA is not an Afrikaner party, nor is it Dutch Reformed in outlook. And, its predominant language is English. So, post-apartheid, the coloureds have a seat at the formerly "white" political table, but most often as part of a party that in culture is predominately "English" and in an overall governance is dominated by blacks.

ASIANS

Later in the nineteenth century, after the end of slavery throughout the British Empire, British entrepreneurs imported large numbers of South Asians as indentured labor to work newly established sugar plantations in the Natal region adjacent to Zululand. When their indenture was completed, most workers stayed, rather than return to South Asia. Some apartheid-era legislation lumped them with the coloureds. However, in general, they were not subject to the same severe restrictions on movement as blacks. Over time, they too evolved into a separate racially defined community, commonly called "asians." Their separate identity initially was based on language, culture, and religion; most of them were Hindu or Muslim. By the twentieth century, however, there was a significant Christian minority among them. Over time, as in Kenya and Uganda, they often became shopkeepers, though the scope of their economic activity was limited under apartheid.[23]

THE RACIAL HIERARCHY

By the late nineteenth century, the racial hierarchy was fixed and increasingly defined by "objective and scientific" characteristics, such as skin color and hair characteristics, and mandated by law. Whites were on top, followed by asians and coloureds, with blacks at the bottom. Whites were divided by language, English and Dutch, later Afrikaans, while blacks were also divided by growing awareness of specific ethnic identities and language.[24] Whites often used coloureds and asians as "bosses" over Africans and extended to them certain privileges locally within a framework of increasingly rigid racial segregation. Africans, in turn, often resented the two intermediary peoples, sentiments encouraged by white divide-and-rule strategies.

However, in the predominately rural environment of South Africa before the mid- and late nineteenth-century diamond and gold rushes, as a practical matter whites dominated the other races primarily through what the Afrikaners called *baaskap* or "mastership." They exercised surveillance and control through personal contact and the threat of violence, rather than through institutions established by law. The slave codes that regulated relations in the American South between masters and slaves had only an underdeveloped equivalent in South Africa.

THE GREAT TREK AND THE COMING OF THE BOER WAR

Afrikaners were in many respects a people of the frontier who chafed against outside authority.[25] The British sought to integrate the Cape into their worldwide empire after they seized it from the Dutch. Early on, British law and regulation restricted owners' rights over slaves and apprentices. The British Empire finally outlawed slavery altogether in

1833. The law took effect in South Africa in 1834. Afrikaner grievances against the British ranged from what they saw as inadequate compensation for their slaves freed under British law to alleged British indifference to their border wars against black ethnic groups.

An Afrikaner response to ever more intrusive British rule was the Great Trek. This was a folk migration of some twelve thousand Boers in the 1830s recalling on a small scale American westward expansion at about the same time. Afrikaners moved in wagon trains hundreds of miles inland and established two small, Dutch-speaking Boer republics, outside the British Empire based on universal white male suffrage and the rule of law. These two states, Transvaal and the Orange Free State, outlawed slavery but enshrined rigid racial segregation, with no political participation for blacks.

Farmer republics on the frontier, Transvaal and the Orange Free State existed on the margins of the international economy until diamonds were discovered in the Cape around Kimberley in 1867 and a few years later gold in the Boer republic of Transvaal around newly founded Johannesburg. There was a diamond and gold rush of adventurers from all over the world. English, the language of international big business, became the lingua franca of a polyglot population of fortune hunters. Transvaal, especially, was transformed from a small country of only marginal importance to playing an important part in the world economy because of its mines.

Johannesburg, established as a mining camp in Transvaal, developed quickly into one of the most modern cities in sub-Saharan Africa.[26] From the start it was a chaotic intermingling of modern buildings and shantytowns. The trajectory of its development resembled that of Denver and other American "gold rush" cities, but the initial residential racial mixing morphed quickly into more rigid patterns of segregation.

From 1877 on, political crises intensified between the gold-hungry newcomers and the Afrikaner governments in the Boer republics—engineered at least in part by the English imperialist, businessman, and swashbuckler Cecil Rhodes and abetted by a clumsy Boer response to the political and economic demands of foreign gold seekers. Between 1880 and 1902 the British and Boers fought two wars. The most important of these confrontations was the Second Anglo-Boer War of 1899–1902. Indigenous blacks usually did not take sides voluntarily, but thousands were forced to fight or to provide logistical support for both sides. Nevertheless, Afrikaners perceived blacks as generally pro-British.

After a much harder fight than anybody expected, the British finally were victorious, using for the first time tactics such as the establishment of concentration camps to incarcerate Boer civilians, especially women and children, and their African support personnel. Camp conditions were deplorable, and many of those incarcerated died of disease. Such tactics were at high cost to the international reputation of the British Empire and to its hitherto righteous self-image. The uncomfortable reality was that the world's mightiest empire conquered two small states and rounded up their citizens in concentration camps. The international focus was almost entirely on the suffering of the Boers, whose sense of grievance against the British Empire only intensified; blacks were ignored.

With international moral support, British shame, and the political skill of their leaders, the Afrikaners won the peace in the subsequent political settlement. The outcome was that they came to govern all of South Africa, not only Transvaal and Orange Free State but also the hitherto British Cape Province, more than half of the new country's geographical area, now reconstituted as the Union of South Africa.

THE UNION OF SOUTH AFRICA

The British Empire and the Afrikaner leadership concluded a bargain at the expense of the nonwhite populations. In return for continued "English" domination of the modern economy, including the gold, diamond, coal, and (later) platinum mines, the British ceded to the Afrikaners control of political life, including "native policy." All of the British territories and the two former independent Afrikaner republics were amalgamated into a new entity, the Union of South Africa. In 1910 it became a self-governing dominion similar to Canada and Australia. Like the two "old dominions," Westminster expected South Africa to be a close diplomatic and security partner of the rest of the British Empire.

South African Democracy and White Supremacy

Demography ensured that "one white man, one vote" meant Afrikaner domination of South African politics and the government. There were limited exceptions for coloureds and certain black Africans in only one province, the formerly British Cape. Those exceptions were themselves further limited by property and education stipulations. Over time the Afrikaner-dominated South African government eroded them away.[27] (Governments of the American southern states also revised their constitutions after 1890 to disenfranchise nonwhites.) South Africa had become a parliamentary democracy, but for white males only. White women were admitted to the suffrage only in 1930, a decade after universal female suffrage in the United States but only two years after the United Kingdom.

The institutional triumph of white supremacy in the American South and in South Africa around the turn of the twentieth century appears to have had similar drivers. The federal government defeated the Confederate states in 1865, abolished slavery, instituted wide-ranging reforms, and largely excluded from government the traditional elites. Ex-slaves won the right to vote, and some gained elective office. This process, known as Reconstruction, ended abruptly in 1877 when federal troops were withdrawn from the southern states as part of a political deal between southern Democrats and predominately northern Republicans that enabled the Republican presidential candidate, Rutherford B. Hayes, to prevail following contested election results. Thereafter, the traditional elites rapidly regained control of southern state governments. The region was urbanizing and industrializing, a process driven by railway construction. Urbanization and industrialization eroded the southern version of *baaskap*, and blacks were resented because of their participation in the civil war and Reconstruction on the side of the "Yankees" and were often scapegoated for the Confederate defeat. The white-dominated "redeemed" state governments, with little interference by the federal government, excluded blacks from political life, limited any educational opportunities, and advocated white supremacy. There was a dramatic increase in white-sponsored violence against blacks.[28]

In the former Confederate states and in South Africa by the end of World War I, white supremacy was codified by law, enforced by the state, and was a central concern of public policy. Nonwhites were large-ly excluded from public life and almost entirely from elected office. Few enjoyed the right to vote. The common context was urbanization, modernization, and the development of the state bureaucracies neces-sary for enforcement of white supremacy. In the American South and in South Africa, the role of blacks was solely to provide labor, not to otherwise participate in the nation.

White supremacy in the southern states was largely unchallenged by the federal government until the administration of President Harry S. Truman, who integrated the military forces of the United States. There-after, successive presidential administrations slowly and erratically chal-lenged white supremacy, culminating in the civil rights revolution of the 1960s sponsored by Presidents John F. Kennedy and Lyndon B. John-son. In South Africa, the ideological pillars of white supremacy started to crumble in the aftermath of the Holocaust of World War II, which discredited racism; in the face of indigenous protest and revolt; and under foreign pressure. In both places, white supremacy was also undermined by decisions made by their relatively independent judiciar-ies.[29]

The Afrikaner-dominated Pretoria government proved to be a reli-able British ally in the First and Second World Wars, though there was Boer anti-British backlash that contributed to the National Party's 1948 victory, which, in effect, extended and transformed the post–Boer War bargain by instituting apartheid.

Fueled by diamonds, gold, coal, and, subsequently, other minerals, as well as primary commodities, the South African economy in the late nineteenth and early twentieth centuries evolved into a type of unbri-dled booty capitalism, dominated by big, privately owned corporations seeking quick profits, dependent on cheap black labor, and largely un-regulated by any government entity. Rates of economic growth were high, as was income inequality. South Africa rapidly acquired the infra-structure of a modern industrial state. Though the economy was domi-nated by extractive industries, commercial farming and manufacturing also developed rapidly. It was during this period that South Africa's economy became far more developed than anywhere else in sub-Saha-ran Africa.

The Boer War had severely damaged the Afrikaners' agriculture and thereby probably accelerated their urbanization. In 1904, only 6 percent of Afrikaners were urban; by as early as 1960, that percentage had rocketed to 76 percent. By the time of the transition to "nonracial democracy," South Africa's largest white "tribe" was no longer made up of farmers on family-owned farms, but rather of suburban-based employers and employees of urban-based enterprises.[30]

By the 1920s, it was often said that white South Africans—Afrikaner and English—had a material standard of living comparable to whites in the United States. Some South Africans recognized that the very high white standard of living was directly based on exploitation of cheap black labor. In 1925 an official of the Economic and Wage Commission observed that whites were "enabled to maintain a standard of life approximating rather to that of America than to that of Europe, in a country that is poorer than most of the countries of Central Europe, solely because they have at their disposal these masses of docile, low-paid native laborers."[31]

Apartheid

Though it was a twentieth-century phenomenon, apartheid had deep roots in three hundred years of racial separation and white supremacy practiced by Europeans in North America and Asia as well as in Africa. The desirability of racial segregation was largely unquestioned where a black or brown population was living in proximity to whites. As late as the 1930s, the segregation principle was accepted even by the ANC as a means of protecting blacks from white exploitation, especially in urban areas.[32]

Beginning in the early modern period in Europe and its overseas settlements, "race" came to denote genetically different human populations that could be identified by shared, observable characteristics. To each "race" could be attributed specific behaviors and capacities. Whites, "Negroes,"[33] and Asians constituted fundamentally different human populations with attributable behaviors, capacities, and needs. The differences among the three were not biologically insignificant markers such as skin color or eye shape but in their very essence. Each was a separate, biologically defined population that God (or "nature" or "science" depending on the scholar or commentator) had mandated should be kept separate. That belief was fundamental to the apartheid obsession with interdicting interracial sex and the criminalization of interracial marriage in American southern states.

Race and colonialism were reinforcing feedback loops. In the nineteenth century, white northern Europeans dominated the black, brown, and yellow peoples of Africa and Asia. Their success was "irrefutable" evidence of their racial superiority. Tellingly, even in the twentieth century, many South African whites were identifying themselves as "Europeans," even though their ancestors had arrived in Africa three hundred years previously. Vladimir Lenin and other Marxists described apartheid as "colonialism of a special type," where the colonial power was South African whites, not a foreign power.

Apartheid as a formal system based on elaborate legislation that systematically and meticulously separated the races dates from 1948, when the populist, conservative Afrikaner political party, the Nationalists, narrowly defeated the "establishment" and largely pro-British United Party that had governed the country during World War II. For many Afrikaners, the election was mostly fought over the question of South Africa's relationship to the British Empire. The Nationalists drew upon historic Afrikaner grievances against the British and the rekindling of Afrikaner nationalism in opposition to South Africa's participation in World War II, yet again on the side of the British. There was also Afrikaner unease at growing African assertiveness and a sense that a United Party government might compromise the principles of rigid racial segregation.[34]

Building on the already existing theory and practice of racial segregation and white supremacy, under apartheid the South African government developed an elaborate system, incorporated into official regulations, of characteristics for each racial group, such as skin color or whether their hair was straight or curly.[35] Using those characteristics, there was an official body, the Race Classification Board, empowered to assign an individual to a particular racial category. Right up to the end of legal apartheid, individuals petitioned to have their racial category changed, most often "up," black to coloured or coloured to white.

The fundamental assumption was that whites, blacks, and coloureds were all members of *Homo sapiens*, but each "race" was a different form of *Homo sapiens*. By the mid-twentieth century, apartheid's advocates argued that "separate development" was the best way to manage relations among the races and to foreclose whites exploiting blacks or blacks "overwhelming" whites by their sheer numbers.

However, twentieth-century scientists had shown that race had no taxonomic significance. There were no biological attributes dictated by race to individual behavior or capacities. Far from being a biological reality, racial characteristics had become merely a social construct. In the nineteenth-century understanding of the word, race no longer existed. But it still did in South Africa, in certain respects, and in parts of the American South. Fundamental to most South Africans is the preeminence of their racial identity, defined as it had been under apartheid. Many, perhaps most, still see the racial groups as fundamentally different from each other. And, indeed, they are. But the differences are not the result of inherent biological racial characteristics. They are the result of different educational, medical, vocational, and professional opportunities that are remarkably determined by superficial biological markers such as skin color. So South Africa remains profoundly racial, and, in common parlance, the meaning of "race" has not evolved much beyond its nineteenth-century usage. Racial identity and racial demographics remain the fundamental building blocks of politics, and much else.

The white supremacy that apartheid embodied was common currency internationally during the first half of the twentieth century. A traveler from the American southern states would have seen little practical difference between home and South Africa. In the American southern states and South Africa, the subordination of blacks and other races to whites was questioned only in "progressive," usually left-wing or communist circles and among some Christian churches, notably the Society of Friends (Quakers). However, apartheid did have a dimension that segregation in the United States did not: it was an affirmation of a specific Afrikaner nationalism with a particular emphasis on preservation and expansion of the Afrikaans language. Apartheid South Africa was an Afrikaner state, not just a white state, and white English speakers were largely excluded (or excluded themselves) from political power, even though they were the wealthiest community in the country and dominated big business.

The apartheid system was also shaped by the Afrikaner fear of being demographically swamped by the far larger black population that might politically threaten their race-based privileges, especially should they acquire the right to vote. But a parallel sense of grievance against the British following the Boer War, and two world wars fought in alliance with the empire also played a significant role. From an Afrikaner perspective, blacks and English each in their own way imperiled the survival of Afrikaner identity, the former through their numbers, the latter through their greater wealth, their links to the wider British Empire, and their control of the Union's modern economy. For many Afrikaners, apartheid was their response to these anxieties.

Some Afrikaner politicians justified apartheid as a system based on "Christian values" designed to prevent the "exploitation" of blacks by physically separating them from potentially exploitive whites. However, a scholar of American slavery and the antebellum South, Eugene Genovese, notes that the "Christian" defense of apartheid was underdeveloped and unsophisticated compared to the American "Christian" theological defense of slavery before the 1861–1865 Civil War.[36] Apartheid systematized the exploitation of black labor in the context of rigid racial segregation based on blatant racism. Racial segregation shaped by apartheid completed the destruction of black economic enterprise, thereby foreclosing the opportunity to create personal wealth through capital accumulation, investment, or innovation.

Apartheid was established by law and enforced through the judicial process. Nevertheless, the judiciary retained some independence from the National Party government, though it generally shared the same racist assumptions as white society as a whole. In that respect, it resembled the judiciaries in the American southern states. Implementation of apartheid rarely required official, coercive force, though that threat always remained. South Africa never became a thoroughgoing police state, though when under stress it approached it. However, at times the Bureau of State Security (BOSS) functioned as a secret police above the law.

Unofficial violence against blacks in South Africa was widespread, if poorly documented. However, it does not appear to have approached the magnitude of lynchings in the American South and West and race riots in many urban areas, often with the connivance or active participation of the police and other officials. During the twentieth century, racial violence in the United States likely was greater than in South Africa.[37] Race riots and lynchings were, of course, outside the formal rule of law, adherence to which may have been weaker in parts of the United States than in South Africa.

One of apartheid's goals was to eliminate the poverty of "poor white" Afrikaners by a system of job preferences in the public sector. It largely succeeded, for a time. At apartheid's height, an elaborate system of labor regulation reserved semiskilled and skilled jobs for whites. Often the regulations were absurdly detailed. For example, a black working for a white house painter could carry the cans of paint, open them, and lay out the brushes. But he could not apply the paint. Complementing job reservation for whites, the National Party also developed in effect a publicly financed affirmative-action program for Afrikaners. Afrikaners came to dominate public-sector employment. They staffed government institutions ranging from the post office to the railways, thereby ensuring that the "face" of South Africa was white and largely Afrikaner.

Beginning in 1950 and subsequently extended and amended many times, the Group Areas Act assigned racial groups to different residential and business neighborhoods. To enter white areas, blacks were required to carry passbooks, which resembled internal passports. Members of racial groups living in the "wrong" neighborhoods were removed. It is estimated that in a twenty-year period, some 3.5 million blacks and coloureds were so displaced.[38] Blacks and coloureds living in informal settlements, usually shantytowns, rarely enjoyed any security of tenure. Their informal settlements were usually without electricity and often with limited access to water. For coloureds and asians, reflecting their intermediate racial status, physical conditions in their townships were often better than in those for blacks.[39]

Rural black Africans were increasingly squeezed into lands of marginal fertility, and their market agriculture economy by and large did not survive. Miners were contract employees, housed in barracks-like hostels and separated from their families. Townships and "informal settlements" had existed outside predominantly white cities from the very beginning, and as time went on some of them grew and became permanent. Others, "ink spots" in predominantly white areas, were bulldozed. Unlike the hostels, townships were characterized by family units. They, rather than the homelands, became the center of visible black opposition to apartheid. Hostels, on the other hand, were the more usual venue of violence among ethnic groups.

Under apartheid, segregation involved the physical separation of black and coloured townships by considerable distance from each other and from white areas, including many places of employment. Blacks and coloureds in work routinely faced long commuting times. Those who were fortunate lived near rail lines that ran commuter services into large cities. Train operations were scheduled so that blacks could remain in white areas no later than about 6 p.m. Whether by train or various bus and taxi services, commuting costs were high as a percentage of black and coloured wages.

As apartheid evolved, the National Party government eventually established or expanded tribally defined "self-governing homelands" for blacks. Over time, the expectation was that they would become fully independent states. The result would be a smaller South Africa geographically, but one in which the majority of the population would be white, with coloured and Asian minorities. Africans would be stripped of their South African citizenship and assume that of the independent homeland to which they ostensibly belonged. However, millions of black sojourners would provide the cheap labor the economy needed; their movements and residence would be regulated by pass laws.[40] In fact, full-time residents of the homelands were disproportionately women, children, and the elderly. Husbands and fathers were at work in white areas.

In the late apartheid period, a few "homelands" were granted a sham independence by South Africa, and their nominal residents were stripped of their South African nationality. The independence of these states was recognized only by South Africa and each other.[41] The so-called independent and self-governing homelands recall in some ways the tribal lands of Native Americans. Both were characterized by rural poverty and rule by local elites who often exploited those whom they governed. An important difference, however, is that Native Americans were not stripped of their American citizenship, while those South Africans living in the independent homelands usually were.[42]

With an ideology that was anticommunist, overtly racist, and suffused with a sense of colonial grievance against the English, Afrikaner apartheid contained few ideas new to South Africa. What was new was that apartheid was systematically organized and rigidly enforced. Its primary feature was the physical separation of races into different geographical territories ranging from neighborhoods to states, while at the same time ensuring the availability of cheap labor for an industrial state and commercial agriculture.

If apartheid physically separated the races through the Group Areas Act, in the United States, residential segregation in urban and suburban areas was routinely achieved locally by means such as restrictive covenants on property use and ownership. There was no American equivalent of the Group Areas Act. In South Africa and the southern part of the United States all public facilities—ranging from water fountains to schools—were segregated. Ironically, the establishment of a separate black state in the territory of the former Confederate states that would have resembled in some ways a South African homeland was long advocated by American black separatists.

Apartheid, the distortions in national life that it promoted, its personal tragedies, its challenges to the achievement of a democracy, and the struggle against it have shaped post-1948 South Africa. Its significance for South Africa is of a magnitude similar to that of the Civil War and its aftermath in the former Confederate states, especially from 1865 to 1898.[43]

Apartheid's Twilight

In the United States, the end of segregation was opposed by the majority of whites in the South. But, in the United States as a whole, a majority of whites appear to have favored the end of segregation based on law. Nevertheless, the process was driven by the judiciary rather than by the executive or legislative branches of government. The Supreme Court found school segregation based on race to be unconstitutional in 1954; it was a decade before Congress passed the Civil Rights Act, which outlawed discrimination based on race, in the emotional aftermath of the assassination of President John F. Kennedy, who had supported the Civil Rights Act. In South Africa, right to the end, many whites supported apartheid, even if many of them had lost confidence in it. But there was white opposition to apartheid that included English-speaking liberals, Christians, civil society organizations, and communists. In the last two decades of apartheid, there were also Afrikaner voices against apartheid. Big business increasingly also opposed apartheid because it inhibited skills transfer and the mobility of labor.

South African apartheid and American segregation ended through court intervention, public demonstrations, and political pressure at home and from abroad. In the United States, segregation was embarrassing in the Cold War context when District of Columbia, Maryland, and Virginia state law enforced it with respect to diplomats from newly independent African countries. Hence at least some politicians and federal officials came to oppose segregation because they saw it as undermining national security in the context of Cold War rivalry with the Soviet Union and China in which Africa could be the venue of proxy wars.

In the United States, pressure to dismantle segregation came from African American victims of segregation often working through organizations, such as the National Association for the Advancement of Colored People (NAACP) or the Southern Christian Leadership Conference (SCLC). With often white, progressive allies, they used the court system whose judgments were enforced by the federal government. Following the lead of Martin Luther King Jr. and influenced by Mahatma Gandhi's successful campaign for India's independence, the American civil rights movement was powered by nonviolence.

In South Africa the struggle against apartheid was also waged by the system's victims, especially in the townships, and by their sympathizers, often white, at home and in the outside world. Unlike the American civil rights movement, the South African anti-apartheid struggle had a violent dimension. The armed struggle carried out by the liberation movements beginning in 1961 never threatened the apartheid state, but it did undermine white confidence in the durability of apartheid.[44] Probably more important to undermining the apartheid state was its increasing inability to govern the black townships. Narrow Afrikaner policies, such as requirements for the use of Afrikaans in state schools, combined with police brutality, provoked violence. A multiracial coalition, the United Democratic Front (UDF), often led by religious leaders, mounted public protests.

South African black opposition movements to segregation and labor exploitation date from the early twentieth century. Before and after the formal establishment of apartheid, black resistance was widespread and often informal. However, it was usually nonviolent. The ANC, probably the largest liberation movement throughout the period, was founded in 1912. It was multiracial in its early years and dominated by middle-class black professionals. It was a movement rather than a political party. In some respects, it resembled the NAACP of the same era in the United States, though the latter never embraced an armed struggle or evolved into a political party.

Protests, often violent, against apartheid were continuous, but each decade there was a larger, more dramatic uprising, usually punctuated by security service violence that increasingly drew international attention and opprobrium. In 1952 there were mass protests over passbooks. In 1960 a demonstration against passbooks at Sharpeville resulted in sixty-nine being killed. In 1976, there was an uprising in Soweto, a Johannesburg township, over efforts to impose Afrikaans as the medium of instruction in the schools. In 1961 the ANC established an armed wing, Umkhonto we Sizwe, often called MK. The Pan Africanist Congress (PAC), a rival liberation movement, also established an armed wing, Poqo.

In 1955, as a statement of its core principles, the ANC issued its Freedom Charter following prolonged discussion with representatives of many nonwhite groups. (White organizations declined to participate.) The charter affirmed as its goals a democratic, socialist, nonracial South Africa, with protection of human rights, land reform, and nationalization of big enterprises. While many of the charter's provisions were to be incorporated into South Africa's post-apartheid constitution, the Freedom Charter has never had legal standing under South African law.

The UDF, a multiracial umbrella of civic organizations opposed to apartheid, was organized in 1983. Eventually, it included up to six hundred organizations involving women, youth, and civil organizations. Black trade unions by and large did not participate in it. The apartheid government tended to see the UDF as the internal wing of the ANC, though in fact it maintained a separate, though friendly, identity.[45]

Rivalry within the liberation movements could be intense and, on occasion, bloody. The PAC split from the ANC essentially over the question of whether whites could genuinely participate in black liberation; the PAC argued that they should not because their presence was a distraction from the struggle to liberate oppressed black people. While the PAC has been marginalized by the ANC, especially after the coming of nonracial democracy in 1994, it played an important role in the "internal liberation" of some blacks from the feelings of inferiority and subordination fostered by "scientific racism" and the dominant white culture. In the last decade of apartheid, its armed wing was more violent than that of the ANC.[46]

Also important for "internal liberation" was the Black Consciousness Movement (BCM). In 1968, when there was little organized black opposition to apartheid, students organized the South African Students Organization (SASO). SASO came to embody BCM. Its focus was on black self-worth and black activism, with economic self-reliance. BCM included as "black" all victims of apartheid, especially the coloureds. Steve Biko, perhaps the most prominent BCM figure, was murdered in "police custody" in 1977. The mother of his children was Mamphela Ramphele, a medical doctor and later a post-apartheid businesswoman and political leader.

THE STRUGGLE

The anarchic quality of black resistance in the first decade of apartheid and the refusal of the National Party government to negotiate is cited by some ANC leaders now as having contributed to Nelson Mandela's decision to launch the armed struggle, which, it was thought, would be disciplined by the political goals of the Freedom Charter.[47]

Nelson Mandela, who had already emerged as a liberation leader, and other ANC leaders who were also members of the South African Communist Party (SACP) launched the armed struggle in 1961. Mandela said that the goal was only sabotage, not killing, with the goal of forcing the National Party government to the negotiating table. But, in the face of accelerating pressure by the apartheid government, the ANC soon employed terrorist tactics. It sought help from abroad, and received it from the Soviet Union and the Eastern bloc. Over time, numerous ANC operatives received military training in the Soviet Union, and the East German secret police, the Stasi, shaped ANC counter-intelligence.

These developments aligned the liberation struggle with the Soviets in a Cold War setting.[48] That foreclosed possible support from London or Washington and undercut potential support from liberal South African whites. The SACP had a leading, often the dominant, role in the armed struggle, especially in exile. Many of its leaders were trained in

Moscow. Mandela was always silent on whether he was a member of the party. However, his membership and his service on the Central Committee were confirmed by official SACP and ANC statements upon his death.[49] The apartheid government, on the other hand, increasingly represented itself as a "bulwark" against Soviet communism in southern Africa and as an ally with the West.[50]

Divisions

Far from monolithic, white South Africa was riddled with fissures that contributed to intense debate within the National Party and in parliament. Big business still tended to be "English," while the white working class was heavily "Afrikaner." Commercial cities such as Johannesburg and Cape Town were more "English" than the Afrikaner-dominated administrative and judicial centers of government, Pretoria and Bloemfontein. Afrikaners also dominated many rural areas. Fissures between white management and white labor organized into trade unions could be deep.

Before 1948 the National Party itself was no monolith. There were fissures based on individual power rivalries as well as policy differences. For example, before World War II, some National Party leaders supported South Africa's continued participation in the Commonwealth and, with the coming of war, its participation on the Allied side. Others, however, expressed admiration for Adolf Hitler and opposition to fighting yet another war for the British. But the most fundamental division was over race relations, with some insisting on the exclusion of non-whites from all aspects of national life, while others advocated a marginally more flexible approach.

Government and party policy making lacked transparency. A secret organization, the Afrikaner Broederbond (AB), included virtually all the leaders of the National Party and was the venue where many policy issues were thrashed out. Members of the AB were the principal architects of the legal framework for apartheid. The AB played a role in Nationalist politics comparable in some ways to that of another secret organization, the SACP, in the ANC.

After 1948, the National Party slowly enlarged its electoral base by attracting increased "English" support. The longer it remained in office, the more it became "the party of government," a source of lucrative contracts, and a font of patronage. Most English initially acquiesced to or shared the radical racial segregation principles that were at its core. But, over time, white opposition developed, driven in part by security service violence and the foreign opprobrium apartheid generated. For its part, the later apartheid regime under P. W. Botha and F. W. de Klerk showed some tactical flexibility. For example, the National government significantly increased spending on black education and urban housing, even if it remained far below what was needed for participation in a modern economy (as desired by many business leaders) or what was allocated to whites.[51] But a central principle of apartheid was to deny blacks participation in the modern economy except under the most controlled of circumstances. That policy was increasingly contrary to the economic interest of big business in the mobility and flexibility of labor.

Whites were prominent in the UDF, which had significant clergy leadership and included human rights nongovernmental organizations. One was Black Sash, largely made up of middle-class white women. It was organized in 1955 initially to protest against the removal of coloureds from the Cape's voting rolls and subsequently the authorities' removal of blacks and coloureds from white areas as mandated by the Group Areas Act. They soon expanded their activities more generally to protest human rights abuses.

By apartheid's last decade, sophisticated white public opinion was moving against it. Clergy, especially from the Anglican and Roman Catholic churches, became increasingly vocal in their criticism of apartheid. Some Dutch Reformed clergy, influenced by the consequences of racism as demonstrated by the Holocaust, became anti-apartheid activists. Helen Suzman, who represented the wealthy, largely English-speaking constituency of Houghton outside of Johannesburg, was a parliamentary thorn in the side of the National Party and apartheid. Some white lawyers and judges also actively sought with success to undermine the legal basis of apartheid.

Many of the small number of white activists in the anti-apartheid movement were "English," especially from Johannesburg's large and liberal Jewish community.[52] Ironically, the apartheid regime had a close and clandestine relationship with Israel, based in part on shared pariah status and similar nuclear goals.

Earlier, whites opposed to apartheid had gravitated to the SACP, which also attracted support from all the other racial groups. The SACP, reflecting its Marxist-Leninist orientation, was firmly nonracist, and has remained so.

White as well as black anti-apartheid activists faced opprobrium and sometimes violence. Black Sash demonstrators could be beaten, despite their gender and relatively privileged status. Other activists received letter bombs of uncertain origin. However, many more blacks than whites were victims of terror that could often be traced back to the security services.

The black liberation movements were also riddled with divisions. The most important was between those who went into exile to join the armed struggle and those who remained behind, the "exiles" versus the "inziles." There was division between those who saw the liberation struggle as exclusively black and those, especially in the SACP, who argued that liberation was nonracial. There was the rivalry between the PAC, with its orientation toward Beijing, and the ANC and the SACP, which looked to Moscow in the days of the Sino-Soviet split. Nevertheless, until the late 1980s, these opposition groups had in common a vision that a socialist or communist economy was the key to ending apartheid and establishing a nonracial democracy, and their ideological stance was strengthened by the significant material support they received from the Soviet bloc through the SACP. Among many in the anti-apartheid movement, there was particular admiration for the German Democratic Republic (East Germany) as a developed yet socialist economy.

The apartheid security services thoroughly penetrated the liberation movements and conducted military operations against MK camps outside South Africa. In response, some ANC leaders in exile became increasingly authoritarian and intolerant of dissent, even to the point of committing human rights abuses against suspected "traitors." Mandela and his fellow prisoners isolated at Robben Island avoided the taint.

The Struggle: The International Dimension

The liberation movements, especially the ANC, also received material and political support from liberal, democratic European states, especially in Scandinavia and the Netherlands. The World Council of

Churches, based in Geneva, rallied opposition to apartheid as fundamentally contrary to the teachings of Christianity. The Scandinavians and the churches played an important role in achieving United Nations condemnation of apartheid and sanctions against South Africa.

Private individuals organized a consumer boycott of South African goods in the United Kingdom beginning in 1959. Anti-apartheid sentiment swelled within the Commonwealth, from which South Africa withdrew in 1969. Thereafter, every Commonwealth heads of government meeting featured a discussion of how to bring about the demise of apartheid. In the 1960s the United Nations imposed an arms embargo on South Africa, and in 1973, the Organization of Petroleum Exporting Countries imposed an oil embargo. Beginning in 1985, the then–European Community (EC) imposed limited trade and financial sanctions, and the Commonwealth followed suit. Thereafter, many states imposed bans on South African exports, but they were tailored to the specific needs of the country involved. Hence, for example, the EC banned South African gold coins, but not South African gold and diamonds.

The effectiveness of the economic sanctions in bringing about the end of apartheid is still debated.[53] One estimate is that the marginal cost of sanctions to the South African economy was as low as 0.5 percent of gross national product (GNP).[54] The decisions made by private firms to disinvest from South Africa or to cease lending were often made because of market factors not directly related to the anti-apartheid campaign. Nevertheless, during the final act of the struggle against apartheid, the ANC and others saw sanctions as essential, and there was deep concern that they would be lifted too soon. At present, it is almost conventional wisdom to see sanctions and the armed struggle as the principal causes of the collapse of apartheid rather than loss of confidence in the system, recognition of its economic dysfunction, the collapse of the Soviet Union, and the guaranteed preservation of white wealth.

Probably the greatest impact on most white South Africans was the country's progressive expulsion from international sporting competition. As early as 1968, the United Nations General Assembly called on member states to suspend cultural, education, sporting, and other exchanges with South Africa. The Olympic Committee suspended South

Africa from the 1964 Tokyo Olympics and expelled the country altogether from the Olympic movement in 1970.

The liberation movements received some support from the United States, though not as much as Americans often assume. As in South Africa, clergy and human rights activists were prominent in the American anti-apartheid movement. After the passage of the Comprehensive Anti-Apartheid Act, many U.S. corporations divested their South African assets, often at fire-sale prices, ironically benefiting well-connected pillars of the apartheid state who had the capital to buy. The American diplomatic mission in South Africa promoted a wide range of exchanges and other educational opportunities for those opposed to apartheid. It also provided a venue where representatives of all political views could meet.[55]

The apartheid state recognized black trade unions in 1979 as part of its efforts to ameliorate the negative apartheid impact on labor mobility.[56] From its founding in 1985, the Congress of South African Trade Unions (COSATU) also politically mobilized working Africans. Many leaders of the unions that made up COSATU were also clandestine members of the SACP. Black organized labor played an important role in the struggle against apartheid and wrested with difficulty concessions for its members. White, highly skilled workers organized their own trade unions, which were not usually sympathetic to expansion of black employment opportunities. Working-class white Afrikaners often supported apartheid and were a bedrock of support for the National Party.

THE END OF APARTHEID

During the 1980s it was increasingly clear to the National Party leadership that apartheid was not working. Apartheid's rigidities became economically dysfunctional, especially as the modern economy developed. Apartheid restricted education and training opportunities for blacks, contributing to high levels of unemployment in a modernizing economy facing global competition yet paradoxically plagued by labor shortages. Their poverty stunted the growth of a market for goods and services. Apartheid legislation, such as the Group Areas Act, limited where blacks could live, thereby interfering with labor mobility. From the perspective of large-scale employers, apartheid resulted in high labor costs and inefficiencies. Though there were many exceptions, much of the leadership of big business came to favor the reduction or even elimination of apartheid structures. Foreign pressure played a role. It demoralized many South Africans that their country had become the world's polecat, a reality brought home by international sporting sanctions.

Throughout their tenure in power, the National Party government responded to the anti-apartheid movement with inefficient if often brutal repression. Popular insurrections were met with bullets and escalation of government repression. That, in turn, promoted increased violence in the townships, especially against those residents seen to have "sold out" to the apartheid regime. Nevertheless, apartheid South Africa never became a "totalitarian" state. Its judiciary retained some independence, and press censorship was clumsy and sporadic. Many of the most notorious human rights abuses were committed by out-of-control security operatives in the last years of apartheid, from which the government appears to have looked away rather than sponsored.

Nevertheless, public opinion in Western, democratic nations came to associate apartheid with official violence. European aid agencies and many private organizations increased their levels of funding for the liberation movements, though the Soviet bloc continued to provide the highest levels of international aid.

The apartheid structure entered a decadelong, fits-and-starts process of collapse in the 1980s. P. W. Botha (prime minister, 1978–1984, and subsequently president, 1984–1989) and F. W. de Klerk (president 1989–1994) unilaterally ended some aspects as confidence in apartheid ebbed. Pressure from the liberation movements also played a role. For example, in the aftermath of the Soweto riots, the regime backed away from requiring instruction in township schools to be in Afrikaans rather than the much more popular English. Western countries intensified a variety of economic and athletic sanctions against South Africa. For whites especially, exclusion from international sporting competitions was a bitter pill. Meanwhile, the UDF and other black and multiracial organizations fueled township unrest. Police stations along the borders of ungovernable townships were fortresses from which few ventured out.[57]

Whites gradually came to acquiesce to the National government of F. W. de Klerk's unbanning of the liberation movements in 1990 and the release of their imprisoned leaders, including Nelson Mandela, who already had iconic status. The collapse of the Soviet Union ended the pretense that apartheid was somehow a bulwark in southern Africa against communism and "atheism." F. W. de Klerk skillfully neutralized far-right Afrikaner opposition to compromise, taking advantage of the Soviet collapse and also of the successful transition to nonracial democracy in neighboring Namibia in 1990 that preserved white wealth. The Afrikaner "lunatic fringe" further discredited itself by its armed support of a 1994 attempted coup in the "independent homeland" of Bophuthatswana. Of the white politicians involved in the dismantling of apartheid and the move toward nonracial democracy, nearly all were Afrikaners. In part this reflected the historic exclusion or nonparticipation in politics by the "English" minority.

The political transition was negotiated by all parties from 1990 to 1993 at Kempton Park, a convention center near the Johannesburg airport. The process was called the Convention for a Democratic South Africa (CODESA).There were many ups and downs in the negotiations, which were sometimes set back by specific acts of violence, such as the murder of Chris Hani, a charismatic leader of the SACP. The most prominent negotiators were Cyril Ramaphosa for the liberation movements and Roelf Meyer for the National Party, but there was broad participation on both sides. The Inkatha Freedom Party (IFP), a cultural and political Zulu organization led by Mangosuthu Buthelezi and a rival of the ANC in KwaZulu, up to the last minute threatened to play a spoiler role. While the successful negotiations were the achievements of South Africans themselves and both Nelson Mandela and F. W. de Klerk were awarded Nobel Peace Prizes after their successful completion, the international community, especially the United States, played a facilitative role by politically supporting the process and making available constitutional and legal expertise when so requested.[58]

"Nonracial" Elections and Their Aftermath

South Africa's elections in 1994 were the culmination of the Kempton Park process. For the first time, there was no racially designated voter's roll. The poll resulted in a black majority government under President Nelson Mandela, but during a transition period there was substantial participation by the National Party and the IFP. De Klerk served as second deputy president until he resigned in 1996, while Mangosuthu Buthelezi was a cabinet minister until 2004. The transition arrangements, in effect, ended with de Klerk's resignation when the Mandela administration indicated that it would not extend the transition arrangements past the already fixed end date.

Under the new constitution, the state was somewhat decentralized, and newly created provinces enjoyed some authority. The last two white governments before the nonracial elections had privatized certain state-owned enterprises, and de Klerk dismantled South Africa's nuclear weapons capability with the support of the ANC, which had long opposed a South African nuclear weapons program. The National Party's rationale for nuclear weapons had disappeared with the collapse of the Soviet Union.

In anticipation of assuming power, the dominant wing of the ANC, led by Nelson Mandela, gradually abandoned socialism without altogether embracing free-market capitalism. The last Soviet government under Mikhail Gorbachev played a significant role in Mandela's and Thabo Mbeki's partial conversion to the free market. Foreign Minister Anatoly Adamishin told Mandela and Mbeki that communism was a disaster for the USSR and that the new South Africa should avoid it. While President George H. W. Bush and Secretary of State James Baker made the same points, the Soviets were particularly credible because of their long support for the ANC.[59]

Mandela's emphasis on racial reconciliation played a crucial role in assuaging fears and smoothing the path toward nonracial democracy. That was the theme of his presidency. From 1994 to 1999, he left most of the policy initiatives to Deputy President Thabo Mbeki. His administration was marked by the interim power-sharing arrangements and by the achievement of a permanent constitution. To the chagrin of Washington, Mandela maintained close relations with such international pariahs as Cuba's Fidel Castro and Libya's Muammar Gadhafi, both of whom had supported the ANC's anti-apartheid struggle.

AFTER MANDELA

Under Mandela's successors, Thabo Mbeki (1999–2008) and subsequently Jacob Zuma (2009–present), government policy tied South Africa closely to the global, liberal economic system, dubbed the Washington Consensus. The black majority government established Black Economic Empowerment (BEE), later expanded into Broad-Based Black Economic Empowerment (BBBEE), to redress the damages done by apartheid and to facilitate the participation of blacks and coloureds in the modern economy. But these policies did little for the majority of blacks mired in poverty and high unemployment within an environment of globalization and the slow decline of extractive industries. More important for the growth of the black middle class was accelerated access to employment in the public sector. The civil service became predominantly—though not exclusively—black, encouraged by a system of racial preferences. The ANC government significantly improved black housing and facilitated fee-simple ownership and access to water and electricity. (However, the expanded customer base also resulted in significant power shortages that, in turn, have set back economic growth.) In education there was limited progress in overcoming the heritage of apartheid. On the other hand, the already chronically inadequate health services for nonwhites went into free fall in the face of the HIV/AIDS epidemic, which the Mandela and Mbeki governments for too long largely ignored. More recently, however, the Zuma government has been fully engaged with significant assistance from the United States, and the progress in rebuilding the public health system has been dramatic.[60]

LESSONS

This overview of South Africa's history highlights some of the major realities that frame its present and its future. Perhaps the most important is the primacy of racial identification in political, social, and economic spheres, a result of centuries of white supremacy. But, among all races, there are also enduring fissures based on language, ethnic identification, and social class.

Second, since the post–Boer War political settlement, government has operated as an institution limited by law. Unlike nearly all other African states, South Africa had been a democracy, if only for white males, for almost three generations by the time of its 1994 nonracial elections. The struggle against apartheid and the coming of nonracial elections extended democracy to the hitherto excluded parts of the population. But a democratic culture based on law already existed, and it did not have to be created out of whole cloth. Apartheid was established by law, and it was dismantled largely by means of the law.

Third, there is a modern economy—Africa's most advanced.[61] But the benefits accrue largely to whites and to those who are directly linked to the government. Economic growth since the transition has been insufficient to transform the conditions in which most South Africans live.

Fourth, the past century has been characterized by political deals that have averted a seemingly inevitable catastrophe. The English and the Afrikaners came to terms in 1910–1911, at the expense of the other racial groups, with economic power going to the English and political power to the Afrikaners. The successful 1990–1994 negotiations at Kempton Park that led to the transition to nonracial democracy were based on recognition by the liberation movements that they could not overthrow the state and by the National Party that the state could not continue as it had been. The resulting bargain was a constitutional framework that was democratic and based on the rule of law, and that provided extensive protection for individual human rights, including property rights. The "final" constitution, following the liberal principles and human rights protections agreed upon at Kempton Park, went into effect in 1997. The bottom line was a shift of political power to the black majority while the white minority retained its economic power in the framework of the rule of law. South Africa became a predominantly black state with a mostly black government characterized by the rule of law, but one in which white economic privileges are largely preserved for now.

3

TWO INAUGURATIONS AND A FUNERAL

The May 10, 1994, inauguration of Nelson Mandela as the first president of a nonracial, or, more properly, "all races," South Africa focused the soaring hopes of its citizens for a new and just national dispensation. It also captured the imagination of the broader international community. Nelson Mandela's inauguration day made concrete for millions at home and abroad that abstraction, "a peaceful transition to nonracial democracy." Apartheid's nightmare of institutionalized white supremacy based on overt racism maintained through episodic but often egregious violations of human rights was finally over. So, too, for the time being, was anxiety over the possibility of a bloody race war.

While the political deal making that produced the transition occurred in the context of much black-on-black bloodshed, South Africans and international observers largely ignored or downplayed it because white victims were minuscule in number and the country had dodged the widely expected race war that would have pitted blacks against whites.[1] However, one credible estimate is that fourteen thousand people died violently in political unrest during the formal transition's last act, between February 11, 1990, when Mandela was released from prison, and May 10, 1994, when he was inaugurated president.[2] Nearly all of those were killed in a virtual civil war in KwaZulu-Natal between the African National Congress (ANC) and the Inkatha Freedom Party (IFP), the Zulu political and cultural organization.[3] The handful of white victims nationwide did receive extensive media attention. Not so for most of the black victims. If a race war was avoided, the "peaceful" transition was much less peaceful than it is often portrayed.

INAUGURATION I: PARADISE

Despite the violence leading up to the 1994 elections, at home and abroad, the new South Africa promised a democracy free from the scourge of racism and with elaborate protections for human rights, first under an interim constitution negotiated as part of the transition and then subsequently by the "final" constitution that remains in force today. The new South Africa had been achieved through negotiation between the apartheid-era National Party government and the liberation movements. The goal was no losers, only winners, and, for the moment, the success of that process produced a euphoric sense of national unity that transcended the country's historic racial, ethnic, and class divisions. In his inauguration speech, Nelson Mandela said, "We understand it still that there is no easy road to freedom. We know it well that none of us acting alone can achieve success. We must therefore act together as a united people, for national reconciliation, for nation building, for the birth of a new world."[4] Archbishop Desmond Tutu, the Anglican archbishop of Cape Town, caught the popular mood when he said, "We are the rainbow people of God! We are unstoppable!"[5]

The largely unchallenged assumption was that the "rainbow nation" had transcended its dark history. The idealistic if unrealistic assumption in South Africa was that nonracial democracy would attract sufficient foreign direct investment to transform the economy and end the pervasive poverty of the black majority.

Mandela's inauguration ceremony took place on the lawn in front of the Union Buildings in Pretoria, the seat of South Africa's executive (the parliament is in Cape Town; the Supreme Court is in Bloemfontein). The Union Buildings, Sir Herbert Baker's magnificent imperial confection (he also helped design the new imperial capital of New Delhi), provided a suitable backdrop for the pomp and circumstance. A *sangoma* (traditional healer) participated. There were traditional praise singers from Mandela's native Eastern Cape. The oath was administered by a white, Afrikaner justice. There was a flyover by jets of the South African air force, thereby signifying to the crowd the subordination of the military to the new, "nonracial" dispensation. Six thousand official guests included dignitaries from 140 countries, and 60,000 others assembled on the lawn at the base of the Union Buildings. They were a kaleidoscope of celebrities and the merely famous, not just of South Africa but from all over the world. They ranged from numerous African heads of state including Libya's Muammar Gadhafi; Vice President Al Gore; First Lady Hillary Clinton; Betty Shabazz, widow of American civil rights activist and martyr Malcolm X; and Anglican archbishop Trevor Huddleston from the monastic Mirfield Community of the Resurrection in Yorkshire (he had been a major anti-apartheid activist). Ladies hatted-and-gloved as though for a garden party or Pucci'd-and-Gucci'd for cocktails mixed with traditional rulers in long robes.[6] Such was the good feeling among the crowd that outgoing president F. W. de Klerk, an implacable anticommunist, was seen shaking hands with Fidel Castro.

Eleven jets belonging to visiting chiefs of state were parked at the airport. The U.S. delegation was transported around town in American limousines flown in for the occasion.

Then-president of Ireland Mary Robinson recalled the ceremony eighteen years later: "Everything about it was special: the taking of the oath by the country's beloved Mandela, the rows upon rows of South Africans of all races singing as one, and the military fly-past and salute that caused a huge, visceral roar from the crowd below."[7]

The morning after, as mandated by the country's political settlement, President Mandela convened his new government that included the leaders of all three of the principal political parties. The first deputy president was Thabo Mbeki, a longtime leader of the ANC in exile, and later the 1999 successor to Mandela as president. Outgoing president F. W. de Klerk from the National Party that had been the originator of apartheid and the voice of most of the Afrikaners was second deputy president. Mangosuthu Buthelezi, the head of the Zulu IFP that had battled the ANC in KwaZulu-Natal, was in the cabinet as the minister of home affairs. His participation marked the end of the civil war in KwaZulu-Natal.

Of course, the majority of the cabinet came from the ANC, which had won about two-thirds of the popular vote in credible elections the previous month. The ANC under Mandela's leadership emphasized that it was nonracial, even if its electoral support was overwhelmingly black. ANC ministers included asians, coloureds, and whites as well as blacks.

There was at this moment a spirit of reconciliation between former enemies, seeing each other, perhaps for the first time, as fellow human beings despite ethnic and religious divisions. The special quality of that spirit was captured by Archbishop Tutu: "Forgiving is not forgetting; it is actually remembering—remembering, not using your right to hit back. It is a second chance for a new beginning. And the remembering part is particularly important. Especially if you don't want to repeat what happened."[8]

In the weeks following the inauguration, South Africa rejoined the Commonwealth of Nations in a glittering ceremony at Westminster Abbey in the presence of Queen Elizabeth II. South Africa became once again a full participant in the United Nations and was elected promptly to one of the rotating seats on the Security Council. International anti-apartheid sanctions were dismantled, though how quickly depended on the political entity that had imposed them. In the United States, for example, most federal trade and investment sanctions were quickly removed; but, for procedural reasons, it often took much longer for state and local governments to do so.[9]

Mandela and others pursued a policy of racial reconciliation. Mandela shrewdly used the politics of symbolism. In 1995, the South African Springboks defeated the New Zealand All Blacks for the world rugby championship. Rugby is a white sport in South Africa, and the Springboks register included a sole coloured player—no blacks. Nevertheless, President Mandela presented the trophy to the team wearing the jersey of the Springboks captain, Francois Pinaar. The predominantly Afrikaner crowd went wild with adulation at the president's appearance.[10] Nelson Mandela and rugby had bridged the chasm between Afrikaners and a "nonracial" South Africa. A few white supremacists remained, but by the time of the Springbok victory, most whites had accepted the new nonracial democracy.

Nevertheless, in 1994, few whites saw apartheid as a "crime against humanity." Instead, for many of them, it was a system that had not worked, not a system that was a methodical attack on human dignity. However, twenty years later, polling data show that a majority of whites now accept the "crime against humanity" designation.[11]

It was morning in South Africa, without clouds. For the moment, nobody wanted to be anywhere else. Many talented black, coloured, and asian professionals who had pursued successful careers abroad free of the constraints of apartheid came home, often encouraged by an imaginative UN program that provided a temporary bridge between their high salaries abroad and the lower ones payable in South Africa. Many whites who had left because of distaste for apartheid and mandatory military conscription also came back.[12]

The transition to nonracial democracy, the administration of Nelson Mandela with its emphasis on reconciliation, and subsequently a "final" constitution with its thoroughgoing protection of human rights drew on and reflected the spirit of the Enlightenment and the universality of humankind, much as had the American Declaration of Independence, the subsequent Constitution of 1789, and the French Declaration of the Rights of Man in the same year. The focus on human rights is a tribute to the leadership of the ANC shaped by some of the lawyers who had defended Mandela at the Rivonia Trial in 1963–1964, as well as constitutional experts from a variety of backgrounds and places, including the United States. Its human rights provisions provide the basis for gay marriage, the right to abortion, and the elimination of the death penalty. All were unpopular among the ANC's core constituency at the time and have remained so. Yet the constitution seems sacrosanct enough that the ANC has made no serious move to eliminate those provisions, even when it has had the necessary support in parliament to do so.

If the civil rights revolution in the United States was stalled by the persistence of racial discrimination, black poverty, and lack of a political consensus about what to do, South Africa seemed to point the way forward toward a democracy free of racism. From that perspective, especially in the West, the transition belonged to all humanity, not just South Africans. But the worm in the apple was the persistence of poverty, largely defined by race, and a hitherto autarkic economy now challenged by globalization and pushed into conformity with the liberal economic theories of the Washington Consensus. The post-1994 economy grew fast in statistical terms, but not fast enough to sop up unemployment, which only seemed to increase.

INAUGURATION 2: PARADISE LOST

Mountaintop experiences do not last forever.

The atmosphere was different in 2009, fifteen years after Jacob Zuma was inaugurated as South Africa's fourth president (Thabo Mbeki served as president from 1999 to 2008, and Kgalema Motlanthe was acting president from 2008 to 2009). There were nevertheless similarities with the Mandela inauguration, such as the flyover by South African air force jets and the presence of Mandela and Mbeki. The former was by then an elderly icon, the latter a politician discredited at the hands of Zuma himself. Official guests numbered five thousand, about the same as at Mandela's. The crowd, at thirty thousand, was about half the size of that at Mandela's inauguration. The cost of the event was estimated at USD 9 million (it would have occurred to few even to ask how much Mandela's cost). Unlike 1994, all of the heads of state present were African, and included Zimbabwe's Robert Mugabe and Libya's Muammar Gadhafi. If Mandela's inauguration had been the "event of the decade," Zuma's was at most the "event of the week."

Rather than drawing on the universal themes of the Enlightenment, Zuma's ceremony was African, even specifically Zulu in tone, with less of the universality and inclusiveness of Mandela's. The hatted-and-gloved and the Gucci'd-and-Pucci'd were scarce, while African traditional dress could be seen in abundance. Zuma himself, openly a polygamist, was escorted only by his senior wife.

Zuma's administration, like Mandela's and that of his successor, Thabo Mbeki, was dominated by the ANC. However, because of proportional representation, there were some junior members of the cabinet from other parties—though not from the Democratic Alliance (DA), the official opposition.[13] Power-sharing provisions of Mandela's transitional administration had expired or had been repealed. Zuma's government was that of the ANC, and it was mostly—though not entirely—black in its composition. Unlike Mandela's first cabinet, there was no particular effort to be inclusive of the many strains that make up South Africa. Indeed, Zulus appeared particularly dominant, with Zuma and Blade Nzimande, the general secretary of the allied South African Communist Party, being part of that ethnic group. (The current president of the Congress of South African Trade Unions [COSATU], Sdumo Dlamini, and Nkosazana Dlamini-Zuma, chair of the African Union Commission and Zuma's ex-wife, are both Zulu.)[14]

Mandela had been trained as a lawyer and was one of the earliest black South Africans to be admitted to the bar. Subsequently, he followed a highly disciplined regime of self-education while imprisoned on Robben Island, including correspondence courses through the University of South Africa, an "open university," in his later years of imprisonment. Mandela had supported personally as his successor the highly sophisticated Cyril Ramaphosa. Mandela, however, deferred to majority opinion within the ANC and accepted their choice in Thabo Mbeki.

Mbeki had been educated abroad, at the University of Sussex, and later received military training in the Soviet Union. In contrast to Mandela's aristocratic, Xhosa bearing, Mbeki's mannerisms and dress were those of a British intellectual. He favored tweeds and expensive Scotch whiskey. He was criticized within the ANC for being too distant from township dwellers, an ANC core constituency. Nevertheless, despite their differences, Mandela and Mbeki shared good educations and sophisticated and cosmopolitan outlooks.

Unlike Mandela and Mbeki, Zuma had little formal education and served as an ANC counterintelligence operative in the bush during the liberation struggle. While he could be charming, there is little of the cosmopolitan in his personality. With a street fighter's pugnaciousness, his political skills are formidable. As president, he cultivates a brand of Afro-populism, wearing a traditional Zulu leopard skin, practicing polygamy, and often using the Zulu language. However, he makes most of his speeches in English when he is addressing the nation as a whole. He knows when to change his image if it is to his advantage. During the 1994 transition negotiations, when he called on the American ambassador, he appeared in three-piece suits.

Some fifteen years separate the Mandela and Zuma inaugurations. Institutionally, that was a period of legal and political consolidation; all-race democracy conducted according to the rule of law is probably stronger under Zuma than it had been under Mandela, not least because it now has a record of practice and success. Indeed, "democracy" has displaced "apartheid" as the primary characteristic of the state. The economy was transformed from an autarky solely benefiting a racial minority into one characterized by free markets and globalization. With the reincorporation of the homelands into South Africa, the population appeared to increase rapidly. Black unemployment was probably higher in 2014 than it had been in 1994. The rate of population growth is now about 1.6 percent, while the economy continues to grow at about 2 percent.[15]

The black majority determines the government through universal suffrage, and the striking lack of economic and social progress for blacks impels the ANC toward becoming more "African" in its rhetoric, its symbols, and its organization by patronage/clientage networks. That in turn makes South Africa less exceptional in Africa now than it was under President Mandela. Looking over their shoulders at the large postcolonial African states north of the Kalahari Desert feeds anxiety, especially among whites and those outside the ANC, about whether South Africa's democratic institutions can withstand populist pressure for dramatic social and economic change. Many South Africans cite pervasive corruption, declining quality of government services, and a bloated public sector as evidence that the country is becoming more like its neighbors. On the other hand, slower black population growth reflects the growing rate of urbanization among blacks; higher levels of education, especially among women; and a decline in levels of absolute poverty.

If virtually nobody wanted to leave South Africa on Mandela's inauguration day, polling data in 2008 showed that the percentage of each racial group that would emigrate now if possible is high: 42 percent of coloureds, 38 percent of blacks, 30 percent of asians, and 41 percent of whites.[16] Many whites because of their relative wealth have the means to leave, and "white flight" is widely assumed; in fact, however, the white population is slightly larger in number in 2014 than it was in 1994, though it is a smaller percentage of the nation's population as a whole.[17]

The coming of nonracial democracy marked by Mandela's inauguration was a historic turning point in governance. But South Africa's current social and economic realities—with poverty declining only slowly and blatant racial inequality as salient as in the apartheid past—are the product of a historical trajectory that is hard to change. South Africa remains, in the words of Mamphela Ramphele, "a nation of wounded people."[18]

A FUNERAL: PARADISE REMEMBERED,
BUT NOT REGAINED

Nelson Mandela died on December 5, 2013, at his home in Houghton, an apartheid-era, leafy, once whites-only suburb of Johannesburg that had been the constituency of the anti-apartheid activist Helen Suzman. He was ninety-five. Though constitutionally entitled to do so, he had declined to run for a second term in 1999. After retirement, he devoted much of his energy to charitable work focused on the two foundations he had established. In 2004, he "retired from retirement" and thereafter avoided the public eye. If for the previous nine years he had become more distant from the South African people, his decline and death seemed to bring him back—if only for the moment—along with the spirit of the 1994 mountaintop. If de Klerk had shaken hands with Castro in 1994, President Barack Obama, at Mandela's state memorial service, did the same with Castro's successor, his brother Raul.

Heads of state in attendance at Mandela's funeral exceeded in numbers those of John F. Kennedy and Pope John Paul II.[19] At Mandela's 1994 inauguration, the United States had been represented by Vice President Al Gore, First Lady Hillary Clinton, and a large congressional delegation. At his funeral, both President Obama and First Lady Michelle Obama were present, again transported to events in armored limousines flown in from Washington. Also part of the American delegation were former presidents Jimmy Carter, Bill Clinton, and George W. Bush. Memories stirred by the funeral reignited American enthusiasm, but the focus was on Mandela the man, not the South African experiment in nonracial democracy. Nevertheless, if not the "event of the decade," as his inauguration had been, Nelson Mandela's funeral was the "event of the year"—at least in Africa.

The inauguration of Nelson Mandela in 1994 had been skillful in its marshaling of inclusive symbolism and well organized in its logistics. Not so the Mandela state funeral. The First National Bank (FNB) stadium in Soweto where the state memorial took place was only half full, with fewer working-class South Africans present than anticipated.[20] The government failed to make the day a public holiday, apparently through oversight, and made no provision for additional transport from central Johannesburg to the FNB stadium. The ANC appeared to have organized transport for many of those who did make it. Many ANC speakers at the ceremony were overtly political, urging ANC votes in the 2015 elections as a fitting tribute to Mandela.[21] Then there was the strange episode involving a sign-language interpreter who did not know how to sign and subsequently claimed to be schizophrenic. He was steps away from the visiting heads of state, including President Obama, raising questions about the efficacy of South African security arrangements.

Astonishingly, the crowd that did make it to the stadium booed President Jacob Zuma. According to a local news channel, "the large monitors in the stadium were turned off to stop the boos every time a camera rested on Zuma." As the crowd appeared to be heavily ANC in affiliation, the booing was taken as an indication of Zuma's unpopularity with the party's rank and file.

The crowd cheered almost everybody else who has played a major role in post-apartheid South Africa: former chief of state Thabo Mbeki, whom Zuma defeated for ANC party leader in 2008; Kgalema Motlanthe, also defeated by Zuma in a contest for ANC party leadership earlier in the year; Winnie Mandela, Nelson Mandela's former wife and Zuma's critic from the left; George Bizos, Mandela's lawyer; Graca Machel, Mandela's widow, who kissed Winnie Mandela; and even F. W. de Klerk, the last white president of South Africa. The loudest cheers of all were for President Barack Obama and for Zimbabwe's Robert Mugabe.

A few days later, there was a smaller ceremony in Mandela's home village of Qunu where he was interred. For months the South African press had been reporting on a division in Mandela's extended family as to where the patriarch should be buried. At base the quarrel appeared to outsiders to be about who the keeper of the flame would be after the former president's death. It was also anticipated that the burial site would become a place of pilgrimage, generating significant revenue for the locality. In the end, the family came together on the location of the burial site, and relations appeared to be harmonious, at least in public.

The funeral was a mixture of traditional African and Methodist Christian rites. As mandated by Xhosa tradition, a bull was sacrificed to accompany the former president on his last journey. Though most of the leaders of the ANC were present, it was much less of a formal, state occasion than the event at the FNB stadium had been, and foreign dignitaries were not encouraged to attend. However, the Prince of Wales and Oprah Winfrey were present. Not so for most of the Qunu villagers, who watched the service on television, as did most South Africans. Even (now retired) Anglican archbishop Desmond Tutu was at first not invited to the Qunu ceremony. The Zuma administration later claimed this was an oversight.

Some Methodists in South Africa and the United States sought to claim Mandela as one of their own after his death. Mandela was educated at Methodist institutions, and his third wife, Graca Machel, is a Methodist laywoman. She and Mandela were married in a Methodist ceremony, assisted by Archbishop Desmond Tutu and following a blessing by a rabbi.[22] In keeping with his emphasis on inclusion rather than exclusion as chief of state, Mandela never paraded his religious beliefs or his denominational affiliation, if he had any. Like most South Africans, he readily used religious, even Christian, rhetoric. But he had also been a member of the Communist Party and the Central Committee at one stage of his struggle against apartheid.

The boos directed toward Zuma at the FNB stadium demonstrated clearly that South Africa is a free country with its absolute, constitutional guarantees of freedom of speech. The crowd's anger may have reflected dissatisfaction with service delivery in the townships. That was the conventional analysis at the time. However, it is at least as likely that the boos reflected the yawning gap between the Mandela vision being celebrated at the event and the Zuma reality. Mandela was being remembered for his integrity and his all-inclusive leadership. Everybody knew that Mandela left office after one term as chief of state, almost alone among African leaders. His lifestyle in retirement, while appropriate for a former chief of state, was not lavish. Methodist bishop Ivan Abrahams captured the mood of the crowd when he stated that "what brings us here today is not so much grief but love." ANC efforts to turn the funeral into a campaign rally were widely disliked, including by many ANC stalwarts.

In his later years, Mandela's personal life had been beyond reproach.[23] His divorce from Winnie Mandela six years after he left prison resulted from her personal and public misbehavior.[24] Though she remained popular in the townships, divorce did nothing to diminish Nelson Mandela's reputation, even among evangelical and increasingly Pentecostal blacks. His marriage to Graca Machel, the widow of the former head of state of Mozambique, was encouraged by Archbishop

Tutu and was very popular. South Africans regarded her behavior as the Mozambican wife of the national icon as impeccable.[25]

Zuma, by contrast, has faced rape charges, is still subject to an ongoing judicial procedure involving his alleged corruption, and is credibly accused of authorizing the spending of large amounts of public money on his private compound, Nkandla, in Zululand, much of which is ostensibly for "security." How much public money is spent to maintain his multiple wives is a contentious issue. His government is also perceived in some quarters as Zulu dominated, and he apparently has displaced the Xhosas, the ethnic group of Mandela, Mbeki, and other leaders of the anti-apartheid struggle. Moeletsi Mbeki, brother of Thabo and known for the independence of his views, told the British Broadcasting Corporation that "he wasn't surprised by the crowd's actions" at the funeral. "South Africans expect their leaders to keep to the straight and narrow, and would take whatever chance they had to tell them when they didn't."[26]

Mandela's funeral highlighted that the country was a new South Africa, if not meeting the ideal hoped for in 1994. The booing of a sitting president at a state funeral without retribution was a reminder of the strength of South African liberties. If Zuma is no Mandela, his South Africa is no authoritarian state of the African "big man" model. In that sense, South Africa remains as truly exceptional as it was in 1994, and, for now, "the rainbow nation" has indeed transcended its dark history.

Reflecting his own broad spirit, and also the practical advice he received from Mozambican icon and chief of state Samora Machel, Mandela encouraged whites not only to stay in South Africa but to actively participate in national life. An urban legend that rings true is that Machel told Mandela that if the liberation movement drove the whites out, the economy would collapse, and the black majority would suffer more than anybody else. Whites continue to be active in national politics, especially in the opposition DA. The ANC also continues to employ white ministers, albeit in reduced percentages since Mandela's administration. But South Africa is no Malaysia, where the rich Chinese minority is tolerated but at the price of their exclusion from national politics.

However, Zuma's administration is increasingly narrow, dominated by Zulus, displacing the Xhosas, and with shrinking numbers of whites and asians. ANC-dominated local authorities' wholesale abolition of Afrikaner place-names and their replacement with those of various African languages undermines the inclusiveness of Mandela's vision. The Zuma administration's increasingly "African" style in a multiracial country where available investment capital is largely in white hands also has practical consequences: whites, especially Afrikaners, appear increasingly unwilling to invest locally.

Mandela's formal policy of racial reconciliation was not repudiated by Thabo Mbeki and Jacob Zuma, and it is a basis for Zimbabwe president Robert Mugabe's criticism that Mandela cared more about whites than blacks. Julius Malema, the youthful firebrand now expelled from the ANC, makes the same criticism as Mugabe. Accordingly it is no surprise that Mandela's death led to an upsurge of anxiety among whites, many of whom were visible participants in the national mourning.

By the time he died, Mandela had been absent from South African politics and ANC party matters for many years. There have been a few signs that the ANC mainstream seeks to change course with respect to racial reconciliation. The "Africanists" in the ANC and elsewhere increasingly use antiwhite rhetoric. However, instead of destroying the white-dominated economic establishment, the black oligarchs of the ANC seek to join it. A significant number of them have done so. But, what about the millions still trapped in poverty in the townships and in rural areas? Up until now they have been relatively voiceless, or their leadership, including Winnie Mandela and Julius Malema, has been largely self-serving and irresponsible. But high levels of poverty and a lack of economic opportunity mean that prosperity for the majority of South Africans remains only an aspiration for most blacks in post-Mandela South Africa.

4

THE BENCHMARK

Where Is South Africa after "Nonracial Democracy"?

May 10, 2015, marked the twenty-first anniversary of Nelson Mandela's inauguration as president of post-apartheid South Africa. What has changed during those two decades? The African National Congress (ANC) 2014 election campaign materials took pride in the claimed three million housing units built since it came into office. Though the quality of the housing is poor and much of it is far from places of employment, it is significantly better than the shacks it replaced. Government policy, incompletely implemented, is to hand over the houses to its occupants, who eventually will enjoy fee-simple ownership of them. In 1994, about half of all households had access to electricity; in 2014, that had increased to 85 percent, though all income classes are subject to power shortages. More than 90 percent of the population now have access to potable water. All-race access to educational opportunities has expanded, even if the transformation of apartheid-era "Bantu education" has been painfully slow.

Blacks now make up a significant part of the middle class. According to a report by Goldman Sachs, the black proportion of the middle class has grown from 7 percent in 1993 to 14 percent in 2008; while whites were 81 percent of the middle class in 1993, they were 67 percent in 2008. It should be noted that the black increase reflects the overall growth in the size of the middle class; by and large, it was not at the "expense" of whites.[1]

The mass of South Africans, not just the elites, now have a higher standard of living than in other large African countries. This mostly reflects the growth of the economy rather than redistribution from one race or class to another.[2] Gross national income (GNI) has grown from USD 142.5 billion in 1993 to USD 349.82 billion in 2015. However, the number of recipients of welfare grants has grown from an estimated 4 million in 1994 to 16.3 million in 2015. This does represent a redistribution from income and other taxpayers to those who usually only pay sales tax—value-added tax (VAT).[3]

Legal segregation is entirely dismantled, and government institutions are racially integrated. Government personnel directly serving the public reflect South African demographics. The same is true of the media. If the ownership remains mostly white, the presenters are largely black. Racial identities remain paramount. At the same time, however, popular attitudes are undergoing an evolution toward the values of nonracial democracy, which potentially provides an additional bulwark for the rule of law. However, for now, the process remains incomplete.

One of the governance challenges remains the overlap between the ANC and the state and the extent to which the former is still evolving from a liberation movement into a political party. Jacob Zuma and other ANC leaders sometimes resort to populist, antiwhite, and antiforeign appeals in the face of the unaddressed poverty of its core constituency. Poverty potentially generates anger that could become a threat to the human rights guarantees and the rule of law enshrined in the constitution. As elsewhere in Africa, the quality of political leadership remains a wildcard in South Africa's future. Arguably it has steadily declined, with the Zuma administration weaker than Mbeki's and Mbeki's weaker than Mandela's. South African democracy and maintenance of the rule of law is ever more dependent on the strength of the institutions put into place at the time of the transition, rather than the personalities of the country's leaders. From the perspective of state building, this is a positive development, even if it results in anxiety in the short term.

Obviously a South African's racial identity is not the sole determinant of whether he or she will live a long life and do well. But it is a powerful driver, and after a history of white supremacy culminating in apartheid, racial identity remains central to the personal destinies of most South Africans and also to the way they see themselves and others. Demographic surveys show that in terms of life span, education, economic opportunity, and disease burden, the future of white infants is much brighter than those who are coloured or black.

RACE—AGAIN

In today's South Africa, it is a commonplace that class is replacing race as the principal divider of South Africans. According to a credible survey in 2012, one in four South Africans cited the gap between rich and poor as the most important fault line, while only 13 percent identified race.[4] Archbishop Tutu captured the vision of post-apartheid, nonracial South Africa's change from even the recent past: "When you think for instance we had something called the Immorality Act and the Mixed Marriage Act that said no to any intimate relationship between whites and people of other races, and I mean you look around and you . . . see mixed couples walking hand in hand, or more often they are in a clinch, you wouldn't get a razor blade between them."[5]

Indeed, there are a few well-known interracial couples in South Africa today, such as Matthew Booth, a now-retired, white soccer player for Ajax Cape Town, and his wife, Sonia Bonneventia, a black international model. (Soccer is a "black" sport, and Booth was at one time the only white player on the South Africa national team.) The leader of the official opposition, the Democratic Alliance (DA), Mmusi Maimane, is married to a white woman. Like Archbishop Tutu, many South Africans hopeful about the future cite interracial marriage as evidence that the country is overcoming its racist, segregationist legacy. But, notwithstanding the examples of Booth and Maimane, interracial marriage involving whites is rare.

Observers also often cite the emergence of the black middle class and the few high-profile black oligarchs as evidence of twenty years of progress. Their visibility and the black presence at formerly segregated institutions and public accommodations would have been almost unimaginable a generation ago, just as it would have been in the southern states of the United States. The multiracial public presence is a new reality different from apartheid South Africa, enhancing black self-esteem and helping shape how South Africans see each other. Nevertheless, the reality remains that 41.9 percent of blacks continue to live below the national poverty line.[6] Race no longer rigidly determines the opportunities available to a South African child. But, for most blacks, opportunities remain far more limited than for most whites. However, the anger of the marginalized is directed at least as much against those blacks who have become privileged as against whites.

RACIAL DEFINITIONS

Under apartheid, race was defined by law and regulation. It still is. Since 2006, the Ministry of Labor has required private companies above a certain size to classify their employees by race using the former apartheid categories—white, coloured, black, and asian. The purpose was the implementation of Black Economic Empowerment (BEE), now called Broad-Based Black Economic Empowerment (BBBEE), a type of affirmative action for those disadvantaged under apartheid. The ministry required the employee to affirm his racial identity. If he refused to do so, and some did, seeing the question as a throwback to apartheid, then it was the employer who was required to make the classification using the apartheid categories.

Persons of all races are to be found all over the country. Even the most expensive "white" suburbs have a large number of resident black domestic workers, and in the predominantly black rural areas, there are usually a few white farmers. An "Afrikaner homeland," Orania, is exclusively white, with ten thousand "supporters" but an unknown number of residents, all of whom must speak Afrikaans. Its purpose would appear to be the preservation of Afrikaner culture rather than isolation from contact with nonwhites.

RACE AND CLASS

The post-apartheid reality is that race and class remain inextricably linked, just as they do in the United States. Many, perhaps most, South Africans confine their contact with other races to the public sphere, especially their workplace. There is little interaction in private residences. In the public sphere such as church services, theaters, and shopping malls, racial integration has indeed increased. Nevertheless, survey data indicate that South Africans of all age groups and races "felt non-racialism and greater integration were an unlikely prospect for 'their generation.'"[7] Despite Archbishop Tutu's observations on love across racial boundaries, interracial marriage remains rare, ranging from 1 to 4 percent of South Africans under the age of thirty-five depending on the racial group.[8] Among South African whites, it is perhaps 2 percent. In the United States, 3.9 percent of married couples were interracial in 2008, according to the U.S. Bureau of the Census, and white interracial marriage was substantially less than that of Hispanics, blacks, or Asians. Only 2.1 percent of married white women and 2.3 percent of married white men were in an interracial marriage.[9]

The reality is that most South Africans live in separate, remarkably unconnected spheres and come together primarily at the workplace. For example, a credible survey in 2012 found that 43.5 percent of South Africans rarely or never speak to someone of another race. Only about half interact with persons of a different race "always or often" on weekdays, and only 17.8 percent "always or often" have social, rather than work-related, contact with people of other races. More than half "rarely or never" socialize with persons of other races.[10] In South Africa, as in the United States, racial interaction does increase with movement up the socioeconomic scale; the black middle class perforce interacts with other races, not least because whites continue to dominate the economy. Many of those who rarely speak to a person of another race are rural or township dwellers with limited mobility and where few if any persons of a different race are present. However, if many blacks interact little with other races, nearly all whites and asians do, not least because most service personnel are black.

For the present, race is the overwhelming predictor of voting behavior.[11] Despite its historical all-race character, most of the governing ANC's electoral support comes from blacks, and the party is recruiting few new leaders from the other races; indeed, its leadership is increasingly drawn from a single black ethnic group, the Zulus. The opposition Democratic Alliance (DA) is the party of choice of most whites and coloureds. It is seeking black supporters, especially from the black middle class, and is recruiting high-profile nonwhite leadership. It remains to be seen whether this will translate into a DA electoral advantage, though based on the 2014 elections, the trend is positive. In general, younger persons of all races are less likely than older ones to participate in party politics.[12]

What of the "born frees," those nonwhite South Africans born after 1994? The term is usually applied to those nonwhites who are already middle class and, it is thought, may be less burdened by apartheid than their parents. They are a focus of media interest rather like the U.S. fascination with "millennials." The DA sees them as a target of opportunity. It remains to be seen what their electoral behavior will be. Some observers, however, think they may account for the DA's increase in black support.

SOUTH AFRICAN SOCIAL STATISTICS

South Africa's official statistics and those generated by nongovernmental organizations, while hardly flawless, are the best in Africa.[13] Statistics South Africa produces the country's official statistics, and the analysis of them by the South African Institute of Race Relations and other nongovernmental organizations provides the most complete picture of any country in sub-Saharan Africa. They are a starting point for consideration of the current state of the ambiguous transition from apartheid to democracy.[14] Taken together, they provide a credible picture of the major South African racial groups, where they live, and the extent to which they are thriving. Nevertheless, in many cases, they should be taken as indicative of the reality they purport to describe, not as definitive.

Statistics that are readily available are a window into important realities, but they are not necessarily comprehensive. For example, they say little about the persistence and evolution of racial identities, though they certainly chart their consequences. Nor do they tell us much about the religious revival that is sweeping the country, especially in evangelical, Pentecostal, and "African" forms. (Both President Zuma and DA leader Mmusi Maimane are sometime preachers.) Statistics are silent on the growing culture of corruption, now a major preoccupation of South African civil organizations and the media, but they do indicate that South Africans perceive that it is growing. They do not measure the degree to which South Africans regard themselves to be free and active participants in a democratic polity, though they do measure voter participation, from which it can be inferred. Statistics measure best the realities that lend themselves to quantification. Recognizing their limitations, their use is a step toward an understanding of post-apartheid South Africa.

POPULATION

According to the official Statistics South Africa, the country's population in 2014 was 54,001,953. In 1995, less than a year after the coming of nonracial democracy, the population was 41,150,000.[15] Three other sub-Saharan African countries had larger populations: Nigeria, Ethiopia, and the Democratic Republic of the Congo (DRC), as table 4.1 shows.

A half century after UK prime minister Harold Macmillan announced the end of colonialism in his 1960 speech in Cape Town, South Africa is the only large multiracial country remaining in sub-Saharan Africa. Racial, if not ethnic, diversity in sub-Saharan Africa is now rare. In Kenya, another country of high-profile European settlement as late as the aftermath of World War II, the Arab, Asian, and European populations combined are less than 1 percent of the total.[16] Zimbabwe was also once an important venue of colonial settlement, also especially after World War II. Now the population is more than 98 percent black, with about twenty thousand "settlers" left, mostly of British descent.[17] Namibia's population is about 6 percent white, 6 percent coloured, and 87.5 percent black, but its total population is only 2,182,852.[18] Mauritius, with 1,286,051, and Seychelles, with 85,000, are also multiracial, but with very small populations and different histories and political economies than continental Africa.[19]

Table 4.1.   Populations of Select Sub-Saharan African Countries, 2014

Country	Population
Nigeria	177,155,754
Ethiopia	96,633,458
Democratic Republic of the Congo	77,433,744
South Africa	54,001,953

URBANIZATION

South Africa is urbanizing at a steady rate. In 2000, 56.9 percent of the population was urban. As of 2013, the urban population was 62.9 percent, comparable to Ireland, Japan, and neighboring Botswana. As table 4.2 shows, of the four sub-Saharan African nations with the largest populations (Nigeria, Ethiopia, the Democratic Republic of the Congo, and South Africa), South Africa is the most urbanized.[20]

Urbanization in South Africa is also accompanied by intraprovincial population shifts. All of South Africa's provinces have gained population since 1994, but Gauteng (Johannesburg) and the Western Cape (Cape Town) have had a larger increase. The city of Durban has also grown, but its province of Natal has not grown as rapidly as Gauteng and the Western Cape. Nevertheless, in effect, Gauteng, the Western Cape, and Durban, the centers of the modern economy and of entrepreneurship, are pulling ahead of the rest of the country.[21]

By 2014, Gauteng and Western Cape included 35.2 percent of the country's population.[22] KwaZulu-Natal would add an additional 19.8 percent, though much of that province's population is in the former "self-governing" homeland of KwaZulu and is rural; nevertheless, the three provinces that host Johannesburg, Pretoria, Cape Town, and Durban account for more than half of the country's population.

From 2000 to 2013, the populations of the four cities increased by 12 to 15 percent, with Johannesburg having the highest rate of growth. Moreover, their black populations increased by between 30.2 and 79.6 percent, with Cape Town, formerly mostly closed to blacks under apartheid, having the largest black growth. The coloured population in the

Table 4.2. Percentage of Urbanized Populations, 2013

Select Countries	Urbanized (%)
Japan	66.8
South Africa	62.9
Ireland	61.9
Botswana	61.1
Nigeria	49.8
Democratic Republic of the Congo	35
Ethiopia	17

four cities grew by between 6.2 and 60.2 percent from a low base, with Pretoria having the greatest growth. The asian population has increased in three of the four cities, ranging from a 29 percent increase (Cape Town) to 79.3 percent (Pretoria). The asian proportion of the population decreased by 14 percent in Durban, in part because the black population grew significantly in absolute numbers. The white population declined in Johannesburg, Pretoria, and Durban, and it remained the same in Cape Town.[23] However, many of the whites departing urban centers merely moved to adjacent suburbs. The years since 2000 have thus seen a substantial migration of those groups disadvantaged by apartheid from the rural areas or far suburbs into the country's largest cities. Blacks commonly describe Johannesburg as "African," while they see Durban as "asian" or "indian" and Cape Town as "white," though the largest racial group in the latter is coloured, as is the mayor, Patricia de Lille.[24]

Asians

Asians in 2014 totaled 1,341,877, making up 2.5 percent of the population;[25] in 1995 they had numbered 1,024,400, or 2.6 percent of the population.[26] While most are of South Asian descent, there are up to three hundred thousand Chinese, many of relatively recent origin. Fifty-nine percent of asians live in Durban (556,335) and Johannesburg (224,817). The concentration in KwaZulu-Natal of persons of South Asian origin dates from the nineteenth century when they came as indentured laborers to work that province's sugar plantations. The decline in the asian proportion of the total population receives little media attention. The asian birthrate is slightly below replacement level, comparable to that of whites. Their community continues to be augmented by some immigration. Like blacks and coloureds, asians are, for the most part, beneficiaries of Black Economic Empowerment, and they are a significant percentage of the top leadership of the ANC.

Blacks

Not as urbanized as the other racial groups, blacks numbered 43,333,709, making up over 80 percent of the total population in 2012; in 1995, they numbered 30,184,400, about 76.4 percent of the country's total population.[27] They are divided into numerous ethnic groups defined by language. The five largest are the Zulu, Xhosa, Northern Sotho, Tswana, and Sesotho. An additional 21.9 percent of blacks speak other languages, usually Afrikaans or English.[28] Table 4.3 gives the linguistic breakdown.

Despite much internal migration, blacks are still not concentrated in specific geographical locations to the same extent as other racial groups. Dispersed throughout the country, only 20 percent live in Johannesburg, Durban, East Rand, Cape Town, and Pretoria combined, but everywhere except Cape Town they are the largest resident racial group in any urban area.

Coloureds

Coloureds in 2014 numbered 4,771,548, or 8.8 percent of the population, the same percentage of the population they constituted in 1996. The first language of most coloureds is Afrikaans. They, too, are concentrated in a few urban areas. Forty-six percent are concentrated in Cape Town (1,643,397); Johannesburg (256,280); and Port Elizabeth (280,596), in the Eastern Cape. Coloured distribution reflects apartheid-era settlement patterns and also the fact that the former Cape Province (which included the present Western Cape, Eastern Cape, and Northern Cape) was a "coloured preference area," where certain occupations and neighborhoods were opened to them but were closed to blacks under most circumstances.

Coloureds have a higher birthrate than whites, but their population is not significantly increased by immigration, and their disease burden is heavier than that of whites and asians.

Table 4.3.   Languages of Black South Africans

Language	Rate (%)
Zulu	28.1
Xhosa	19.8
Northern Sotho	11.2
Tswana	9.7
Sesotho	9.3
Other	21.9

Whites

In 1995, whites accounted for 11 percent of the population at 4,386,600; in 2014, they numbered 4,554,820, falling to 8.4 percent of the total population even though they had grown in absolute numbers. Whites, like blacks, are not monolithic linguistically; 59.1 percent speak Afrikaans as their first language, 35 percent speak English as their first language, and 5.9 percent speak as their first language a variety of other European tongues. They are concentrated in urban and suburban areas, with altogether 53 percent living in five conurbations: Cape Town (585,953), Johannesburg (529,509), Gauteng's East Rand (487,332), Pretoria (577,995), and Durban (230,456).[29] Most of the others are in smaller cities. There are white farmers, but South Africa's rural population is mostly black except in the Western Cape, where it is coloured.

WHITE FLIGHT?

Real or potential white flight has been a fixture of South African conversation at least since UK prime minister Harold Macmillan's "Winds of Change" speech in 1960. Whether to move to Australia, Canada, the UK, or the United States remains a staple topic of conversation at white social gatherings. There are large white South African expatriate populations in Perth (Australia), London, Los Angeles, and Atlanta, many of whom are convinced that South Africa is "done" and that they are well away. There is anecdotal evidence that a high percentage of the white graduates of, say, Johannesburg's University of the Witwatersrand ("Wits") medical school promptly emigrate upon completing their training. Conventional wisdom in South Africa is that the white population is "declining," and post-apartheid "white flight" is frequently cited as a major cause of South Africa's "skills shortage" that contributes to disappointing rates of economic growth.

Nevertheless, as Statistics South Africa shows, the white population has grown in absolute numbers, not declined, and some white immigration into South Africa continues. As was true in 1994, the white birthrate is below the replacement figure by about the same percentage as in Europe. As for white emigration—"white flight"—there is no clear picture. Holders of South African passports are free to come and go, and they do. There are limited restrictions on individual South African travelers taking money out of the country. It appears that large numbers of young, well-educated whites, especially those who are English speaking, do leave the country of their birth. But after a period of time, many or perhaps most of them return. A medical graduate of Wits who immigrates to Canada can find himself practicing medicine in Nunavut, the Northwest Territories, or the Yukon. (The Canadian government assigns initially immigrant medical practitioners to underserved locales.) After a few Canadian winters, "Sunny South Africa" and its high standard of living for professionals looks attractive, and many—perhaps most—return.

The white population pyramid lends credence to this hypothesis. It shows a "waist" in the 25–34 age group. Often this is ascribed to "white flight." But the decline is reversed by something of a "bulge" in the 45–49 age group, when many or most of those who left have returned.[30] A general pattern of well-educated young people leaving their country of birth to pursue professional opportunities or simply because of itchy feet is also common in the countries of the European Union. Most of them, too, eventually return home. There is anecdotal evidence that among white Afrikaans speakers, the temporary emigration seen among English speakers is less common.

IMMIGRATION

Post-apartheid legal immigration into South Africa has also continued from all over the world. Between 1990 and 2004, there were a total of 110,121 legal immigrants, of whom 29,745, or 27 percent of the total, were African. The African percentage has been increasing, and by 2004 it was almost half. But a large percentage of legal immigrants remained non-African, and white and Asian immigration may mitigate white and asian losses to emigration and lower birthrates.

In addition, there are temporary workers from neighboring African countries. Migrant labor has long been especially important in the mines. In 2006, migrant workers in the gold mines numbered 267,894, of whom about 100,000 were from outside South Africa.[31] Migrant labor is almost entirely black. Those who are not South African citizens are not included in the permanent immigrant statistics because they are temporary sojourners.

The apparent growth of the black population from more than thirty million to more than forty-three million in twenty-one years at first glance looks extraordinary. Many native South Africans believe the country is being "overrun" by illegal immigration from other parts of Africa. They will cite the highly visible Nigerian, Congolese, and Somali communities in Johannesburg. Many South African blacks resent Zimbabweans who, because of their superior primary education, compete successfully for scarce jobs. Rich Nigerians and Congolese, especially, purchase property in South Africa. Their wealth increases the visibility of their communities. Nigerians, Congolese, and Zimbabweans also account for a significant percentage of legal immigrants, but their absolute numbers are small.

In 2013, South Africa's population included 2,399,000 immigrants, only 4.5 percent of the country's population—and that figure included all races.[32] Statistics South Africa estimates that the number of documented and undocumented migrants is in the range of 1.6 million to 6 million.[33] This wide range reflects a lack of statistics on the number of undocumented or illegal migrants in the country. By comparison, the U.S. Census Bureau in January 2010 estimated the number of documented noncitizen immigrants at 17,476,000, or 7.9 percent of the total population, with an additional illegal immigrant population between 10.9 million and 11.9 million, or 3.7 percent of the total population.

Combining these two categories, immigrants make up perhaps 11.6 percent of the population of the United States. In comparison with the United States, South Africa's immigrant population, of whatever origin or legal status, is about the same percentage if the highest estimate for undocumented immigrants is used.

The 10,011 recipients of South African permanent residence permits in 2011 came from 128 different countries. Almost 60 percent came from only eight countries: Zimbabwe, the Democratic Republic of the Congo, China, India, Nigeria, Pakistan, the UK, and Somalia. About 60 percent of the 10,011 recipients came from Africa; the other 40 percent from around the world, including North America, with 149 permanent residence permits, or 1.5 percent of the total.[34]

In the townships, there is widespread resentment that African foreigners are taking jobs from native South Africans, and in 2008 and

2015 there was serious xenophobic rioting. To better control the foreign influx, the Zuma administration proposed new immigration laws, which were passed and implemented in 2014. Their thrust appears to be to increase the role of the Department of Trade and Industry and the Department of Labour. The former "exceptional skills" category has been replaced by "critical skills." There has been an effort to tighten spousal or "life partner" visas. Such visas now require an official interview to determine conjugal status, a development that recalls certain apartheid practices. The new legislation is cumbersome, and it is being implemented in a ragged fashion. Aspects of it have been challenged in the courts.[35]

BLACK POPULATION GROWTH

Despite the myth of white flight from South Africa, official statistics indicate demographic stability among all racial groups—except blacks. Whites, coloureds, and asians increased in absolute numbers between 1996 and 2014, but only by a small percentage.[36] Blacks, however, increased in the same period by more than 25 percent. In fact, it is the growth of the black population that accounts for most of South Africa's demographic growth since 1994.

Immigration from other parts of the African continent does contribute to the growth of the black population. But, in 2011, that legal immigration numbered only slightly more than five thousand. Even if combined with a substantial undocumented population, African immigration is not large enough to account for the growth in the black population.

How then to account for the huge increase? It is true that the birthrate among blacks is significantly higher than among some other racial groups, though it is declining. But the death rate among blacks is higher than that of other groups, too, and the black average life span is much shorter. Blacks carry the heaviest disease burden of any group. HIV/AIDS especially damages the black population. Among the black population as a whole, an estimated 15 percent were HIV positive in 2001–2010; in 2012, among those fifteen to forty-nine years of age, the estimate was that 22.7 percent were HIV positive.[37] In any event, the higher birthrate taking into account the higher death rate is insufficient to account for the black increase.

The most plausible explanation for the seeming dramatic increase since 1994 is that under apartheid, the census undercounted blacks. Even as late as 1994, an estimated 50 percent of the black population lived in rural areas, and many of them were outside of the modern economy. Much of the black population lived in or was assigned to "independent" homelands. According to apartheid theory, they were not part of South Africa. There is also anecdotal evidence that the census in black areas was often cursory. After all, under apartheid it was not in the white supremacist government's interest to amplify black numbers. After the end of apartheid, with rapid migration from rural areas toward the cities, more accurate counts became possible. Accordingly, South Africa's population figures jumped, as did the proportion that was black.

Nevertheless, census undercounts still persist, and it is blacks more than other racial groups who are likely to be left out. In 1996, it is estimated that the undercount was 10 percent; in 2001, it is estimated to have increased to 17 percent, in part because of the increased mobility of people. The Statistician General, Pali Lehohla, believes that lack of accessibility to certain areas contributes to the undercounting. The inaccessibility to which he refers appears to be the result of poor or nonexistent roads and isolation; there are no particular security issues blocking the work of census enumerators. Still, South African under-counting seems very high; in Canada, Australia, and New Zealand, it averages 2.2 percent. In Mozambique, it is 5.2 percent.[38]

It seems likely that there has been relatively little change in South Africa's demographic makeup; it also seems that the country's population including the "independent" and "self-governing" homelands in 1994 was greater than the official estimate at the time and that it has grown since then at a slower rate than conventional wisdom maintains.

LIFE EXPECTANCY

A theme of this book is that racial disparities have changed only slowly since the end of apartheid, even as overt racism has morphed or declined. This is clearly illustrated by life expectancy statistics. As a measure, life expectancy is also useful for comparing the overall well-being of South Africa's population with that of other countries.

For black South Africans, projected life expectancy at birth in 2000 was 58.4 years; in 2015, it is projected to have fallen to 46.9 years, in large part because of the ravages of HIV/AIDS. For coloureds, the comparable statistics were 66.2 years in 2000, falling to 60.6 years in 2015. For asians, it was 70.9 years in 2000, falling to 67.5 years in 2015. For whites it was 74 years in 2000, projected to fall slightly to 72 years in 2015. On average, a white South African lived more than twenty years longer than his black fellow national.[39]

The age profiles of the racial groups are dramatically different, illustrating once again the racial hierarchy of privilege. In 2014, of children up to age fourteen, 13,782,016 were black, 1,294,021 were coloured, 290,072 were asian, and 813,656 were white. Hence there were almost seventeen times as many blacks as whites in that cohort. Of those aged sixty-five and older, however, blacks numbered 2,043,920, coloureds 201,605, asians 88,803, and whites 637,559. In that age cohort, blacks were just over three times as numerous as whites, and the latter were about one out of every five South Africans age sixty-five or older. A much higher percentage of whites, who have access to better health care and a higher standard of living, live to a ripe old age than those in other racial groups.[40]

There are significant geographic differences in South Africa's economic development, with Gauteng (Johannesburg) the wealthiest province in the country, followed by KwaZulu-Natal (Durban) and the Western Cape (Cape Town). The Free State, Limpopo, and the Eastern Cape are significantly poorer. Table 4.4 shows life expectancy by race in a poor province, Free State, and a rich one, Gauteng.

For whites, coloureds, and asians, life expectancy hardly varies between the Free State and Gauteng. However, black Africans living in

Table 4.4.   Life Expectancy by Race in Two Provinces, 2012

Race	Free State	Gauteng
Whites	70.7	70.4
Asians	64.6	65.9
Coloureds	58.2	58.6
Blacks	44.7	48.0

Gauteng can expect to live more than three years longer than black residents of the Free State. There are likely many reasons for the discrepancy. Most black Africans in the Free State live in rural areas, while the black population of Gauteng is predominantly urban. Not only is black poverty less in Gauteng than in the Free State, but it is also likely that black access to medical care is better.[41]

While there are significant racial disparities in life expectancy, the overall average (including all races) for South Africans in 2012 was 56.10, a decline from 62.12 in 1990, mostly the result of HIV/AIDS. Table 4.5 compares South Africa's life expectancy with that of its BRICS partners.

People living in the most developed parts of the world can live almost twenty-five years longer than in the statistically average South Africa.[42] Table 4.6 compares South Africa's average life span with selected developed countries.

Hence, overall South African life expectancy is significantly below that of its BRICS partners and almost thirty years shorter than in the most advanced Western countries—an entire generation. Moreover, even for whites, life expectancy is comparatively low. In 2007, it was similar to that of Egypt (71), Hungary (70), and the Philippines (72). South African black life expectancy was slightly better than the statistical average in Nigeria (47), Mozambique (42), and Zimbabwe (43). It was almost exactly comparable with Botswana (51) and Uganda (51). It was significantly lower than Ghana (60).[43]

For South African whites, life expectancy is comparable to that in poor European countries, including Russia. For blacks, it is comparable to other sub-Saharan African countries, though not nearly as good as Ghana. Asians and coloureds fall in between, with the former living somewhat longer than the latter. In terms of life expectancy, post-apart-

Table 4.5. BRICS Life Expectancy, 2012

Country	Age
China	75.2
Brazil	73.6
Russia	70.5
India	66.2
South Africa	56.1

Table 4.6. Life Expectancy in Selected Developed Countries, 2012

Country	Age
Australia	82.1
Sweden	81.7
United Kingdom	81.5
United States	78.7
South Africa	56.1

heid South Africa is comparable to a poor European country intermixed with a much poorer African one. And the border between these two "countries" is race.

How to account for the overall low life expectancy? As we will see, HIV/AIDS remains a scourge. In 2013, it was estimated that AIDS deaths numbered 196,620, compared with non-AIDS deaths of 419,459. Again, there was considerable regional variation. The HIV prevalence rate was highest in KwaZulu-Natal, at 16 percent, with the Free State and the North West next at 13 percent each. But in the Western Cape it was low at 5 percent. In KwaZulu-Natal, 38 percent of all deaths were a result of HIV/AIDS, while in the Western Cape the figure was 13.7 percent.[44]

The South Africa Survey estimates that in 2010, HIV/AIDS reduced overall life expectancy by 10.4 percent. It also calculates that absent HIV/AIDS, South Africa's population in 2010 would have been 55 million rather than 50.7 million.[45]

The ravages of HIV/AIDS are disproportionately felt by the black population, especially women. If the disease has cut life expectancy by an average of 10 percent of the entire population, it has had an even greater impact on black Africans. Absent HIV/AIDS, the life expectancy of black South Africans would likely be comparable to Ghana's, among the best in Africa.

Beyond HIV/AIDS, however, low life expectancy of blacks also reflects a host of social realities, ranging from poor medical facilities, limited education, and profound poverty that affects diet, housing, and the quality of child care. For example, Baragwanath Hospital in Soweto developed a world-renowned expertise in treating burns because they were so common among children playing around open cooking fires adjacent to shanties without cookstoves.

CRIME

On a personal level, South African pessimism is often exacerbated by the country's very high levels of violent crime; the country has among the highest levels of reported rape in the world. White South African expatriates regularly cite crime as a primary motivation for emigrating.[46] Reported violent crime in 2013/2014 included 17,068 murders, 62,649 sexual offenses, 17,110 attempted murders, 183,173 assaults to cause bodily harm, 167,157 common assaults, 119,351 robberies with aggravating circumstances, and 53,858 common robberies.[47] Yet, despite these statistics, it is commonly assumed that a high percentage of crime goes unreported. Compared to the United States, South Africa is underpoliced. In 2014, South Africa had a population of about fifty-four million and a police force of about 153,000 officers.[48] Thus, South Africa had one law enforcement officer per 346 people. In the United States in 2008, state and local law enforcement agencies employed 1,133,000 persons, making the ratio equivalent of 1 to 268.[49] Compared with their professional counterparts in the United States, South African police are poorly trained and poorly paid.[50]

Comparison of crime statistics from one country to another can be no more than indicative because of a variety of technical and cultural factors. The South African Institute of Race Relations (IRR) and the Centre for Risk Analysis (CRA) use murder rates to compare safety and security levels internationally. Murder is probably less underreported than other crimes, and its definition is relatively close across international boundaries. They record 16,259 murders in South Africa in 2012, a rate of 31 per 100,000. Table 4.7 compares South Africa's murder rate with that of selected countries.

For the United States, with more than six times South Africa's population, murders numbered 14,827. By contrast, nonviolent Denmark had a total of 47 murders in 2012. The highest number of murders occurred in Brazil, with 50,108. The highest rate of murder per one hundred thousand in the world was in Honduras, at 90.4, with 7,172 murders. South Africa's murder rate is comparable to that of the Bahamas and Colombia.[51]

There is a misperception that blacks target whites for murder. In fact, a 2009 analysis of murder dockets showed that 86.9 percent of the murder victims were black. Whites accounted for only 1.8 percent of

Table 4.7.   Murder Rates in Selected Countries, 2012

Country	Rate per 100,000
Honduras	90.4
South Africa	31.0
Colombia	30.8
Bahamas	29.8
Brazil	25.2
United States	4.7
Denmark	0.8

the victims, though they are almost 9 percent of the population.[52] Nevertheless, even the most prominent of South Africans can become crime victims. The celebrated Nobel Prize–winning novelist and long-time anti-apartheid activist Nadine Gordimer was attacked by home invaders in 2006. She had refused to move into a "gated" community.

High levels of violence in South Africa are not new. As we have seen, for more than two centuries after their first arrival, white colonists fought wars with indigenous peoples and used violence to control a slave population. Apartheid South Africa continued to be violent, though then it was probably less well documented than now. Among the apartheid-era Bureau of State Security (BOSS) and South African Police Service (SAPS), human rights abuses were ubiquitous, especially in apartheid's last years, directed against opponents of the regime of any race, but most of the victims were black. BOSS functioned in some ways like a secret police and thoroughly penetrated the liberation movements after the latter launched the armed struggle in 1961. That reality, in turn, fostered paranoia and human rights abuses within the ANC in exile in the search for informants and spies, generating a culture that it has only partly overcome as it has evolved from a liberation movement into a political party. There was ethnic conflict, especially in the mining hostels where workers were housed absent from their families, that was sometimes abetted by the security services as part of a "divide and conquer" strategy, especially during apartheid's last days. While most of the violence was black on black, crimes against whites were widely publicized by a white-owned and clumsily censored press.

Since 1994, South Africa has remained violent. Public frustration with crime is so high that a majority of South Africans of all races favor the restoration of capital punishment, even though it is associated with the apartheid government that hanged freedom fighters. If the organized and repressive security structure of the apartheid state is gone, police brutality continues, as was demonstrated by their massacre of platinum mine workers at Marikana in 2012, the largest since Sharpeville in 1960.

WEALTH AND POVERTY

The differences in wealth among the racial groups are stark. A predominantly white, blue-collar trade union, Solidarity, argues that 10 percent of the white population is "poor," as is 50 percent of the black population.[53] According to the 2014/2015 South Africa Survey, aggregate income in 2013 for whites was South African rand (ZAR) 770 billion; for asians, it was ZAR 124 billion; for coloureds, it was ZAR 161 billion; and for blacks, it was just over ZAR 1 trillion.[54] Table 4.8 shows average individual income by race.[55]

However, such aggregated statistics hide important distinctions. The salaries of educated nonwhites are usually the equivalent of their white counterparts and in some cases may be higher. Nonwhite net worth, however, will almost always be lower, because their parents and grandparents lacked the opportunity to accumulate capital, unlike those of their white counterparts.

South African fiscal policy has sought to address poverty and inequality. In a 2014 report, the World Bank gives it high marks.[56] The report concludes that fiscal policy benefits the poor more than the rich. Taxation and redistribution are progressive, ensuring that the rich pay a higher rate than the poor in income tax. The value-added tax (VAT) rate, a sales tax or tax on expenditure, is fixed. Rich and poor pay the

Table 4.8. Average Individual Income by Race, 2013

Race	Annual Income (ZAR)
Whites	199,726
Asians	107,608
Coloureds	38,811
Blacks	26,594

same. But the rich spend more and therefore pay more VAT. Social spending strongly benefits the poor. In fact, the World Bank concludes that child support, disability grants, old-age pensions, and free basic services caused the overall poverty rate to fall to 39 percent from 46.2 percent—a reduction of 3.6 million people.

The World Bank compared South Africa's fiscal policy to that of eleven other countries. It concluded that South Africa's was the best in addressing poverty, defined as those living on USD 2.50 per day or less, through fiscal policy.[57] In effect, South Africa cut in half its extreme poverty level (defined in this case as living on less than USD 1.25 a day), from 34.4 percent of the population to 16.5 percent. But fiscal policy had little impact on achieving greater income equality. Inequality of household consumption actually increased between 1993 and 2011.[58]

Faced with persistent income inequality, slow economic growth, and rising discontent in the townships, the Zuma administration has sought to strengthen BBBEE and extend its provisions to small companies since 2011. Among other steps, it has also introduced legislation that would impose price and export controls on coal and other minerals. It is seeking to accelerate land reform, and it has introduced legislation that would, in effect, significantly reduce property rights. Most such measures are controversial, and some would seem to violate the constitution. If passed, they are likely to face court challenges.

The proportion of blacks in the top 1 percent of the population by income actually declined from 19.53 percent in 1995 to 16.11 percent in 2008. However, within the top 10 percent of the population by income, blacks have increased from 25.13 percent in 1995 to 36.49 percent in 2008. The increase in the black percentage of the total population helps account for their growing numbers in the top 10 percent of the population, along with their accelerating entry into the civil service and state-owned enterprises. It also helps to account for the widespread view that class is displacing race as the principal fault line in South African society. But their decline in the top 1 percent, even while their numbers overall were increasing, is an indication that whites have consolidated their position at the very top of the South African economy.[59]

Arguably, racial inequalities in wealth and income in the United States are comparable. According to CNNMoney in 2012, white Americans on average had twenty-two times more wealth than blacks. The median household net worth for whites was USD 110,729 in 2010, while for blacks it was USD 4,995. The ratio between white and His-panic wealth was fifteen to one. CNN notes that wealth discrepancy was made much worse by the Great Recession and the housing collapse, which disproportionately affected blacks and Hispanics. In 2005, the height of the most recent boom, whites had twelve times more wealth than blacks and eight times more than Hispanics.[60]

Conventional wisdom holds that the racial wealth gap in the United States demonstrates persistent discrimination in housing, credit, and labor markets. Those factors are also in play in South Africa.

A theme of this book is that more than twenty years after the end of apartheid, the racial economic and social hierarchy remains much the same. But South Africa is changing in other ways. The country's popula-tion is shifting from the countryside into the cities. Since the country industrialized rapidly at the turn of the twentieth century, a first-world country, if relatively poor, has existed cheek by jowl with a developing state. Despite the end of apartheid, this reality continues and contrib-utes fundamentally to the threats to the liberal and democratic political structure that was the great achievement of the transition to nonracial democracy.

RACISM?

Almost a generation after the coming of nonracial democracy, racism continues to be the South African "elephant in the living room." Some racism is straightforward. The crude racism among whites characteristic of apartheid continues to exist, especially in rural areas, even if in its overt forms it is no longer acceptable in elite company. On the other hand, critics of the Mbeki and Zuma governments accuse them of pan-dering or exploiting for their own narrow political interests—if not creating—a similarly crude black racism against whites. Mbeki's eco-nomic policy, so the argument runs, was designed to create a black, "national" bourgeoisie through a set of black preferences that recall aspects of affirmative action in the United States. The instrument was Black Economic Empowerment, later amended as Broad-Based Black Economic Empowerment (BBBEE). Broadly speaking it aimed at cor-recting the injustices and distortions of apartheid by transferring wealth from whites to other racial groups. This program was based on racial categories and definitions, with clear winners and losers. But is it "racist?" Or is it public policy designed to address current South African realities resulting from past history, as was affirmative action in the United States? There is something of a consensus across the spectrum in support of the goals of BBBEE, even if there is often criticism of the implementation.

Clearer examples of racism have been the use of "freedom songs" by black politicians. Julius Malema, that firebrand former head of the ANC Youth League, revived "Kill the Settler, Kill the Boer." President Jacob Zuma performs in public, "Father, Give Me My Machine Gun." South Africa has laws against hate speech, and Malema has been convicted under them. The ANC leadership has also expelled Malema from the party. For his part, Zuma appears to be strengthening his populist credentials by appealing to memories of "struggle" violence.[61] As we have seen, South Africa is a violent country. However, most of that violence does not appear to be tied directly to race. The South African Commercial Farmers' Union (a predominantly white organization) observes that some three thousand white farmers have been murdered since the transition. It sees a relationship between these murders and "freedom songs" and other hate speech. On the other hand, many white farmers were notorious for their harsh treatment of their farmworkers. Accordingly, others have argued that in essence the killings may be better characterized as labor disputes.

IT'S A NEW SOUTH AFRICA

At the time of the 1994 transition, whites generally viewed apartheid as a failure. But, by and large, they did not see it as evil, or a "crime against humanity." There were similarities with the views of white American southerners after the end of legal segregation in the United States: segregation may not have worked, but it was certainly not evil. (In fact, most white southerners opposed racial integration and supported governors who did all they could to prevent it.)

Hence, it is significant that by 2012, a credible poll shows that 83.8 percent of South Africans (including all races) see apartheid as a crime against humanity.[62] A large majority, 82.5 percent, agree that the apartheid state committed atrocities against anti-apartheid activists, and 81.1

percent agree that the apartheid government oppressed the majority of South Africans. A substantial majority of white South Africans also share these views, though by a smaller percentage: the range was 68–74 percent. Nevertheless, the white statistics show them moving away from the apartheid mind-set, if more slowly than other groups.

This same polling data show that there remain significant differences among the races on public policy issues. Most black Africans, 82 percent, see black poverty as a result of apartheid; 73.3 percent of asians agree, as do 61.4 percent of coloureds. However, only about half (50.6 percent) of whites share this view.

Still, these polling data are an indication that a substantial majority of whites have accepted the "new" South Africa. Nonracial South Africa, however, in terms of earning and spending is not so different from the apartheid era, though rates of poverty have declined, and the living conditions for many have undeniably improved.

Even with the racial hierarchy of economic and social privilege, in a democracy numbers count. Set free from the artificial constraints of apartheid, the public square in South Africa has become much more "African" in style. The faces in advertisements and on television reflect the demographics of the country. The agencies of government with whom most people regularly come into contact—the post office, the police, customs and immigration figures, agricultural extension experts—have also come to mirror the demographics of the country in the twenty years since the end of apartheid. That is a major democratic achievement.

5

POVERTY, EDUCATION, AND HEALTH

South Africa's future as a liberal democracy with perhaps the world's most extensive protection for human rights is linked to progress in reducing poverty. Extreme poverty is mostly a black and coloured phenomenon. However, with the end of apartheid's guarantee of employment, up to 10 percent of whites regard themselves as poor, though few live on as little as USD 1.25 per day, an often-cited poverty threshold.[1] The apartheid system not only limited the possibility of black and coloured earnings, but it also made it almost impossible for members of those racial groups to accumulate capital for investment. The post-apartheid government's lack of success in poverty reduction despite numerous initiatives undermines popular confidence in democratic governance based on the rule of law, feeds radical politics that undermine investor confidence, and probably drives the country's very high crime rate.

But there are grounds for hope for the future. With respect to education and public health, there are South African initiatives, both public and private, that could promote future poverty reduction, especially by reducing unemployment. An outstanding question is whether they can be realized quickly enough. South Africa's extensive network of social grants, mostly dating from the post-apartheid era, helps to buy time. So, too, does the safety net provided by the traditional family structure, where it continues to function.[2]

POVERTY

According to UNICEF, about 14 percent of the population lives below the international poverty line of USD 1.25 per day.[3] About half of South Africa's population faces episodes of hunger, and one-third of households even in Cape Town, Johannesburg, and the East Rand face serious hunger. The issue is poverty, not the unavailability of food.[4] Too many South Africans lack the wherewithal to pay for the food they need. With almost two-thirds of South Africa's population now urbanized, most can no longer grow their own food. In informal settlements in townships outside the principal cities, land is too scarce even for small market gardens, and residents rarely have access to low-cost food markets. Urbanization also results in dietary change, especially among the poor. Hence, the age-old picture of stunted children living in rural poverty must be supplemented now by images of township children obese from fast food of low nutritional value. They are prone to a new range of urban diseases including high blood pressure and diabetes.

Hunger and poor nutrition play a major role in South Africa's educational and health shortcomings: hungry children learn more slowly and are prone to illness. So, too, does the deterioration of the traditional family structure, which may leave behind an attitude of contempt for women and the glorification of violence that often accompany rapid urbanization. This deterioration of traditional family structures has been under way for several generations and reflects apartheid's preference for nonwhite male labor living apart from their families that remained in rural areas. Risky or criminal sexual behavior including rape may result in this milieu and too often contributes to South Africa's greatest health challenge, HIV/AIDS. An estimate is that half a million women are raped each year.[5] A Medical Research Council poll in the Eastern Cape revealed that a quarter of the male respondents admitted to committing rape at least once. In a different poll taken among Soweto schoolboys, one-quarter said that "jackrolling"—gang rape—was "fun."[6] The UN Office of Internal Oversight Services reports that South African troops participating in selected UN peacekeeping missions are the worst sexual offenders of any troop-providing nation.[7] In 2014, 36,225 people were jailed for violent crimes against women, and the South African courts sentenced 695 to prison for life for "heinous" crimes against women.[8]

Many of the poor survive on South Africa's system of welfare grants. More than sixteen million of South Africa's fifty-odd million people receive grants of some type. Critics of the grants system will argue that the millions of grant recipients are supported by only five million taxpayers.[9] This is misleading. In 2013, about 56 percent of the government's revenue came from direct tax, including income and property taxes. That was paid by the five million direct tax payers. But anybody in the money economy, now virtually all South Africans, pays indirect tax, including those who receive social grants. Forty-three percent of the government's revenue is from indirect taxation, including value-added tax (VAT), a form of sales tax.

Grant beneficiaries are primarily children, the elderly, and the chronically ill. Seventy percent of the beneficiaries are children under the age of eighteen; 18 percent are old-age pensioners. Grants constitute a safety net that has mitigated some of the most severe poverty. The number of South Africans receiving social grants continues to grow, from 12.4 million in 2007 to 16.1 million in 2012, about 30 percent of the population. Budgetary planning anticipates that this number will rise to 17.1 million by 2016. For many critics, these allowances are palliative rather than transformative of the inherited apartheid system, and transfer payments to the poor are growing at a rate that is unsustainable. However, social grants remain remarkably steady at 3.5 percent of GDP, even with an economic growth rate of less than 2 percent.[10]

How many taxpayers support those who receive social grants? For the period 2014–2015, personal income tax provided 34.5 percent of the state's tax revenue; 19.9 percent came from company tax, 26.4 from value-added tax (VAT), and 19.2 percent from a variety of other taxes, including import duties and fuel taxes.[11] The South African income tax system is progressive: as income and wealth increase, so too does the tax rate. Personal income tax ranges from 18 percent to 41 percent.[12] Company taxes are payable at 28 percent of income.[13] Inheritance taxes are 20 percent; the payment threshold is estates valued at ZAR 3.5 million.[14] Capital gains are taxed at 33.3 percent.

VAT is assessed at 14 percent and is paid by all consumers, regardless of the size of their incomes. Some consumer items are exempt from VAT.[15] However, in 2015, Finance Minister Nhlanhla Nene proposed that the government expand VAT to cover commodities widely used by the poor. VAT is an exception to South Africa's generally progressive tax regime as everyone—rich or poor—pays at the same rate.

If these rates are higher than federal taxes in the United States, provincial and local taxes are far lower. Hence, the tax burden in South Africa is not conspicuously high in comparison with most of the United States.

There are 13.7 million South Africans registered as potential income tax payers with the revenue service, but more than half do not reach the threshold to pay. On the other hand, wealthy South Africans pay income tax, their companies pay company taxes, they are likely to pay capital gains taxes, and ultimately they will be subject to inheritance taxes. Township dwellers and those who live in the rural areas and are very poor will likely pay VAT only on some of their meager purchases. However, for the very poor, taxes, mostly VAT, can consume a larger percentage of their income than do the multiple taxes that the rich pay.[16]

It is estimated that 3.3 million South Africans pay 99 percent of all taxes.[17] That about 5 percent of the population carries most of the tax burden reflects the extreme inequality of income and wealth in South Africa.

Despite low growth rates in the economy after 2008, the country's wealth has increased dramatically since 1994. When Nelson Mandela was inaugurated, the country's nominal per capita income was about USD 3,000. By 2012 it had grown to USD 6,800.[18] But it is the wealthy and near wealthy who have most benefited, not the township and rural poor.

A full-time employed South African of any race is rarely starving, though he or she might be hungry between paychecks. The greatest driver of poverty is unemployment. It is extraordinarily high. As table 5.1 shows, South Africa's unemployment rate is substantially higher than that of its BRICS partners.

South Africa's current unemployment rate is about the same as that of Greece. However, South Africa has had economic growth, if anemic, over the past five years, while Greece has endured economic recession.[19]

Causes of unemployment include a relatively rigid industrial relations system, shortcomings in education and health, and a host of fac-

Table 5.1.   BRICS Unemployment Rates, 2015

Country	Rate (%)
South Africa	26
India	9
Brazil	6
Russia	6
China	4

tors left over from the apartheid era, such as the location of many townships far from employment centers.

Predictably, unemployment varies among the races. See table 5.2.[20]

Unemployment statistics often lack precision. Nevertheless, they indicate that unemployment ranges from an official nationwide figure of about 26 percent of the workforce in 2014 to up to 50 percent in certain townships and rural areas. (These statistics do not include the underemployed.)

Perhaps 20 percent of South Africa's workforce is employed in the informal economy, a lower proportion than any comparable developing country. Most of those who work in the informal economy are female, and 90 percent are black. A large proportion is in domestic service. Their incomes are very low, an indication that they are often the poorest of the poor.[21]

As table 5.3 shows, most of South Africa's unemployed are disproportionately young.

Table 5.4 demonstrates that age improves employment chances.[22]

The key to reducing poverty in South Africa is to reduce unemployment. The key to that is improved education and health and a restructuring of the labor market. Better education and health have the potential for reducing the pervasive shortage of skilled labor combined with a high level of unemployment among the low skilled that together act as a brake on the economic growth needed to reduce poverty.

A better-educated and healthier workforce would address the chronic shortage of skills about which potential employers complain. Higher levels of employment would also have a "spiral up" effect in an economy that is increasingly dominated by domestic consumption; more employed means more customers for South African goods and trade.

Table 5.2.   South African Unemployment Rates by Race, 2014

Race	Rate (%)
Blacks	28.3
Coloureds	25.3
Asians	12.1
Whites	8.1

ECONOMIC GROWTH

South African rates of economic growth have not been as high as in China, India, and Brazil since the coming of nonracial democracy in 1994. Nevertheless, they are respectable in comparison with those of more developed countries to which South Africa's formal economy is similar. Since 2010–2011, the economy has grown at a faster rate than the population.[23] Yet poverty levels have declined very slowly, while the relatively wealthy have become significantly wealthier. Economic growth, increasingly based on information technology, financial services, investments outside South Africa, tourism, and real estate rather than mining and manufacturing, disproportionately benefits the whites who have access to quality education. The uneducated or poorly educated are left behind. Their marginalization feeds the irresponsible radicalism of figures like Julius Malema. Poverty reduction requires addressing unemployment, which in turn requires better educating the workforce so that it can participate in a modern economy no longer based on unskilled labor.

In South Africa, the gulf between white wealth and black poverty was arguably greater in 2013 than it was at the end of apartheid, notwithstanding the end of formal racial wage discrimination, BBBEE, the growth of a black middle class, the emergence of a few black oligarchs, and the reappearance of a small but visible class of poor whites.[24] In a liberal, capitalist economy, whites benefit from generations of capital accumulation, access to good education that prepares them to participate in the modern economy, and much better health. Notwithstanding the visible black elite, the white minority remains the greatest beneficiary of the South African post-apartheid political economy, followed by asians and coloureds, with the black African majority at the bottom.

Table 5.3. Unemployment among South Africans Age 15–24 by Race, 2014

Race	Rate (%)
Blacks	56.3
Coloureds	50.8
Asians	29.7
Whites	17.2

EDUCATION

Employers regularly complain about the shortages of qualified workers. This labor shortage ranges from the most sophisticated sectors, such as in information technology, to the skilled trades, such as carpentry, bricklaying, and office management. With respect to the latter, employers complain that they cannot find receptionists who speak good English and are literate. Hence, they will fill such positions with Zimbabweans, who have benefited from more rigorous primary education in English even under Robert Mugabe. It is widely recognized that the labor shortage in parallel with high unemployment is a significant brake on South Africa's economic development, and it is a magnet that attracts better-educated Africans to south of the Zambezi, fueling periodic outbreaks of xenophobia among South Africans who lose out to the better qualified, often Zimbabwean, in the competition for jobs, especially at the entry level.

It is widely recognized in South Africa that far too many of its citizens are ill equipped by their education to participate in the modern workforce. On this point, there is a consensus across racial, class, and political party lines. But the consensus breaks down as to how to improve education for the black and coloured poor.

Pedagogical questions such as whether primary education should be delivered in a learner's native language or whether it should be in English or Afrikaans are contentious in more than just education circles. Language is central to cultural and ethnic identity; among speakers of Afrikaans and the African languages, there is the fear that the language of globalization, English, will crowd out the others.[25] But English is dominant in business, finance, science, higher education, and information technology, including the Internet. Though an estimated 31 percent of the population speaks some English, it is the first language of

Table 5.4. Unemployment among South Africans Age 25–34 by Race, 2014

Race	Rate (%)
Coloureds	29.3
Blacks	32.3
Asians	11.0
Whites	10.6

only 9.6 percent of the population. By comparison, about a quarter speak Zulu as their first language. Only a small percentage of black and coloured South Africans are proficient in English, while nearly all whites are.[26] Lack of English probably contributes significantly to the high unemployment rates in the townships.

There is a national consensus on the need to spend money on education. During some years, up to one-quarter of the national budget is devoted to education in one form or another. Public spending for education is much higher than for defense.[27] Most of South Africa's education budget goes for personnel; the goal is 80 percent for personnel, 20 percent for nonpersonnel. But this ratio has been achieved in only one province. Elsewhere, the allocation for personnel is higher. In terms of purchasing power parity, South African teachers are among the highest paid in the world.[28] Concern about alleged public-sector corruption is ubiquitous in the South African media. Yet educational expenditure is not a particular focus. Instead, the criticism generally is not that money for education has been stolen, but rather that it has been misspent.

As in many other countries, there is also little consensus about how to measure educational success. In 2014, President Jacob Zuma claimed that the higher "matric pass rate"—the rough equivalent of high school graduation in the United States—was evidence of the success of his administration's education initiatives. Many other commentators, however, strongly disagreed that the "matric pass rate" was a credible and objective measure of educational achievement because of highly publicized instances of rigged statistics.

South African education was profoundly distorted by segregation and apartheid. Separate state education systems from kindergarten through university existed for each recognized racial group. There were additional systems for "independent homelands" and "self-governing" homelands. Levels of funding varied hugely. The white system was generously funded, while "Bantu" education received little.[29] Even within the same racial category there could be little coordination. School calendars could vary from one province to another. For example, the white school calendar for Transvaal (Johannesburg and Pretoria) was different from that of Cape Province (Cape Town). This caused hardship for the families of government officials and politicians who moved from Pretoria to Cape Town when parliament was in session and then back again.

Nevertheless, and despite the organizational and management shortcomings of South African education inherited from apartheid, the post-1994 African National Congress (ANC) government has rationalized administratively and consolidated what had been up to nineteen separate education systems into one. This is a major achievement, though arguably more successful among the universities than at the primary and secondary levels. Even if the quality remained low in many primary schools, enrollment of the general population has increased.[30]

Educational content had been shaped by history and apartheid ideology. In the nineteenth century, apprenticeships were the mechanism for the transition from slave labor to wage labor after the British abolished slavery throughout the empire in 1832. Former slaves owed their erstwhile masters four years of labor as apprentices before becoming legally free. Other, mostly marginal, populations were also subject to mandatory apprenticeships.

For most of apartheid's history, blacks were, in effect, excluded from the skilled trades. The 1922 Apprenticeship Act set educational qualifications for apprenticeships. Few blacks could meet the educational qualification standards. Hence they were ineligible for apprenticeships. However, by the mid-twentieth century, the liberal professions—law, medicine, and the church—were increasingly open to blacks. Nelson Mandela was among the first blacks called to the bar. But universities open to blacks provided few or no course offerings to prepare students for professions such as accounting or engineering. Apartheid's assumption was that blacks were to be confined to manual labor, for which they needed to know little more than how to read and write—ideally in Afrikaans rather than English.

Current education dilemmas often appear in stark relief because bad schools in South Africa are frequently adjacent to schools and universities of the highest quality. South Africa is the only African country that contributes to the journalistic lists of the world's best universities. The *Times Higher Education Magazine* ranking of the top five hundred universities in the world includes the University of Cape Town, the University of Witwatersrand, and Stellenbosch University.[31] Such lists are notoriously problematic and contentious, but they do indicate commonly held perceptions. All three of the cited universities have large international enrollments, from Africa but also from Asia, Europe, and North America, attracted by the quality of their academic programs. These elite institutions are by no means whites only. The majority of students enrolled at Cape Town and Witwatersrand are nonwhite, with the former more than two-thirds nonwhite; only Stellenbosch is majority white, by about two-thirds. But the faculties of all three are mostly white, and whites' enrollment in these institutions far exceeds their percentage of the total population.

There is much the same pattern in secondary education. There are world-class "independent" or private schools in South Africa, usually commanding high fees and largely free of government authority. All (with trifling exceptions) are racially integrated, but the enrollments of all are disproportionately white. Their graduates are to be found not only in elite South African universities but also at Harvard, Princeton, and Yale. "Independent" schools are popular among those who can afford them. On the political left in South Africa, among Julius Malema's Economic Freedom Fighters, for example, it is argued that the resource shortages that plague schools for the majority of the population will only be addressed when private or quasi-private schools are abolished. That would, so the argument goes, give the wealthy elites a stake in improving the quality of the schools. (This sentiment is also to be found on the left in the United Kingdom, where advocates for the abolition of "public schools"—private institutions—see meaningful educational reform as unlikely so long as the elites can escape state schools.)

There is interest in adapting the "independent model" for a poor demographic; the Anglican Church in the Western Cape is considering the establishment of a network of church schools in the townships that would have only rudimentary playing fields and no gothic architecture.[32] Other Christian denominations are reopening "mission" schools in rural areas that apartheid had shut down. The number of independent schools has grown by 75 percent over the past decade. Nevertheless, they still account for only 2.6 percent of enrolled students.

More than 96 percent of South Africa's students are in state schools. The school quality is by no means uniform, and many charge fees. "No fee" schools were started only in 2005, and they now enroll about 40 percent of all students. Even among them, however, there can be daunting expenses for the poor for ubiquitous uniforms and books. Among the formerly whites-only state secondary schools, many are high quality, with faculty and facilities close to equivalent to those of independent schools. These usually charge fees, and most are white oriented in terms of pedagogy and general outlook, though all are racially integrated, and in many cases, nonwhites are the majority. State schools established for whites during the apartheid era continue to have better facilities and better-trained principals who recruit better-qualified teachers. Many of them have been successful in maintaining high standards. Nonwhite students at elite universities and secondary schools often come from the new black elite and the new middle class, though (as in the United States) there are scholarships for poor students. Nevertheless, the educational experience of the children of the new black government and business elite is far more similar to that of their white equivalents than it is to the mass of the black population. Accordingly, they may be derided in the townships as "coconuts, black on the outside, white on the inside." "White" education distances its beneficiaries from those in the townships and rural areas whose interests the ANC says it represents. The excellence of this educational sector also masks in South Africa and abroad just how bad the quality of education is for most South Africans.

The picture is grim among state primary and secondary schools that were black or coloured under apartheid or that were in the "independent" or "self-governing" homelands of that era. Though a few charge fees, the quality in rural areas and in many townships remains very poor. The physical facilities, often a holdover from "Bantu education" during apartheid times, are often bad. More than 90 percent of such schools have no libraries, or, if they do, no books. Sixty percent have no laboratories. More than 80 percent have no computers. Almost one-fifth of all schools either have no toilets or more than fifty pupils per toilet.[33] In some schools in rural areas, mathematics teachers have no more than the American equivalent of a sixth-grade education.[34] It is this sector of the student population that is particularly ill served. Yet it is also the crucial venue where students should be preparing to participate in the modern economy, meeting the labor shortage, reducing unemployment, promoting economic growth, and thereby reducing poverty.

By international standards, these state schools are failing. According to the Organisation for Economic Co-operation and Development (OECD), eleven-year-olds in South Africa score two-thirds below their age cohort in Russia on a reading examination. Sixteen-year-olds in South Africa perform three times less than, say, the fourteen-year-old cohort in Cyprus in mathematics. More than half of all South African children leave the school system before graduation. [35]

In South Africa the quality of education available to a child depends on the ability of his or her parents to pay for it. This is also true in the United States, where there is a huge variation in the quality of state schools, which are largely funded through property taxes: wealthy neighborhoods generate higher property tax revenue that is available to support better schools. In South Africa, most educational costs are met through funds from the central government that are disbursed through the provinces. The difference is in school fees, which are variable. And once a schedule of school fees is set, they are compulsory, though there are exceptions for orphans and other special categories. Therefore in both South Africa and the United States, rich neighborhoods have good schools; poor neighborhoods often have bad ones. The difference is that the United States is a much richer country than South Africa so that the physical condition of the poorest schools is not as bad as that found in South Africa.

As with so much else in South Africa, this grim reality is part of the heritage of apartheid. The apartheid regime made too little provision for Bantu education. Under apartheid, especially in the rural areas, schools sometimes enrolled up to one hundred pupils in a single class, and teachers often had little more than a primary school level of education. There were only a handful of black, coloured, and asian universities by the end of the apartheid era.

These harsh realities were exacerbated by the role that education issues played in the township struggles against apartheid. These often involved local school boycotts or strikes by black students and teachers against the apartheid authorities. Yet apartheid-era teachers in some

townships, especially around Johannesburg, were often regarded as col-
laborators with the apartheid state. After 1994, teachers from the old
Bantu schools organized into unions and became a powerful part of the
Congress of South African Trade Unions (COSATU). Many became in
essence active local branches of the ANC. "Struggle" characteristics
have persisted. Critics complain that the teachers' unions in effect control schools in some townships and rural areas. Teacher absenteeism is
rife. There is little structure that is conducive to learning. Teacher
strikes are common. (Such strikes occur only rarely in "white" schools.)
Too many teachers, critics claim, are more interested in advancing their
careers as union and ANC local leaders than they are in education.
(Predictably, these union critics are often from the white-dominated
media.) According to many South Africans, part of the impetus toward
the reopening of mission schools and the proposed establishment of an
Anglican school system in the Western Cape is to bypass teachers' unions.

Where are the signs of hope? Perhaps the most important is the
broad-based consensus that South African education is failing to meet
the needs of too many students. This consensus is accompanied by a
willingness to fund education at a high level. In the 2013 budget, education was the largest item, at USD 25.4 billion. In 2010, the Zuma
government added one year to primary school, grade R (reception
year). The Action Plan for 2014 includes ambitious goals to improve
primary education, including guaranteeing universal access to textbooks
and workbooks.

Second, South Africa's federalism still provides space for individual
provinces to experiment and innovate. In Cape Town, for example,
Patricia de Lille has introduced a city apprenticeship system for certain
skilled trades. The city needs plumbers, carpenters, electricians, and
other practitioners of the skilled trades. Her program aims to supply
them. She anticipates that many graduates of the program will leave city
employment after a few years and go into business for themselves,
thereby making their skills available to the larger community.

Third, despite the widespread criticism that educational changes in
South Africa have resulted in a "dumbing down" of the former, excel-
lent white system, in fact South Africa retains some world-class institutions that are now open to all races. The challenge is to extend that
quality to schools that educate the majority of students.

HEALTH SERVICES

In health care, the pattern is similar to that in education: a high-quality system funded mostly by fees covered by private insurance and dating from the apartheid era exists parallel to a nominally free state system that fails too often to meet the needs of its patients. In the apartheid era, there could be some overlap between the two systems, especially in the large state hospitals that admitted patients from all races though segregating them by wards. Hence Groote Schuur Hospital in Cape Town received many black and coloured patients, while Baragwanath Hospital in Soweto treated burn victims of all races.

South Africa has eight medical schools, broadly organized according to British practice. They are high quality and attract an international student body. The percentage of nonwhite matriculation has been steadily growing since 1994. In addition, the government sends South African medical students from rural areas and disadvantaged backgrounds to Cuba to study medicine at little or no cost. In 2014, prospective medical doctors studying in Cuba numbered about one thousand, according to the health minister, Aaron Motsoaledi.[36]

South Africa has a distinguished medical history: Groote Schuur Hospital in Cape Town has long been a major research center and was the venue for the world's first heart transplant, establishing a tradition that continues.[37] Baragwanath Hospital in Soweto, built as a black facility, is an international center for burn research. These are both public hospitals. In addition, there are numerous high-quality private hospitals with patients from all over the world. For example, Americans seeking cosmetic surgery not covered by medical insurance patronize hospitals in the "white" suburbs of Johannesburg. U.S. embassy personnel stationed in sub-Saharan Africa requiring sophisticated medical treatment may be evacuated to private hospitals in Johannesburg rather than to London or the United States. The cost of these world-class facilities is low compared to competitors in Europe or North America. Formerly exclusively white, they now admit patients of all races, though whites are disproportionately represented.

The state public health care sector served forty-two million people in 2011, about 83 percent of the population.[38] It spent about USD 11 billion, 49.2 percent of the national total spent on health.[39] It is organized into provincial health departments, which in turn provide district-based public health care. This is the successor to the old "Bantu" health care system.

The private sector in 2011 served 8.2 million people, or about 17 percent of the population. It accounted for USD 10.5 billion, or 48.5 percent of national total spending on health care.

An estimate is that the 17 percent participating in the private sector are served by almost 60 percent of the nation's medical doctors. Conversely, the 83 percent of the population served by the public sector are cared for by 41 percent of medical doctors.[40]

Private health care is largely funded by private insurance: there are approximately 110 registered medical schemes that enroll some 3.4 million principal members with 7.8 million beneficiaries.

NATIONAL HEALTH INSURANCE

The National Development Plan is blunt in its assessment of the health system: "The overall performance of the health system since 1994 has been poor, despite the development of good policy and relatively high spending as a proportion of GDP. Services are fragmented between the public and private sectors. . . . Imbalances in spending between the public and private sector have skewed the distribution of services. . . . Evidence suggests multiple system failure across a range of programmes. At the heart of this failure is the inability to get primary health care and the district health system to function effectively."[41]

In 2011, the ANC government proposed an overhaul of the current health care delivery system by a National Health Insurance.[42] It aimed to eliminate the current system of underfunded free medical care and private medical care paid for by the individual recipient. Instead, a single health insurance fund would be created in which public and private funding would be pooled. There would be an emphasis on health promotion and prevention services in the individual community and household.

The government envisioned several steps over fourteen years. For the first five years, the emphasis was on strengthening the public health sector in preparation for National Health Insurance following the issuance of a white paper and the necessary legislation by parliament.

In 2014, the government announced that it would be building 43 new hospitals and 213 clinics over the next five years. In addition, the minister of health said, the Department of Health will refurbish 870 clinics. South African medical schools have agreed to enroll 425 additional students, and more Cuban medical specialists are being recruited.[43]

This process remains mostly on track. In 2011, the government described in a green paper the principles of National Health Insurance. A white paper is expected soon that will be the basis for parliamentary legislation. Many details await the white paper and parliamentary legislation, and a national debate has only just started. For example, it is not clear how taxes to pay for the program would be assessed. It is assumed that the rich would, in effect, be subsidizing the poor. Some medical doctors are concerned that the new system will result in a decline in their incomes.

Private medical insurance, however, would seem to be permitted. If so, what is envisaged seems similar to the National Health in the United Kingdom, which transformed public health for the better in that country. Free universal health care is guaranteed for all, but individuals can and do pay for private medical insurance that provides access to fee-based medical care. However, the existence of the National Health alternative keeps down the costs of private medicine.

The process of developing National Health Insurance appears to be a model of South African governance at its best. Widespread consultation was the key. The National Department of Health consulted professional associations, statutory bodies, government departments, academic civil society, and parliament. Input was also invited from the pharmaceutical industry and from medical professionals. There was an international conference to explore the experiences of other countries that have introduced universal health care. Eleven pilot districts were identified. The minister of health visited each and met altogether with over fifteen thousand stakeholders.

HIV/AIDS PROGRESS IN SOUTH AFRICA

South Africa has been the world's ground zero in the HIV/AIDS tragedy. In 2014, about 5.51 million people were HIV positive, about 10 percent of South Africa's population.[44] According to *The Economist*, the HIV/AIDS disease burden was carried disproportionately by blacks, 13 percent of whom were HIV positive. For coloureds it was 3 percent; for whites, less than 1 percent.[45] South African women also carried a disproportionate burden; they are more than half of all new cases of infection.[46]

Health minister Dr. Aaron Motsoaledi commented in February 2014 that the mortality rate doubled in the country between 2006 and 2007, a statistic characteristic of a war zone.[47] In 2014, he went on, 49 percent of maternal deaths were attributable to HIV/AIDS; the child mortality rate (children who die by the age of five) was 35 percent because of HIV/AIDS. The disease also makes people vulnerable to other diseases. "A lot of cancers . . . diseases like leprosy and TB, which we thought had been defeated, came back because of HIV/AIDS." He also commented that 43 percent of people who were HIV positive "developed mental health problems."[48]

Despite the trends in previous years, a recent report released by Statistics South Africa in December 2014 revealed that the mortality rate in South Africa was at its lowest in over a decade; 458,933 people died in 2013 (6.5 percent down from 491,100 deaths in 2012).[49] The vast majority of deaths were due to preventable diseases. Tuberculosis remained the leading cause of death among South Africans (8.8 percent of total deaths), followed by influenza and pneumonia (5.2 percent), HIV (5.1 percent), cerebrovascular diseases (4.9 percent), and diabetes mellitus (4.8 percent). Nevertheless, HIV had risen to become the third leading cause of death in the country. Medical professionals also gained expertise in accurately reporting deaths due to HIV/AIDS, rather than other coinfectious diseases, such as TB.[50] The stigma around HIV/AIDS has diminished in South Africa due to enhanced public health programs and national discussion on the disease. On World AIDS Day, December 1, 2014, South Africa attempted to break the record for the number of people tested for HIV/AIDS.[51] Despite promising and more accurate statistics, the Statistics South Africa report exhibits some worrying trends: tuberculosis and HIV/AIDS remain widespread, diabetes has become a "prominent killer," and malnutrition still kills 7 percent of children who died at one to four years old. With a renewed focus on public health initiatives, the Department of Health has decided to make these health statistics available on a quarterly basis in the hopes that this downward trend continues.[52]

The slow and unscientific response to HIV/AIDS by the administrations of Nelson Mandela and Thabo Mbeki was one of the greatest failures of the early years of post-apartheid, nonracial democracy. But, in the Zuma administration, there has been a turnaround. According to a South African Institute of Race Relations (IRR) spokesperson, the Department of Health distributed almost four hundred million condoms (male and female) in 2011/2012.[53] Condom use at first sex increased from 18 percent to 66 percent between 1996 and 2012. According to the IRR, those who use condoms at first sex are likely to continue to do so.[54] The Department of Health also launched a campaign to convince as many men as possible to choose circumcision. According to Dr. Motsoaledi, "We have circumcised one million men—we are going to quadruple it and circumcise four million men by 2016."[55] (Circumcision significantly reduces the male risk of contracting HIV.[56]) He said that the campaign to reduce mother-to-child transmission of HIV is working: "It is now markedly low at 2.7 percent. At one stage, it was 8 percent. We want it to go below 1 percent or if possible 0 percent."[57] According to the IRR, the new infection rate has decreased by more than 50 percent since 1999.[58]

There has also been a dramatic increase in the number of South African HIV/AIDS victims receiving antiretroviral treatment (ART). Here, the United States has been an important partner. According to the American embassy in Pretoria, the President's Emergency Plan for AIDS Relief (PEPFAR) has invested more than USD 4.2 billion in South Africa's HIV and TB programs. Unusual for PEPFAR partners, the South African government has assumed greater managerial and financial responsibilities for these programs, now investing about USD 1.5 billion annually of its own revenue in countering HIV and AIDS.[59]

The payoff can be seen in South Africa's significant increase in life expectancy, from 51.56 years in 2005 to 56.10 years in 2012.[60] South Africa still carries a heavy HIV/AIDS burden and will do so for a long time. But the South African government's recent campaigns against HIV/AIDS are a major achievement.

South Africa's approach to health issues other than the HIV/AIDS disaster under presidents Mandela and Mbeki had been engaged and practical, and that approach has continued under President Zuma. Thus far, it has been remarkably nonpolemical, and discussion and process have not been distorted by the country's history of racial division. Though the disease burden remains very high, HIV/AIDS has been contained, and the life spans of South Africans are increasing, though they are not yet at pre-HIV/AIDS levels. The establishment of a National Health Insurance is proceeding and, thus far, appears to be largely accepted, at least in principle. That would appear to be a consequence of provisions for the continuation of private medicine and private medical insurance to pay for it. There have also, as yet, been few details about how the National Health Insurance program will be paid for. It is anticipated, however, that the upper and middle classes, who pay most of the direct taxes, will carry much of that burden.

CONCLUSION

South African institutions are responding successfully to health issues. With respect to education, the assessment must be mixed. Certainly there have been achievements. For example, in 1996, 22.5 percent of five-year-olds were enrolled in early childhood development; by 2007, that percentage had grown to over 80 percent. Racial segregation has been dismantled; in historically white schools, about 56 percent of students are black. In 1990, about a third of all students enrolled in higher education were black; now that percentage has increased to two-thirds.[61]

But the education quality for those in public-sector primary schools remains low. The annual national assessment of fifth-graders in 2013 showed that only 46 percent were literate and 33 percent were numerate.[62]

With respect to primary and secondary education, especially in the townships, change is constrained by attitudes toward education, shaped in part by the struggle against apartheid. South Africa's powerful teachers' union, an important element in the governing coalition, also works against change. Moreover, perhaps even more important, the fact that a world-class education sector already exists and is accessible to the new elites mitigates against radical reform.

It may be significant that on the left, there is already discussion of the possibility of eventually abolishing private education to free resources for educational reform across the board, but also to generate the energy and the political will for meaningful change. If health is a matter of science and organization, perhaps education in South Africa is shaped to a greater extent by political realities. If so, further dramatic progress on education may await the emergence of a genuine left-wing political party, perhaps by the 2019 elections.

So, South Africa can foresee a healthier population that lives longer than it does now. The National Development Plan's goal of an average male life expectancy of seventy years would certainly seem to be realistic, especially given the progress in fighting HIV/AIDS. But, with an educational system that continues to prepare too few to participate fully in the new, knowledge-based economy, economic growth is likely to remain relatively low and poverty is likely to be an enduring reality. While education for too many blacks in South Africa has stagnated, elsewhere in Africa education is improving. South Africa's hitherto comparative advantage of having the most skilled workforce on the continent may be eroding, making it difficult for the undereducated to break out of the cycle of poverty.

Whites continue to have access to first-world-quality education, yet educational standards for most blacks remain below those of Robert Mugabe's Zimbabwe. Clearly apartheid and its restrictions on black access to education and the tradition of school boycotts and strikes promoted by leaders of the anti-apartheid struggle have caused long-lasting damage. Yet improvement in education is vital if South Africa is to grow its economy and address poverty.

Health care also reflects a legacy of apartheid not yet overcome. There are parallel health care systems. South African medicine has a modern sector. Yet for township dwellers, medical care is poor, and in rural areas, often nonexistent. HIV/AIDS remains a scourge, so much so that the average life span of nonwhite South Africans is about the same as for Nigerians; for whites it is broadly comparable to Americans (if the data are aggregated from both genders and all races).[63] The disease burden, like educational shortcomings, is an important barrier to economic growth and reflects the enduring apartheid legacy.

6

LAND

In 1996, two years after Nelson Mandela's inauguration, white commercial farmers owned 70 percent of the land and leased an additional 17 percent, mostly from the government and tribal authorities.[1] Then, as now, South Africa had the most developed commercial agricultural sector in sub-Saharan Africa and was an important food exporter, including wine, meat, sugar, and grain. Who possesses land in South Africa is inextricably linked to history and race. Whites' ownership of land is disproportionately far greater than their share of the population. Among many black and coloured South Africans, white ownership is seen as the result of almost four hundred years of white supremacy mandated by law and enforced with violence. Blacks frequently view disproportionate white ownership of land as a root cause of their poverty.[2]

Related to the land question is the issue of where people live. South Africa is rapidly urbanizing, a process that accelerated with the ending of apartheid legislation that sought to confine blacks to homelands. People are streaming into the large South African cities, as they had into Johannesburg even under apartheid. But they are also moving to smaller urban centers. Many, even most, of the new arrivals are too poor to buy land, most of which is privately owned.

In the rural areas of some parts of the country, black and coloured farmworkers are tenants with little security of tenure. It has long been the policy of the governing African National Congress (ANC) to secure for them regularization or security of tenure or, ideally, to facilitate their purchase of the land they work. That goal has not been achieved.

Especially in the former "homelands," individual land ownership is relatively rare. The more usual practice is communal ownership by the tribe or the clan. In those areas, it is often the traditional rulers who have the ultimate authority. It has long been recognized that reform is needed, but traditional rulers are part of the constituency of Jacob Zuma's faction within the ANC.[3]

So land issues in South Africa involve more than restitution to those who lost their land because of apartheid social engineering or increasing the surface area of the country owned by blacks.

In many postcolonial societies, unresolved land issues have undermined new democracies. Many South Africans of all races express concern that the failure of the post-1994 government to impose an equitable land settlement feeds popular discontent that potentially undermines the constitution and the rule of law, the heart of the 1994 transition to nonracial democracy. Those who are pessimistic about the future will cite black farmworker murders of white employers as evidence of the consequences of the failure to carry out redistribution of land, and they will argue that South Africa is following the disastrous trajectory of Zimbabwe.

South African discussion across racial lines of rural land ownership issues is often framed in terms of justice and equity but also the need to mitigate unemployment and the poverty it fosters. Many politicians—not just radicals—argue that white-owned farmland should be provided to landless blacks who would, in effect, operate family farms. The assumption of many such advocates is that family farms would absorb some amount of black unemployment and thereby alleviate poverty.

Rural dwellers by and large are very poor. One estimate is that almost 40 percent of rural households survive on less than USD 1.50/day, with the poor spending more than 40 percent of their income on food.[4] Like the rural poor elsewhere in Africa, they are largely voiceless. But their legitimate grievances have been exploited by political figures, now with an urban base, such as Winnie Mandela and Julius Malema, to advance their own ambitions by advocating the expropriation of white property without compensation. Their articulation of this possibility lends a sense of urgency among many South Africans regardless of race for the significant transfer of land from whites to blacks.

Continuing poverty among rural dwellers does make them a potential pool for radical movements that if in power would destroy South Africa's commercial agricultural sector. However, their proportion of the population is declining because of urbanization. Too many residents of new townships live in shacks on plots too small for them to grow their own food and with the local authorities providing little more than water and electricity points. Better education and training opportunities would open the door to employment for both the rural and urban jobless. That would more likely lift the rural poor out of poverty than the transfer of a percentage of South Africa's land surface from people of one race to people of another. This view is held disproportionately by whites, but that does not reduce its validity.

With its juxtaposition of history, emotion, race, poverty, and economics, land is perhaps the most difficult issue South Africa's successive post-apartheid governments have faced. Nevertheless, at present, landholding issues remain within the purview of the law, the courts, and parliamentary politics, not the "revolutionary justice" of Julius Malema's rhetoric or the thuggish practice of Robert Mugabe's Zimbabwe. The management of land issues, including open and free public debate in a free media and in parliament, with all their complexities and ambiguities explored, is clear evidence of the relative maturity of South Africa's democracy. With rapid urbanization and the restructuring of the economy away from mining and agriculture, it remains to be seen how long and to what extent white-to-black land transfers will continue to be a significant issue for the majority of the population. The government has built more than three million houses since the end of apartheid. It has, literally, given them away to their occupants who eventually will own them fee simple. Already, some have been bought, sold, and mortgaged. Such houses become a store of wealth over time and could transform for the better a significant percentage of township residents.

WHO OWNS THE LAND?

Information about the current racial breakdown of land ownership in South Africa is largely anecdotal, though the conventional wisdom remains that it is overwhelmingly white. In 1911 and subsequently, the political settlement between the British and the Afrikaners that created the Union of South Africa set aside 87 percent of the land for whites. Much of the 13 percent remaining to blacks consisted of "tribal" lands under the control of traditional rulers, rather than individually owned holdings.

From the early days of Dutch settlement to 1994, South Africa's government was entirely white except in the apartheid-created "independent" and "self-governing" homelands for blacks. During that period it made sense to see government-owned land as "white." Most other land was owned by individual, white proprietors. Hence, the statement that whites "owned" 87 percent of the land described a reality. It no longer does.

Post-apartheid, and with the coming of nonracial democracy, the application of racial categories to land ownership works less well. Government-owned land, which accounts for 14 percent of South African territory, is no longer "white"; government land, like the government itself, is "nonracial."[5] The same is true of land owned by corporations, an increasingly large percentage. That land is not "white owned" because corporations are not defined by race. Private land sales by whites to blacks, and vice versa, are also not recorded by race. However, government-sponsored transfers of land from whites to blacks as restitution for seizures under apartheid are usually recorded by race. Taking such factors into consideration, the conventional wisdom is credible that private white individuals own about half of the productive land in South Africa.[6]

A spokesman for the Department of Land Affairs notes that while the Deeds Registry Database does not record land ownership according to race, he estimated that blacks owned 13 percent of the country's surface area in 1994. Most of this presumably was in the former "independent" and "self-governing" homelands that were subsequently reincorporated into South Africa. Such land was held by tribal trusts and similar instruments, rather than individual fee-simple ownership. Since then, he said, blacks had acquired an additional 4.9 million hectares, or 4.69 percent of the country's surface area, the result of government-mandated land reform and land restitution programs.[7]

These figures would indicate that blacks currently own approximately 18 percent of the surface area. Nevertheless, at present, the debate over the number and amount of such transactions is largely based on speculation.

Much of South Africa is semiarid and not good agricultural land. So, the quality of the land that one group or another owns is as much an issue as the quantity. The percent of ownership by race also varies by location, as statistics in KwaZulu-Natal, Mpumalanga, and the Northwest show white land ownership as low as 24 percent.[8] On the other hand, in the capital-intensive wine country of the Western Cape, most of the productive land is white owned and worked by coloureds.

Commercial agriculture is declining in importance to the economy. It is now only 3 percent, as opposed to 20 percent of Zimbabwe's economy before Mugabe expropriated white-owned commercial farms.[9] Still, whites clearly own a disproportionate share of the land, just as they own and control a disproportionate share of all other market-based activities. This is an issue easily exploited by African populists when the overall economy is growing slowly and the conditions of the black and coloured poor are slow to change.

After the Boer War, land "reserved" for blacks resembled in some way the contemporary "Indian reservations" established in the American West. In the United States the vast majority of vacant land was owned by the federal government, which oversaw its sale or distribution to private corporations (particularly the railways) or its sale to individuals, especially by the provisions of the Homestead Act (1863). In effect, what was left over became "Indian reservations," usually through treaties between the federal government and Native American tribes. As in the South African "homelands," much of the land was of marginal productivity, and in modern times Indian reservations became a byword for rural poverty and social dysfunction, especially alcoholism.

Throughout the twentieth century, Native Americans voted with their feet, moving off the reservations to live among the general population, usually in urban areas. A similar process appears to be under way in post-apartheid South Africa, where there are high levels of migration from the former "independent" and "self-governing" homelands into those areas formerly reserved for whites and coloureds.

American Indian reservations and South African homelands were both supposed to be "self-governing." The quality of governance in the homelands was variable but often corrupt, as it was on the U.S. reservations. In both situations corruption was a reflection of pervasive poverty and the limited scope for genuine governance that Washington and Pretoria respectively allowed.

A significant difference between reservations in the United States and homelands in South Africa is that the latter were designed to ensure a readily available pool of black labor to the big industrial cities and commercial farming operations. Male labor was increasingly housed "temporarily" in hostels near places of employment while workers' families remained in the homelands. Reservations, often in geographically remote areas, rarely had the function of providing a pool of labor for factories and mines, though many Native Americans did work on white-owned farms and ranches.

The apartheid-era agricultural sector was heavily dependent on government subsidies. Starting under Mandela's administration, successive ANC governments have been reducing or eliminating these subsidies. Accordingly the number of commercial farmers has declined from about sixty thousand to some forty thousand even as efficiency and production have increased. Of the remaining farms, only about half have an annual turnover of more than USD 32,000.[10] As in the United States, with the decline of the "family farm" and the rise of the "factory farm," corporate land ownership is growing significantly. Commercial agriculture is also growing in scale and, as in the United States, is increasingly a corporate enterprise characterized by high levels of investment and technology.

In the former homelands, there remains much underused land potentially available for labor-intensive agriculture. The land is black owned, but not by individuals. Instead, much of it is held by tribal trusts that are controlled by traditional rulers. By and large, traditional rulers oppose changes in the status of tribal trust land, a major source of their local power and influence. They are often political allies of Jacob Zuma, who has been reluctant to address tribal land issues.

LAND AND POVERTY

South Africans of all races regularly identify poverty, the burden of HIV/AIDS, crime, and corruption as the nation's most important problems. Especially for many whites, land redistribution is largely irrelevant to meeting these challenges or, if it were to be implemented on a large scale, has serious trade-offs. For example, replacement of Africa's most efficient commercial farms by small units operated by individual proprietors might reduce unemployment but could also reduce food security throughout the southern African region because of its inherent inefficiencies and likely lower levels of investment. That would result in lower levels of production and likely higher food prices. Instead of land redistribution, so the argument runs, it is the expansion of South Africa's technological and industrial base that could lead to a reduction of unemployment and poverty. That, in turn, argues for greater attention to education.

Many in the ANC and the South African Communist Party (SACP) have long accepted this argument. Joe Slovo, Nelson Mandela's housing minister and a SACP icon, is famously said to have maintained that he had no intention of destroying Africa's most efficient agricultural sector to create a class of African peasant farmers.[11] For him as a Marxist-Leninist, the issue was how to promote modernization and industrialization of the economy with accompanying urbanization. That process manifestly required domestic and foreign investment that could be threatened if land redistribution failed to respect the property rights guaranteed in the constitution. Hence, a confirmed Marxist-Leninist argued pragmatically for respect of property rights as promoting economic growth that would reduce poverty. But other South African communists at various times seemed to envisage a system of state-owned agricultural enterprises that would retain the benefits of large-scale farming and a high level of investment.

However, for many vocal black and coloured South Africans, Slovo's argument is beside the point. For them, land is not primarily an economic issue related to poverty reduction. Instead, it is about justice and recovery of self-esteem destroyed by centuries of white supremacy.[12]

There is no consensus among South Africans as to what genuine land redistribution and tenure reform would look like or who should pay for it, only a deeply felt, popular consensus that it needs to occur. It is a cause embraced in theory by political and opinion leaders right across the racial spectrum, including white politicians in the Democratic Alliance (DA).

COMPLEXITIES AND THE SHORTCOMINGS OF CONVENTIONAL WISDOM

It is conventional wisdom that land redistribution from whites to blacks, accepted in principle by the ANC and the opposition DA, is proceeding too slowly. When Nelson Mandela was president, his national plan stated that blacks would own 30 percent of the land by 2014. It has been the failure to even approach that target that is behind the argument that land reform has not worked.

Where did the target come from, and is it a valid baseline for judging success or failure? The 30 percent target has always had an arbitrary air about it. It emerged at a meeting of experts convened by the World Bank at the request of the ANC in 1993, looking toward the 1994 transition. According to one participant, the experts considered three scenarios for future land redistribution from whites to blacks: 10 percent, 30 percent, and 50 percent. They concluded that the first alternative was politically unacceptable, the 50 percent option was impractical, and the 30 percent was "reasonable." So, from the beginning the land target was governed by political calculation rather than by historical or economic factors or the pursuit of post-apartheid justice.[13]

Nevertheless, the goal has acquired a mystique and legitimacy. For some blacks, the failure to carry out meaningful agricultural land reform is the cause of their enduring poverty, even if they are urban township dwellers. In that sense, the slow pace of land redistribution is symbolic of the post-apartheid state's failure to transform the conditions of the poor.

Julius Malema's demands for the seizure without compensation of white-owned land, usually in conjunction with the nationalization of the mines, have also been floated in various factions of the ANC, the SACP, and COSATU. The presumption is that such a view resonates among the black poor. Malema's Economic Freedom Fighters (EFF) contested the 2014 elections on the signature issue of expropriation of white-owned property. The relatively low level of its electoral support may call into question the extent to which land redistribution remains a defining issue in black politics. On the other hand, the EFF is a new political party, its supporters will argue, and its campaign was poorly organized. Nevertheless, for now, the EFF does not define the debate over land reform.

LAND AFTER APARTHEID

Under the ANC, land reform has had three dimensions: restitution to those who lost their land under apartheid, a process mandated by the constitution; redistribution of land from those who possess it (mostly whites) to those who do not (mostly blacks), but taking into account the private property guarantees in the constitution; and reform of land tenure to protect the interests of farmworkers on privately owned land and those working land held by tribal trusts and not owned by individuals.

In the aftermath of apartheid, the governing ANC's stated land policy has centered on the redress of historical injustices, including restitution to those whose land was seized as part of the effort to separate the races geographically; more equitable distribution of agricultural land among the races; and greater rural development, including its prerequisite, land tenure reform. These goals, sloganized as "restitution, redistribution, and tenure reform," are broadly accepted by the opposition parties. Their general acceptance plays an important part in inoculating the land issue against violence.

But implementation is difficult, expensive, and contentious. Should the government spend scarce resources on land transfer from one race to another or on urban development in a now urban-majority country?

The nagging persistence of the land question unsettles potential international and domestic investors who too often conflate Zimbabwe and South Africa despite their very different political and social realities. The radical rhetoric of Julius Malema and a few others also almost certainly acts as a brake on foreign investment.

RESTITUTION

Under successive ANC governments, restitution of land seized by the apartheid regime has been a separate process from land redistribution.

In 2014 the cutoff date for lodging a claim for restitution was extended to the end of 2019 to mop up remaining cases. The legislation was also extended to cover the period before the 1913 land legislation. The government accepts a broad range of evidence in support of claims, and there have been few complaints about the process, except for its slow pace. Of the cases settled by 2006, more than 80 percent related to urban land. Most beneficiaries, 92 percent of them, opted for financial compensation. In those cases where the government had to purchase land, much of it had a specific historical or cultural dimension. It was expensive because under the provisions of "willing seller, willing buyer," the government had little negotiating power with the owners. In a February 2013 speech in parliament, Minister of Rural Development and Land Reform Gugile Nkwinti said that altogether the government spent USD 1.2 billion on 1.44 million hectares.[14]

Critics of the restitution process argue that many claimants were steered toward accepting financial compensation rather than recovery of the land itself by ignorance of the bureaucratic process. And, undeniably, financial compensation was cheaper for the government than buying land for restitution. Both current and past owners had a right to compensation: those who currently owned the land (usually whites) received compensation at market prices, whereas past owners (mostly blacks) were given a symbolic compensation reflecting the value of the land at the time it was seized, known as the Standard Settlement Offer.[15] Further, in numerous cases the land seized under apartheid was assigned only a nominal value. Often, too, because the financial compensation was divided among the often numerous descendants of those whose land was taken, an individual received only a small amount, too small to be transformative. Accordingly, claimants often erected tombstones or made improvements in the houses that they already owned with the money they received.[16] Though the evidence is anecdotal, few recipients appear to have used the payments they received to start businesses.

Whites whose land had been taken as the result of apartheid were also eligible for restitution. In an ironic twist, between 1994 and 2013, the government spent over USD 1 billion for restitution to whites and only about USD 600 million for working-class black claimants. Whites usually opted for land, while blacks chose financial compensation.[17]

As the restitution process enters its second stage, there are proposals to make the claimant process more straightforward and to provide counseling for the beneficiaries on the choices that might be available. However, the issue remains that the government faces serious financial constraints.[18]

REDISTRIBUTION

South Africa's transition to nonracial democracy was a political compromise between the National Party government and the liberation movements. Hence, South Africa's constitution and law are not straightforward on land issues. For example, Section 25.5 of the constitution guarantees property rights but obliges the state "to enable citizens to gain access to land on an equitable basis." So long as the principle of "willing seller, willing buyer" was in effect, some whites were reluctant to sell to the government for subsequent redistribution. When they did so, there were often whispers of collusion between appraisers and sellers that resulted in very high selling prices.[19]

Accordingly, in his 2013 state of the nation address to parliament, President Zuma announced that his government is dropping the "willing seller, willing buyer" principle to accelerate land redistribution.[20] Presumably to square the constitutional rights to private property, it would be replaced by "the just and equitable principle of compensation," as also provided for by the constitution. What this will mean is unclear. Necessary legislation will be subject to amendment and doubtlessly will be the subject of extensive litigation. The proposed legislation allows the state to expropriate property "for a public purpose" or "in the public interest." It provides for compensation that should reflect "an equitable balance between the public interest and the interests of the former owner." It also established the Office of the Valuer General to value property identified for land reform or expropriation. In March 2010, Minister of Rural Development and Land Reform Gugile Nkwinti reaffirmed a "use it or lose it" policy that those who received redistributed land would "lose it if they did not use it."[21] It is by no means certain that the cost of acquiring land for redistribution would decline. However, there is anecdotal evidence that in some parts of the country, particularly KwaZulu-Natal, the uncertainties generated by the current debate over land reform, including the Zuma administration's abandonment of the "willing seller, willing buyer" principle, is encouraging whites to sell out to private black buyers.[22]

The opposition DA opposes abandoning "willing seller, willing buyer." It acknowledges the need for land reform: "We believe that the current patterns of land ownership are skewed and it is a moral imperative that they are changed." It argues that the shortcomings of the land redistribution program have not been the result of the failure of "market forces," as claimed by the ANC, but rather of government administrative incompetence. It argues for a "market-oriented approach," the meaning of which is unclear.[23] An MP from the Freedom Front Plus, a white, rural-based, tiny political party, stated in a parliamentary debate that the government's land reform proposals were "whipping up emotions" and threatened to create a "Zimbabwe situation."[24] That is a view held by many in the white commercial agricultural community.

Given the huge ANC majority in parliament and the general consensus in South Africa that the current pattern of land ownership requires reform, Zuma's proposed legislation is likely to become law. However, given the DA's strong opposition to eliminating "willing seller, willing buyer," something approximating the principle may well be retained. Once passed, any legislation is bound to be challenged in the courts.

Perhaps more significant than white reluctance to sell, the slow pace of government land purchases for redistribution has been dependent on the availability of government funding. Under the Mandela, Mbeki, and Zuma administrations, the economy has been managed according to the liberal principles of the Washington Consensus, which has meant a disciplined approach to foreign borrowing, currency stability, protection of private property, and encouragement of foreign investment. Hence, land redistribution has not been funded by wholesale borrowing. Were public authorities to have expropriated privately owned land without compensation, there would likely have been deleterious consequences for both domestic and international investment in the broader South African economy. Hence, the government has never had a realistic option of expropriation without compensation.

Righting specific historic injustices tied to post-1948 apartheid has proved to be easier than transforming the racial distribution of land to reflect the demographics of contemporary South Africa. In no year since the institution of nonracial democracy in 1994 has the government devoted more than 1 percent of the budget for purchasing land for redistribution, including land for restitution.[25] Put another way, the government has spent an estimated total USD 3.2 billion on land reform during the nineteen-year period between 1994 and 2013. That is equal to the budget for urban housing development in a single year.[26] Beyond the land question, South Africa does little to help new farmers.

South Africa spends just 2 percent of its national budget on agriculture, among the lowest on the continent.[27]

This may be changing. In March 2014, Minister for Economic Development Ebrahim Patel announced that the ANC government had acquired, redistributed, restituted, or restored 4,301,005 acres from 2009 to 2013. The cost, he said, was ZAR 20 billion, the equivalent, at that time, of about USD 1.8 billion. He also said that the government was providing assistance to some seven hundred thousand smallholders, including access to finance and the provision of irrigation. The payoff of land reform, the minister said, was that agricultural-sector employment grew by sixty-five thousand from 2009 to 2013. If this trend is sustained, it would be a reversal of the trend since 1994 of the decline in the number of agricultural workers.[28]

On balance, redistribution thus far may have had a negative, if marginal, economic impact, despite the minister's claim that it has created agricultural employment. However, the evidence is contradictory. In 2009, Minister Gugile Nkwinti told parliament that more than half of the farms acquired by the government for redistribution had failed or were failing. The government estimated in 2010 that 90 percent of the redistributed land was "no longer productive." This assessment was based on a comparison with the former use of the land. The new owners often lacked the capital and agricultural skills of the former owners. However, a government study before 2006 showed that perhaps half of the new farmers were, indeed, earning income from agriculture.[29]

LAND TENURE REFORM

Land tenure reform is also moving slowly. Numerous different tenure arrangements exist, and often modern and traditional land tenure arrangements collide, especially in the former "independent" or "self-governing" homelands. Fee-simple ownership and other forms of land tenure associated with the modern economy rub against more traditional tenure arrangements that may be collective in spirit. Traditional tenure often reflects how the land is used rather than who owns it, and it is operated by traditional rulers and indigenous institutions according to local law and custom. Additionally, in areas dominated by white commercial farming, there are many black agricultural laborers and tenants.

The consensus is that these laborers have few rights and are often subject to abuse, as they have been in the past. Almost one million black and coloured people were forcibly removed from commercial farms between 1994 and 2004, more than in the final decade of apartheid.[30] Many of them likely joined the exodus from rural areas to shantytowns around cities. Legislation was passed in 1996 and 1997 to provide some security of tenure for those living on privately owned land, but the consensus is that it has not been well enforced due to bureaucratic weaknesses and shortages of funding.

The ANC government has sought to address some of these issues through legislation. The 2004 Communal Land Rights Act sought to shift land tenure arrangements in communal areas from the state to traditional institutions. It would have greatly increased the power of traditional rulers over their subjects. One estimate is that up to twenty-one million people, mostly in the former "independent" or "self-govern-ing" homelands, would have been subject to its provisions.[31] That is more than a third of the country's population. The South African Constitutional Court subsequently declared it unconstitutional because it vested authority in unelected traditional rulers, violated the principle of gender equality enshrined in the constitution but not in indigenous practice, and undermined some forms of existing tenure. A new government policy on land tenure in communal areas is promised.

For most blacks and many coloureds, land policy should take into account the injustices and sufferings of the past. Most whites do not want to take into account the past beyond righting the post-1948 wrongs of apartheid, or, at most, post-1913 white land seizures.

MTHATHA

An October 2011 land invasion may provide some insight about the popular status of land redistribution. In that episode, hundreds of local people invaded and seized about 141 acres of land belonging to a congregation of the Uniting Reformed Church outside of Mthatha in the Eastern Cape.[32] According to press reports at the time, the invaders divided the land into tiny parcels, and its leadership committee promised to sell each of them for seven thousand rand (then about USD 860).[33] The division of the land into small plots is an indication that the invaders intended to build shacks rather than to farm. The invasion appears to have reflected housing shortages resulting from the pressures of urbanization rather than rural land hunger.

The Mthatha invasion of land belonging to a religious institution was unusual in South Africa and may have reflected specifically local factors. The more frequent practice has been for squatters to occupy land they thought belonged to a public authority rather than to private individuals or institutions.

The church applied to the court for an eviction order, which a judge promptly served. Unlike in the Zimbabwean land invasions, the occupiers then departed peacefully. There was no violence or continuing public protest despite the Eastern Cape's tradition of political activism. If the police were present, there were no media reports of complaints about their behavior.

It is likely that the land invaders were united by at least nominal allegiance to the ANC, even if they were of varied ethnicities. The Eastern Cape where Mthatha is located has a tradition of political radicalism rooted in the anti-apartheid movement. Fort Hare, probably the most distinguished black university under apartheid, is nearby. So, too, is the Mandela ancestral homestead. The Mbeki family, which provided multigenerational leadership for the ANC, also hailed from the Eastern Cape. But there is no evidence that ANC elites played any role in the Mthatha land invasion.

Did this incident have shades of the land grabs from white farmers in Zimbabwe by President Robert Mugabe's "war veteran" thugs? The invaders' rhetoric did recall Mugabe's and Malema's. For example, a spokesman for the invaders' committee said the community was reoccupying land "taken by force and grabbed by missionaries. People have taken the decision to go back and occupy their forefathers' land as beneficiaries."[34]

In Zimbabwe, land seizures were at least in part initially orchestrated by black elites operating within the ruling political party who then lost control to "war veterans" and land-hungry rural masses. By contrast, the Mthatha incident was locally instigated rather than having been encouraged by the national government or the ANC, even though the Eastern Cape is a party stronghold. Mthatha did not spark a larger popular movement to seize land.

Perhaps the greatest difference between Mthatha and the Zimbabwe land invasions was that the South Africa drama was framed by the rule of law. The judiciary, known to be independent and thorough, promptly issued an eviction order that the occupiers accepted, even if they did not agree with it, and there was no violence. That behavior fits polling data that show that while a substantial minority of blacks and coloureds favor expropriation of white-owned land without compensation, a substantial majority believe land policy must be based on the rule of law.[35]

Hence, the real significance of the Mthatha episode is that it did not foreshadow an adoption of the Zimbabwe approach to land redistribution, but rather it demonstrated popular acceptance of the judicial process and the rule of law in contemporary South Africa. The style of the Mthatha invasion was not that of the guerrilla warfare that marked the end of the colonial regime in Zimbabwe and that shaped the land invasions.[36] Mthatha reflects the South African tradition of using popular protest rather than terrorism to bring about political and social change.

Mthatha is also a reminder that land is as much an urban as it is a rural issue. Squatter settlements existed in many places even during apartheid times when pass laws were designed to ensure population "influx control." Then as now, most "informal settlements" were outside big cities. So, too, were squatter invasions of vacant land, to which, under apartheid, the police response was often brutal. On occasion, however, during apartheid the local authorities accommodated the squatters, and white landowners could profit from selling tiny plots at very high prices. Twenty years after apartheid, land for poor blacks remains in short supply in close proximity to nearly all South African cities. Mthatha is one of those numerous medium-sized urban areas that have grown quickly over the past decade as people have moved out of impoverished rural areas, and the construction of housing for the poor, even at the most minimal standard, has not kept up.

CHALLENGES TO REFORM

Some international investors see the South African government's approach to land reform and mineral rights as together a kind of litmus test as to its commitment to private property rights and hence whether to invest in South Africa. The Zuma government is acutely aware of this and is thereby constrained from the wholesale violation of property rights that radicals such as Malema advocate. The emergence of a black entrepreneurial and investment class closely tied to the ANC leadership has probably strengthened the ruling party's commitment to private property and diminished those still within the party and its communist and trade union partners who advocate socialist ideals and methods.

Some South Africans continue to see a mystical tie between the land that contains the graves of their ancestors and those displaced from it during apartheid. Their numbers are difficult to judge. Compensation to those who lost their land due to apartheid measures has overwhelmingly been, by the recipients' often uninformed choice, monetary rather than the return of the land itself.[37] Rural land reform appears increasingly to be a matter of symbols and sentiment, rather than of farmer livelihood.

On the other hand, rural black unemployment is estimated to be about 52 percent.[38] Some advocates for the rural poor see the African peasant agricultural sector as having the potential to greatly reduce rural unemployment and poverty. However, doing it right, with the technical and financial support that such farmers would need from the government, would be very expensive. Despite the party's strongholds in rural KwaZulu-Natal and the Eastern Cape, the ANC's core constituency is becoming urban as well as including the rural poor. Its immediate concerns are education, jobs, health, and housing—not farmland or even perhaps how much of South Africa's surface is owned by members of what race. Further, within the ANC and more broadly, there is the strong sense that it is commercial agriculture with its high levels of investment that guarantees South Africa's food security. Hence many of those who advocate for land redistribution to more closely reflect the country's racial demographics resist breaking up large enterprises into small farms. Some large commercial farms have therefore been distributed to black collectives rather than being broken up into individual plots. These have not been notably successful.[39]

OUTLOOK FOR LAND REFORM

Restitution of land seized under apartheid is likely to continue its slow but positive trajectory. The transfer of land from whites to blacks through government intervention is likely to continue to be slow. So, too, is the reform of land tenure laws, especially in the former "independent" or "self-governing" homelands where tenure is based on tradition.

Meanwhile, the demands on the government to meet the immediate needs of a growing population—above all, schools, health services, and the creation of jobs—mean that the resources and energy available for land transfer are small. Further, beyond rhetoric, the highly pragmatic South African people show little evidence of wishing to return to the land as independent peasant farmers. The simple transfer of land from whites to blacks may increasingly be yesterday's issue.

What about the related issue of rural development? The need in this case is great, with high unemployment in rural areas and with a tradition of the exploitation of labor by white commercial farmers within a lingering tradition of racism.

Abuse of farm laborers has been addressed by legislation. The difficulty is that the state is short of the resources needed for enforcement. Educational initiatives above all are essential for the genuine transformation of rural laborers' lives. These, however, are expensive. The outlook here is at best for slow amelioration rather than sudden change.

To some extent, land tenure reform is the prisoner of ANC politics. Jacob Zuma has cultivated close ties with traditional rulers, and his land tenure proposals, rendered void by the Constitutional Court, would have strengthened traditional rulers and tied them more closely to the ANC. New proposals for land tenure reform are likely to diminish the authority of traditional rulers; therefore it is likely that the government will move with caution.

Meanwhile, land issues do retain the potential for rallying the poor against the 1994 settlement. While it is unlikely that South Africa will become a new Zimbabwe, countries are hostage to events and the quality of their leadership. So, a radical restructuring of land ownership and the accompanying destruction of commercial agriculture is always possible. So far, however, there are few signs of this.

Why, in South Africa, does the land question not threaten the 1994 transition arrangements, given that whites still own a disproportionate amount and there has been so little redistribution?

First, the land question has not been ignored. Restitution of apartheid wrongs has been under way for some years and is continuing.

Second, land redistribution continues to be an active political issue, with general agreement as to its necessity and lively debate as to how it could be best achieved. The democratic political process conducted according to the rule of law is seen as providing a framework for addressing this issue. For South Africans, it is unnecessary to go outside that framework.

Third, as the country's demography shifts from rural to urban, the land issue in the countryside would appear to be of less importance now than it once was. As time passes, the heirs of individual claimants multiply. This makes the size of payouts of less significance to individual beneficiaries.

South Africa may be moving from land reform to a focus on agricultural reform, how to strengthen the agricultural sector, and how it might create additional employment. This places a premium on issues such as land tenure rather than land ownership.

Finally, South Africans of all races have exceptional opportunity for home ownership. According to Statistics South Africa, 75.8 percent of South African households owned or partly owned a dwelling in 2009. That figure has been growing steadily: in 2007 it was 68.3 percent. For the sake of comparison, in 2009, home ownership in the United States was 67.5 percent. In Brazil, it was 75 percent in 2009.[40] Home ownership even among the poor can be attributed to a system of social grants, housing subsidies, and free basic services, such as electricity and water.

Though it is difficult to measure objectively, the fact that an increasingly urban population has ready access to home ownership—even if the units themselves are modest—likely reduces the salience of land redistribution.

Even a private mortgage market for houses built and distributed by the government is beginning to emerge. Already there have been a few sales of houses that had been distributed by the government to occupants, who, in effect, have traded up. Unlike almost anywhere else in Africa, owner-occupied housing built by the government is becoming a store of value, a means by which some blacks and coloureds can accumulate capital on the American model. The process by which government-built housing becomes private is reminiscent of Thatcherite Britain, where the transfer of ownership from the local government authority to owner-occupiers not only transformed the housing market, but it also largely transformed the British working class into a lower middle class.

If, as is likely, urbanization continues, and owner occupation grows, the traditional South African land question may wither away.

7

GOVERNANCE

South Africa, with some fifty million people, and Ghana, with twenty-five million, are the only two large states in Africa that are democratic in the sense that the opposition consistently has a reasonable chance of winning power through credible elections. Nigeria, where for the first time the opposition won the 2015 elections, may join that group if a new pattern has been established. Time will tell. At present, South Africa, Ghana, and Nigeria are joined by four other African electoral democracies, all small states with relatively ethnically homogeneous populations: Botswana, Cape Verde, Lesotho, and Mauritius. Of the states with larger populations than South Africa, Nigeria is hopeful; Ethiopia and the Democratic Republic of the Congo are autocracies of variable efficiencies.

In comparison with the rest of sub-Saharan Africa, South Africa is a relative success, with the continent's most modern economy and strongest protection of human rights. Nevertheless, the question remains whether the country's democratic culture and institutions can continue to flourish in a context in which the economic development of the black and coloured communities continues to lag far behind that of whites and asians.

The economic transformation needed to lift the majority out of poverty, largely by the provision of low-skilled jobs, did not accompany South Africa's political democratization. This has led to South Africa's paradox: a democratic state in which for much of the population economic progress has been slow, while a small racial minority continues to enjoy a relatively high and rising standard of living, now joined by a small black elite.

THE AFRICAN NATIONAL CONGRESS

In the years following the democratic transition and Mandela's presidency with its theme of reconciliation, some of its democratic, "nonracial" ideals have been compromised. The ruling African National Congress (ANC) was a liberation movement that has haltingly and incompletely transformed itself into a political party. The ANC's senior leadership has abandoned any pretense to Marxism-Leninism other than the stray rhetorical salvo. Especially under Mandela and Mbeki, government economic policy followed the free-market principles associated with international financial institutions, supported by the so-called Washington Consensus. This was far from socialism, whether of the Marxist-Leninist or of an "African" variety, with its emphasis on the collective good.

But Washington Consensus economic policy was incompletely implemented. The privatization of state-owned enterprises stalled. If not dominant, left-wing or statist advocates remained influential, providing an alternative to the mainstream free-market principles. For example, the New Growth Path, developed in part by the Department of Economic Development in 2010, envisaged the creation of five million new jobs by 2020. It saw a major role for the state in the economy to promote job growth, including by infrastructure improvements. The National Development Plan, drafted by the National Planning Commission, is a more comprehensive blueprint for the economy, education, and health over a much longer time frame, from 2012 to 2030. It reflects the principles of the Washington Consensus. However, its projections for the growth of the economy have thus far been overly optimistic. As slow economic growth and gross inequality persist, statist advocates are growing in strength within the party.

Many blacks are angry over the poor delivery of government services, with township rioting on a daily basis in one part of the country or another. Black labor unrest is on the rise in some industries. The violent police response to an August 2012 labor dispute at the Marikana platinum mine recalled the massacres at Sharpeville (1960) and Soweto

(1976) by the then-apartheid government's security services. In 2015, university students, mostly black and coloured but joined by some whites, rioted against proposed tuition increases, forcing the Zuma government to back down.

Almost a generation after Nelson Mandela's inauguration as president, it should come as no surprise that there are demands for radical change, sometimes even at the expense of the rule of law and in violation of constitutional protections. The rhetoric of some black politicians, notably Julius Malema, is increasingly hostile to whites, and he identifies them with "the West," especially the United States, rather than "Mother Africa."

At the same time, many South Africans are asking if the ANC really retains a commitment to social change and "nonracial" democracy, or whether it has become primarily an instrument of personal enrichment for its leaders and their clients, as ruling parties often are in other African countries. Of the five richest black South Africans identified by *Timeslive*, three have obvious, close connections to the ANC: Patrice Motsepe, "South Africa's first black billionaire," is a major contributor to the ANC;[1] Cyril Ramaphosa was a negotiator of the 1994 transition and is now the deputy president; and Tokyo Sexwale was the minister of human settlements and is a veteran of Robben Island.[2]

For some of the disillusioned within the ANC, the current leadership follows the watchword of "I did not join the struggle to remain poor." The result, its critics say, is an ANC that is itself corrupt and fosters corruption within the larger South African society. Such criticism is even widespread among the ANC's putative allies on the left, the Congress of South African Trade Unions (COSATU) and the South African Communist Party (SACP).

The ANC prides itself on being a "big tent," and even its critics accept that the would-be oligarchs do not have it entirely their own way. With competing personalities and tendencies, infighting, largely out of the public eye, reportedly can be vicious.

ANC "Democrats"

An important element in the party continues to be democratic, with close links to civil society. It seeks to maintain the nonracial values associated with Nelson Mandela. It opposes efforts by the Zuma leadership to compromise the constitution, and it is a vocal critic of seemingly accelerating corruption.

For such party activists, the ANC should become a grassroots democracy in which political legitimacy flows from the people, rather than down from the leadership. Broadly speaking, this was the approach of Nelson Mandela, though it was leavened by his absolute loyalty to the ANC as a liberation movement. This approach is also characteristic of such anti-apartheid religious leaders as Frank Chikane, a secretary general of the South African Council of Churches and a founder of the United Democratic Front (UDF). Among many of these "democrats" are to be found the most stringent critics of Zuma's government as having betrayed the democratic ideals of the ANC and the 1994 transition to democracy. They accuse the ANC leadership of fostering a spirit of gross materialism that promotes the culture of corruption. Many voices from South African civil society also make this criticism.

The "democrats" complain that the party is losing touch with its grassroots and that internal democracy is giving way to overcentralization at the party headquarters, Luthuli House in Johannesburg, and in the office of the president. Mbeki, especially, centralized as much party authority as he could in his own office. Democrats and others are also uneasy about the growing role of Chancellor House, the corporate and business arm of the ANC. In 2015, a specific concern was Chancellor House's role in the purchase of some South African media by Indian and Chinese allies of President Zuma.

ANC "Marxists"

South Africans often say that the ANC is slow in making the transition from a liberation movement to a political party (it registered itself as a political party only in 1994, just before the first nonracial elections). As a movement, some in the ANC identified it with the nation and made little distinction between itself and the government: for them, the ANC, the government, and the nation were essentially the same. (That could imply that opposition to the ANC approached being treasonous to the state.) For many in the SACP, this was reminiscent of the position of the Communist Party in the former Soviet Union. Similar to Leninists, some advocated democratic centralism: absolute obedience once the ANC made a decision and a harsh response to internal criticism.

This outlook was most pronounced among those in exile during the armed struggle; they may have been more influenced by Marxist-Leninist ideology than those who stayed at home. Their authoritarian approach also reflected their fear of penetration by agents of the apartheid state. The security services of post-apartheid South Africa reflect in many ways an "exile" mind-set hostile to any criticism. Yet, though influenced by Marxist-Leninist patterns of thinking, many ANC leaders nevertheless quickly and easily accommodated themselves to South African big business. The implication might be that the Soviet brand of Marxism-Leninism had only superficial appeal, even among the ANC in exile.

ANC "Africanists"

Another tendency within the ANC can be labeled "Africanist." It is particularly concerned with righting the wrongs of apartheid against the black majority. It draws on and supports traditional African elements in South African society and culture, such as rule by chiefs. Where constitutional protections of individual rights collide with African custom, for example over gender equality, gay rights, or land tenure, the Africanists tilt the scale toward tradition.

President Zuma appeals directly to this constituency by his open practice of Zulu custom, such as having multiple wives. His style of governance and personal behavior are increasingly "African." Nkandla, his personal compound, is built in an exaggerated Zulu style. He emphasizes "solidarity" with other African chiefs of state, including Robert Mugabe and Omar al-Bashir. Yet there are limits. His speeches are always in English, and he wears Western dress. But, in his rape trial, he insisted on speaking Zulu, as is permitted under South African law.

ANC "Disaffected"

As disillusionment with the ANC government has grown, some blacks, especially, have looked for an alternative. An ANC breakaway group opposed to Jacob Zuma and including supporters of Thabo Mbeki, the Congress of the People (COPE), contested the 2009 elections. It took just under 8 percent of the vote, thereby winning thirty seats under South Africa's system of proportional representation. However, in 2014, its electoral support collapsed to less than 1 percent of the vote. Mamphela Ramphele, a medical doctor, the mother of liberation martyr Steve Biko's children, a former chancellor of the University of Cape Town and a businesswoman, organized a new political party, Agang-SA, to contest the 2014 elections. Her particular focus was on support for the constitution and the rule of law, a platform similar to that of the Democratic Alliance (DA). In addition to personality differences and ambitions, a proposed merger of the two parties failed in part because Agang-SA was perceived as a black political party, while the DA historically has been white, and the racial divide could not be bridged in the short time available. On its own, Agang-SA failed to take off and won less than half a percent of the vote in 2014. Two months later, Ramphele announced that she was withdrawing from politics to return to civil society work.[3]

Post-Mandela, no major ANC leader has been able to articulate the hopes and aspirations of township residents and to use them as the basis of a coherent political program. A youthful and corrupt firebrand, Julius Malema, first tried to position himself within the ANC as a successor to Winnie Mandela as the leading township advocate. His political program was based on envy and emotion rather than strategies for growing the economy and creating jobs. Further, he thumbed his nose at the ANC senior leadership. Accordingly, his ever-growing enemies within the party destroyed any future for him within the ANC power structure. In 2013, he founded a new political party, the Economic Freedom Fighters (EFF), with a platform of expropriation of white-owned property without compensation. In effect, Malema moved the voice for radical redistribution out of the ANC and into his fringe party.

Nevertheless, some of South Africa's institutions of governance underpinned by the constitution and the rule of law have strengthened over the past twenty years. They make it possible to address economic and social issues within a plural, democratic context. The National Union of Metalworkers (NUMSA) is the largest and richest union in South Africa. Its interest in establishing a left-wing political party that would operate within the bounds of the constitution is an example of growing political pluralism. Another example is the far-right, overwhelmingly white, Afrikaner Freedom Front, which has seats in parliament. It participates in cabinets, thanks to proportional representation.

The ANC in Parliament

Up to now, elections have resembled a racial census, thereby guaranteeing ANC control of the government at the national level. As the ANC has continued to control the parliament and the presidency, a consequence has been the growth of crony capitalism to the benefit of a small number of insiders at the expense of broad-based economic growth. Critics charge that the party is becoming unresponsive to its constituencies and increasingly oligarchic in character. Nevertheless, the ANC parliamentary delegation has not split and is unlikely to do so.

At the time of the transition, South Africa adopted a system of proportional representation with a "closed list" system. Parties rank order their candidates. Voters vote for a party, not an individual. If a party's share of the vote translates into, say, one hundred seats, the top one hundred on the party's list enter parliament. Under South Africa's proportional representation system, if a legislator resigns from a party, he loses his seat. That arrangement preserves the party as an entity, but not necessarily its policy coherence.

The list system, whereby voters choose a party rather than an MP, endows the party leadership with considerable power because the leadership determines where on the list a particular candidate is placed. Legislators are not accountable to a specific constituency to secure election or reelection. Constituencies, in turn, lack a parliamentary advocate, though some parties do assign legislators to specific constituencies to fill that function.

Proportional representation does ensure that all races are represented, but without seats reserved according to race. The system also ensures the presence in parliament of small parties. The official opposition, the DA, now regularly wins control of scattered local governments, the Cape Town municipality, and the Western Cape provincial government.[4]

Under proportional representation, the ANC holds the lion's share of elected offices at all levels of government. However, its permanent, majoritarian electoral status is checked by legal and constitutional guarantees and by an energetic parliamentary opposition that is slowly gaining votes.

THE TRIPLE ALLIANCE

The ANC government is a triple alliance consisting of the ANC, the SACP, and the COSATU. All candidates for elective office from the alliance run on the ANC ticket; SACP and COSATU are not registered political parties and their candidates do not appear under those labels on the ballot. The Triple Alliance is internally united by little other than an anti-apartheid commitment and advocacy of "democracy," though what the latter means in practice is highly contentious.

The SACP and the democrats within the ANC insist that South Africa must be nonracial. The Africanists, however, overtly seek to transfer resources from whites to blacks, using the racial definitions developed under apartheid. But they are divided on the issue of transferring assets from rich to poor. Successful black businessmen will argue for more "Africans" in the upper reaches of corporations and more ownership and control of corporations by blacks. However, they do not necessarily support restructuring the economy away from the liberal, capitalist Washington Consensus for the benefit of the rural and township poor. It is Julius Malema and his EFF who advocate this latter perspective, though with many inconsistencies.

There are those under the ANC umbrella who do argue for the radical restructuring of South Africa's economy to reduce unemployment and poverty. But they do not have a loud—let alone dominant—voice. At present, only the EFF is genuinely left wing (in the European or American sense), not the ANC or the SACP.

The relative power of the tendencies within the ANC and the Triple Alliance varies from time to time, often reflecting the personality of the chief of state. Hence, under Nelson Mandela, the ANC emphasized nonracial democracy, and the chief architects of the constitution included his own defense attorney from the Rivonia Trial, George Bizos, who was of Greek origin. However, Mandela's successor, Thabo Mbeki, sought to create a "national bourgeoisie," made up of blacks, who would be natural allies of the ANC government. Jacob Zuma openly encourages and supports traditional African governance and culture.

THE SOUTH AFRICAN COMMUNIST PARTY

Over the years, and especially when the ANC leadership was in exile, the SACP was probably more influential than the number of its supporters would warrant. Many of its members were well-educated whites from the middle class. Party members sometimes had a sophisticated worldliness that ANC operatives such as Zuma lacked. But the longer the ANC remains in power, the more the SACP's advantages fade.

In terms of its stated ideology, the SACP is a conventional Marxist-Leninist party. The SACP remains a clandestine organization. The ANC Youth Wing, formerly headed by Nelson Mandela and later Julius Malema, also identifies itself as the Young Communist League. According to the ANC's eulogy, Nelson Mandela was an SACP member and served on the party's Central Committee.[5] The SACP served as the link between the ANC and the Soviet Union when the latter was a major source of funding during the armed struggle. Since 1994, in governance policy and practice, it has been highly pragmatic and nonideological. Committed to "nonracialism and anti-imperialism," it is a check on an "African" bias in the government. It also claims to be a check on the crony capitalism of certain ANC leaders. Members of the SACP serve in the cabinet and also in the leadership of COSATU. With the collapse of the Soviet Union, it has come to be dependent on the ANC for its funding, which limits its independence and influence.

THE CONGRESS OF SOUTH AFRICAN TRADE UNIONS

COSATU is the largest of South Africa's trade union federations, with twenty-one affiliated unions and perhaps 1.8 million workers before the departure of NUMSA. There are points of similarity to the American Federation of Labor–Congress of Industrial Organizations (AFL-CIO). Organized in 1985, it played a major role in the anti-apartheid struggle by organizing strikes and providing crowds for demonstrations. Though it is part of the governing triple alliance, its leadership is frequently critical of the Zuma government for its crony capitalism and subordination of working South Africans to big business.

Its now-removed secretary general, Zwelinzima Vavi, opposed Jacob Zuma's bid for a second term as president. Relations between the secretary general and COSATU president Sdumo Dlamini were bad; Dlamini supported Zuma. Cyril Ramaphosa has reportedly tried but failed to bring about reconciliation. Vavi, a member of the SACP, has predicted a steady erosion of COSATU influence over the government.

The federation's hitherto largest and wealthiest union, NUMSA, in 2013 ceased providing financial support for COSATU. In 2014, NUMSA broke with the ANC and with the SACP and ceased its financial support for both of them. The breach appears to have been caused by policy differences but also personal rivalries. NUMSA had said that it would not withdraw voluntarily from COSATU. Accordingly, COSATU expelled it in November 2014. NUMSA has announced that it will organize a genuine left-wing national political party to contest the 2019 elections.[6] In its rhetoric, it says it will be "responsible," adhering to the constitution and the rule of law as it seeks to establish a "socialist" polity. Its goals include higher taxes on the rich, with the revenue devoted to education and health, and likely the nationalization of parts of the economy. It would seek the transformation of the South African economy outside of the parameters of the liberal Washington Consensus. If the party does emerge, it is likely to be well organized and well financed. It could draw electoral support away from the ANC and the EFF.

The relationships between the ANC, the SACP, and COSATU are shifting and often acrimonious. None of the three is monolithic; the SACP has perhaps the most internal cohesion. However, all three profess and act with reverence toward the constitution and the rule of law.

BROAD-BASED BLACK ECONOMIC EMPOWERMENT

A central theme of South African governance is poverty alleviation through black economic empowerment. There is general recognition that the mass of the population needs to participate in the modern economy and that achieving that goal requires various affirmative-action strategies. The policy's antecedents can be found in the last days of the de Klerk National Party administration during the waning days of apartheid. There is a consensus across racial lines that supports the goals of Black Economic Empowerment (BEE), now, after various amendments, called Broad-Based Black Economic Empowerment

(BBBEE). The consensus appears broader and deeper than the American equivalent for affirmative action. BBBEE is now a signature policy of the ANC. South Africans tend to judge the quality of ANC governance by the progress made in poverty alleviation and service delivery, making BBBEE and black economic empowerment in general a focus of political discourse.

The new South African government implemented the Reconstruction and Development Program (RDP) in 1994 and the Growth, Employment and Redistribution policies (GEAR) in 1996. These programs developed under the leadership of the Treasury and the Central Bank firmly tied government economic policy to free-market capitalism. Within the government, Washington Consensus policies advocated by the Treasury and the Central Bank have often been opposed by the Department of Labour and the Department of Trade and Industry. Those two ministries led the advocates for BEE and BBBEE and in the development of a variety of affirmative-action strategies.[7]

Under apartheid, it was all but impossible for blacks to accumulate capital for investment. Given that reality, under pressure from the post-1994 government, companies sell stakes at a discount to blacks. These companies often used this to their advantage. The original companies could spin off unprofitable sectors into new companies, which were then sold to black investors who purchased them with money borrowed from the original company itself. Companies frequently used BEE to ingratiate themselves with influential ANC political figures. For some of those, in turn, BEE provided a way not "to remain poor."

However, more recently, BBBEE is beginning to focus more on benefiting the poor and the non–politically connected rather than on the creation of a "national bourgeoisie." There is a greater emphasis on persuading companies to adopt affirmative-action employment and training policies through a mix of incentives and penalties.

Throughout BBBEE, the definition of "black owned" is tightening. Monitoring of progress toward goals is increasingly strict, and penalties for avoidance or noncompliance are severe. The Employment Equity Act of 1998 requires larger enterprises to make their workforces representative of the country's demography. Companies that employ more than fifty workers report every other year on progress toward making the workforce 75 percent black, 10 percent coloured, and 3 percent asian. Other legislation requires larger companies to set targets for black ownership as well as the promotion and training of blacks. Yet employers often complain that the workforce lacks the skills that meeting such targets would require and that BBBEE is becoming progressively less voluntary and more coercive.

Many critics see BBBEE in practice, though not in theory, as a new form of the old apartheid-era crony capitalism where the politically connected benefited, not the poor. Many whites believe that they will be largely excluded from corporate jobs, now and in the future. Hence, they focus on entrepreneurial economic endeavors.[8] As these are often the most dynamic part of the economy, they may help to account for the widening wealth gap between whites and the other races.

BBBEE is not expropriation. Shares transferred to black investors are paid for, though often at a discount. Black investors are vulnerable to economic slowdowns and falls in the stock market. In such an event, many investors are subsequently unable to service the debt incurred when they purchased the shares. During the current downturn, some observers have called for the nationalization of mines and other extractive enterprises as a way of bailing out investors who borrowed too much against assets of declining value.

BEE and BBBEE have had little impact on the mass of the black population residing in rural areas of townships lacking the political connections or the capital necessary to participate in it. Indeed, BBBEE may have had a stifling influence on the growth of black entrepreneurship. Few blacks have started new businesses or invested in the prime growth sectors of the economy, especially technology. Instead, critics suggest, it is much easier in the short run for the politically well connected to take advantage of BBBEE.

BEE and subsequently BBBEE contributes to the general atmosphere of corruption. *The Economist*, in 2014, ran a story in which Mamphela Ramphele, once the chairwoman of Gold Fields, a mining firm, complained that the government forced the company to sell a stake in the business to a consortium with ties to the ANC, including the party's chairperson and an attorney who defended President Zuma against rape charges.[9] On the other hand, an American businessman commented that he regarded BBBEE as simply a "tax," and not a heavy one.[10]

BBBEE also conjures up the ghosts of apartheid. Eligibility to participate in it is determined by race: only blacks, coloureds, and asians (mostly indians) may participate. The definitions that determine eligibility date from apartheid. BBBEE is an exception to "nonracial" democracy.

In the United States there is a lively debate as to whether affirmative-action policies are still necessary. In South Africa, with growing, not declining, racial inequality, the debate is about the groups that benefit. Few question black and coloured beneficiaries. The issue is asians, whose social and economic statistics are better than those of blacks and coloureds.

IS SOUTH AFRICA MOVING TOWARD A ONE-PARTY STATE?

Many disillusioned South Africans express concern about the ANC seeing itself as identical to the state and, in effect, pursuing an agenda of one-party governance. They express alarm that the country is being governed from Luthuli House, the ANC national headquarters in Johannesburg, rather than from the Union Buildings, the seat of the executive of the South African government in Pretoria. The concern is that major policy decisions are reached in a party venue and then imposed on the government.

The concern about an ANC trajectory toward one-party authoritarianism receives a boost from President Zuma's deferential policy toward China. Three times his government has, in effect, denied the Dalai Lama entry to South Africa.[11] Many old-line ANC personalities were outraged, and Archbishop Desmond Tutu denounced the ANC as little better than the old National Party. Few believe government protestations that Beijing pressure played no role.

Zuma's trumpeting of South Africa's membership in the BRICS, two of which are authoritarian states, also causes unease, even as China has become South Africa's largest trading partner.[12] Like Pretoria's deferring to Beijing over a visa for the Dalai Lama, the close ties between the Mbeki and Zuma governments and Robert Mugabe's tyranny in Zimbabwe also reduce confidence in the ANC's dedication to the rule of law. In fact, Mugabe on occasion shows open contempt for the South African government and has been publicly rude to Jacob Zuma. He visibly resented Nelson Mandela's celebrity status and post-apartheid South Africa's leadership role in southern Africa. In return, Mbeki pursued a policy toward Zimbabwe that he called "quiet diplomacy," while early in his presidency Zuma appeared to be willing to take a stronger line on Mugabe's human rights and other abuses. But "quiet diplomacy" achieved little or nothing, and Zuma accepted Mugabe's 2014 fraudulent reelection. He even removed from office his Zimbabwe policy coordinator, the well-regarded Ambassador Lindiwe Zulu, upon Mugabe's insistence. The ANC advocacy of democracy appears to stop at the Zimbabwe border.

Rian Malan, an Afrikaner from a prominent white clan, is celebrated for his 1990 *My Traitor's Heart*, a scathing and personal analysis of apartheid and those, such as himself, who were beneficiaries of it. But his 2013 *The Lion Sleeps Tonight and Other Stories of Africa* includes a devastating critique of the ANC and the "liberal" willingness, especially among non–South African whites, to look the other way and give the ruling party the benefit of every doubt.[13] For him, as for Archbishop Tutu and numerous other earlier leaders of the liberation movement, not only is the country's liberal, democratic future far from assured, but the trend line under Thabo Mbeki and Jacob Zuma is moving in the wrong direction. The novelist Nadine Gordimer has sounded similar themes of disappointment, even despair, in her recent fiction, especially *No Time Like the Present* (2012). Their themes do much to shape the pessimism about South Africa's future found within the country but also among many of its friends abroad.

OPPOSITION PARTIES

The Democratic Alliance (DA) is the official opposition in parliament. In the 2014 elections, it won 22.23 percent of the vote, which translated into eighty-nine of the four hundred seats in parliament. Its leadership is skilled in parliamentary procedure, and it is an active and formidable opposition. It has controlled the government of the Western Cape, South Africa's second-richest province, and the city government of Cape Town since 2009. South African media regularly present the Western Cape and Cape Town as the best-governed entities in South Africa. The DA benefits from that reputation nationally. Though it did not win, in the 2014 elections the DA strengthened its position in Gauteng, where Johannesburg is located.

The DA's antecedents are various liberal, English-speaking, anti-apartheid groups that emerged after the National Party victory in 1948. It counts itself as the heir of such famous anti-apartheid activists as Helen Suzman, long a thorn in the side of the apartheid state from her seat in parliament representing Houghton, a wealthy Johannesburg suburb. The chairperson of the party has been Helen Zille, the premier of the Western Cape. Before politics, she was a journalist. She was one of those who broke the story of the police murder of Steve Biko, a founder of the Black Consciousness Movement. Also with a national reputation and recognition is Patricia de Lille, the mayor of Cape Town. In 2015, the DA chose a new party leader, Mmusi Maimane, a black businessman from Soweto who also serves on the Johannesburg city council.

The DA is broadly center-right in its policies. It strongly asserts the inviolability of the constitution, the rule of law, the independence of constitutionally mandated positions such as the public protector that limit the power of any administration, and the independence of the judiciary. It has had considerable success in pushing back various initiatives that could modify constitutionally guaranteed rights, such as that to private property. With its anti-apartheid antecedents, it has close ties with South African civic groups.

The party's electoral base includes most whites, a majority of coloureds, and many asians. As together those groups make up only about 20 percent of South Africa's population, if the party is to become a genuine alternative party of government to the ANC, it must attract more black votes. Zille has followed a strategy to shed the DA's "white" image.

To make the party more attractive to black voters, Zille sponsored as the DA floor leader in the National Assembly a young black woman, Lindiwe Mazibuko. After the May 2014 elections, Mazibuko resigned to study for an advanced degree at Harvard University.[14] Zille had said that when she stepped down as party leader, her successor should be black, preparing the way for the 2015 DA selection of Maimane. Zille remains the premier of the Western Cape.

Following the 2014 elections, the third-largest party in parliament is the Economic Freedom Fighters (EFF). Running on a radical platform that included calls for the expropriation of white-owned property, it received more than 6 percent of the vote and twenty-five seats in parliament. Julius Malema, its founder and leader, now regularly disrupts the National Assembly by violating parliamentary procedure.

The Inkatha Freedom Party was once the third-largest political grouping during the transition and participated in Mandela's administration. Since then, it has declined, from forty-three seats in the National Assembly in 1994 to eighteen following the 2009 elections to winning only ten seats in 2014. Always a Zulu cultural organization as well as a political party and the vehicle for Zulu chief Mangosuthu Buthelezi's personal ambitions, its cultural clothes have been stolen under Zuma by his increasingly Zulu ANC. Its remnant often cooperates with the DA in parliament.

The Freedom Front Plus, the Afrikaner political party of Constans Viljoen, also still survives. It won nine seats in 1994, declining to four in 2009. In 2014, it again won four seats. It continues to advocate for the establishment of a "white homeland."

The use of racial labels is perhaps greater now than it was during Mandela's administration, as is the overt appeal to racial and ethnic identity politics. Politically, rather than being the rainbow nation, South Africa has a black government and a largely white and coloured opposition. The country was probably more polarized racially at Zuma's 2009 and 2014 inaugurations than it had been at Mandela's. In style, Zuma's South Africa is more "African" and less "universal" in its aspirations and ideals than Mandela's was, as the different styles of the two inaugurations illustrate.

POLITICAL CONSEQUENCES OF PERSISTENT INEQUALITY

Failure to address fundamental social inequality has led not only to a resurgence of black radicalism but a more general concern over the government's ability to address legitimate grievances within the framework of democracy and the rule of law. Nevertheless, while township service-delivery riots are lawless, serious debates, both within the ANC and among the government's critics, continue to be framed by the rule of law. The NUMSA-proposed left-wing political party would likely have more staying power than the EFF, which is tied specifically to Julius Malema.

The ANC, the DA, and smaller parties conduct themselves in parliament according to democratic principles. On the other hand, since entering parliament in 2014, the EFF's obstructionist behavior has been fundamentally antidemocratic. As such, the EFF is a threat to South Africa's democratic polity, though at a low level. If a new, left-wing political party challenges the EFF, the latter may well embrace even more closely its current tactics of parliamentary disruption to strengthen its brand in the face of competition, or, more likely, it will disappear.

Despite the antics of the EFF, rather than being under siege, there are signs that South Africa's democratic political culture based on the rule of law is strengthening. There is the remarkable unwillingness to change the constitution, which is popularly associated with Nelson Mandela and the transition to nonracial democracy. Polling data shows that a majority of South Africans favor the reintroduction of the death penalty, the curtailment of gay rights, and the abolition of gay marriage. The ANC has had sufficient votes in the parliament to initiate the necessary constitutional amendments. Not only has it not done so, but the rewording of the constitution has never been up for serious debate. The ANC government has consistently enforced Constitutional Court judgments against it. The principle of limits to presidential power was established by Nelson Mandela and sustained by Thabo Mbeki, who left the presidency when he no longer had the confidence of the ANC, and those precedents will almost certainly be followed by Jacob Zuma if he loses the confidence of his party or is impeached before the end of his term.

THE SOUTH AFRICAN CONSTITUTION

The vehicle for South Africa's democratic transition was the negotiations over a new constitution. The formal negotiations were held at Kempton Park, a conference center near the Johannesburg airport. They started in December 1991 and continued with fits and starts for two years. The process was called the Convention for a Democratic South Africa (CODESA). While the negotiations were "multiparty," they were dominated by the ruling National Party and the ANC. The course of the negotiations reflected the roughly equal balance of power between the governing establishment and the liberation movements, with the National Party government in full control of the military, the police, and other security services that the liberation movements had been unable to defeat.

In very broad terms, the Nationalists focused in the negotiations on minority rights, a reflection that for the first time in South Africa's history the future would no longer be dominated politically by whites. Minority rights involved guarantees for private property. Though the apartheid state had been highly centralized, the Nationalists also looked for a robust federalism as a way to limit the power of a future black government.

The ANC argued for "democracy": one person, one vote. Its leaders fully understood that voting was likely to be, in effect, a racial census and that for the foreseeable future the ANC would dominate a black government. The ANC advocated a powerful, centralized government that could bring about social change.

Reflecting its general position, the ANC wanted the constitution to be drafted by a democratically elected constitutional assembly. The National Party, concerned that such a constitutional assembly could be indifferent to minority rights, argued that the constitution should be negotiated among the parties and then put to a popular referendum.

Starting in 1993, the parties negotiated a highly imaginative compromise that set the standard for democracy and the rule of law in contemporary South Africa. Instead of negotiating a final constitution, the delegates drew up a temporary constitution that established the structure of a nonracial government with guarantees of minority and property rights within a quasi-federal structure. This was the essence of what the Nationalist negotiators had wanted. It also established a Constitutional Court. This court was to ensure that the final constitution adhered to the democratic principles with the protection of minority rights enshrined in the temporary constitution, but otherwise gave a democratically elected constitutional assembly more or less free rein in other areas, as the ANC had wanted. Hence, the Constitutional Court predates the permanent constitution and is a primary guarantor of it.

It was under the interim constitution that South Africa's first nonracial elections took place in 1994. During President Mandela's first term, a constitutional assembly was duly elected under the new "nonracial" suffrage and drafted the permanent constitution. The Constitutional Court ensured that the permanent constitution adhered to the constitutional principles in the interim constitution with which it was required to comply.

The permanent constitution included a bill of rights providing perhaps the most extensive guarantees of human rights of any in the world. These guarantees included equality before the law; freedom from discrimination, including race, gender, pregnancy, marital status, ethnic or social origin, sexual orientation, and religion; and the right to life.

Chapter 9 of the constitution established institutions or commissions to protect democracy.[15] Among these was the Public Protector. The office has enviable independence, and its power has probably increased. President Jacob Zuma appointed Thuli Madonsela to a seven-year term in 2009. A longtime member of the ANC, she had participated in the drafting of the final constitution and served on the South African Law Reform Commission. Far from being a Zuma party hack, in 2014 she determined that the government had improperly used public money on improvements of President Zuma's private house, Nkandla. Zuma's ANC supporters in turn accused her of rendering a "partisan" decision, questioned her authority, and called for her resignation. They also launched ad hominem attacks. In response, support for her and her office grew in the media, in the trade unions, and among civil society. She did not back down.

The bill of rights was drafted after Nelson Mandela became president. The drafting was led by Kader Asmal, a Cape Town human rights lawyer who served on the ANC constitution committee from 1986; Albert ("Albie") Sachs, also a Cape Town human rights lawyer, who defended many in the liberation movement and lost an eye and an arm to a bomb probably planted by the apartheid security services; and George Bizos, a Johannesburg human rights lawyer who defended Nelson Mandela at the 1963–1964 Rivonia Trial. All three were strong advocates for human rights as protected by the rule of law. Unusually, perhaps, none of the three was of black, Afrikaner, or of British descent. Asmal was an asian born in South Africa, Sachs was a Jew born in Johannesburg to Lithuanian parents, and Bizos was a Greek whose family fled to South Africa during the Nazi occupation.

South Africa's constitution is widely celebrated outside of Africa for being the basis for the elimination of the death penalty and the protection of gay rights. During the interim constitution period, in 1995, the Constitutional Court held that the death penalty violated the principle that every human being, no matter how abominable, has a right to life. The court also noted that it had been shown no evidence that the death penalty deters or prevents murder to any greater extent than other penalties, such as life imprisonment.

President Mandela appointed Albie Sachs to the Constitutional Court in 1994. In 1996, Sachs wrote the court's unanimous decision overthrowing the statute that restricted marriage to one man and one woman. The court found that the statute violated the constitution's provision for equal protection of all of its citizens and its ban on discrimination based on sexual orientation. For most of its history South Africa had been behind the developed world with respect to human rights; with respect to the death penalty and gay rights, it is now a world leader.

Hence, the constitution has become an integral part of the identity of a democratic, nonracial South Africa. Unlike in many other African states, it was not imposed by the military or other elites on an indifferent population. In comparison with other countries on the continent, the sense of South African national identity is very strong, and an aspect of that identification is with the constitution. Popular acceptance of it as the fundamental framework for government is similar to that of Americans for their constitution of 1789.

The DA has positioned itself as a vocal defender of the constitution. However, the DA's new party leader, Mmusi Maimane, in 2015 raised the possibility of a national referendum on gay marriage and capital punishment. Mmusi Maimane's suggestion, which is not DA party policy, may have been part of a strategy to make the DA more attractive to black voters. However, his proposal, if implemented, could open the door to other referenda with respect to property rights or freedom of speech that the DA would almost certainly oppose.

CHALLENGES

There has been much domestic and international media alarm over ANC initiatives that would restrict criticism of the government and limit the transparency of official acts and expenditures. A 2014–2015 media focus was on public expenditure on Zuma's private compound, Nkandla, in KwaZulu-Natal. There, for example, a swimming pool constructed at government expense is officially represented as being a "fire safety feature." Many domestic critics see a comprehensive ANC campaign to cover up the corruption of senior ANC political leaders, not solely President Jacob Zuma. Part of that campaign, they allege, is restriction on media criticism of the government. Others see such proposals as muscle flexing by the security services and reminiscent of apartheid days. Examples of these proposals are the ANC's introduction in parliament of the Intelligence General Laws Amendment, the Protection of State Information, and a Media Tribunal Bill. Taken together, this legislation would weaken public access to government information, increase government powers of surveillance, and impose harsh punishment on those who disclose public information related to state security.

Especially after the 2014 elections, there has been growing concern in South Africa about the Zuma administration's political manipulation of such institutions as the National Prosecuting Authority, the police, the revenue service, and the national broadcaster. There is fear that the independence of the Public Protector and the Human Rights Commission could be compromised. There is also concern that the media, especially print, which is dependent on government advertising, is subject to pressure when it criticizes the administration. However, it should be noted that none of these Zuma administration initiatives have yet been passed by parliament, nor have they been subject to review by the Constitutional Court.

With respect to the rule of law, the ANC government introduced in 2013 a Legal Practice Bill that would have extended executive powers over the legal profession. When finally signed into law, the text had been substantially revised. There was also a Traditional Courts Bill that would have strengthened the power of chiefs while undermining gender equality, which is enshrined in the constitution but not in the tribal system. The chiefs are important allies of Jacob Zuma, and, as we have seen, the "African" bloc is an important part of the ANC's core constituency.

Also in 2013, the Zuma government introduced the Promotion and Protection of Investment Bill. This would replace South Africa's bilateral investment treaties with various European states. It also has a provision whereby the state would pay no compensation on the loss of property provided the state takes it not as the owner but as a "custodian" for the disadvantaged.

However, each of these pieces of legislation provoked media coverage, subsequent public outcry, and intense lobbying by civil society groups. They have also attracted unfavorable comment from human rights groups outside of South Africa. In consequence, each piece of such proposed legislation has been put on hold or so modified that it hardly resembles the original draft. However, these episodes also underscore the importance of continued vigilance by South African civil society, a free media, and an independent judiciary.

To its critics, the current Zuma administration lacks vision. In response, the administration and its defenders point to its National Development Plan 2030 (NDP). In 2010, President Zuma appointed twenty-six members of the National Planning Commission, under Minister Trevor Manuel, to draft a plan for consideration by the cabinet and, ultimately, the country. The NDP's broad goals were endorsed by the ANC at its Manguang Conference in December 2012.[16] The plan focused on poverty and the eradication of inequality. The document established two specific targets: no household living below a per-person monthly income of ZAR 419 (USD 55.00 in 2010) and the reduction of economic inequality through higher rates of economic growth. These goals will require improving infrastructure, better access to basic services, jobs creation, and reforming the public service to fight corruption. More specifically, the NDP seeks average economic growth rates of 5.4 percent in gross domestic product (GDP) from 2011 to 2030. Such economic growth would, it was anticipated, absorb the high numbers of unemployed. The NDP also looked to reform the education system to create a modern workforce. It envisaged capacity building for state institutions to ensure better delivery of services.

The NDP has now been formally adopted by the Zuma government and by the ANC. Initial reaction to it has been that the economic growth projections are highly optimistic, but that many elements of the NDP could be implemented even if the economy does not grow as fast as it had foreseen.[17]

ELECTIONS

The country has held credible national elections in 1994, 1999, 2004, 2009, and 2014. Twenty-nine separate parties ran in the elections of

2014, compared with twenty-six in 2009. Thirteen parties won seats in the National Assembly, the same number as in 2009.

With a voting-age population of 25,388,082, South Africa's voting turnout was about 18,650,000, or 73.48 percent of registered voters. As is true in other democratic states, voter turnout among the young was less than among the middle-aged and the elderly. Of the 1.9 million "born frees," that is, persons born after the 1994 transition, only one-third of those eligible to vote registered to do so.[18] Expatriates were also able to vote for the first time in national elections in 2014.

In 2014, the post-1994 electoral dominance of the ANC continued but had started to unravel. The ANC received 62.15 percent of the vote, down from 65.9 percent in 2009. That decline translated into a loss of fifteen seats. The party still retained an overwhelming majority of 249 seats out of the 400 seats in the National Assembly. However, the party fell short of the two-thirds majority, the stated goal of President Zuma, which would coincidentally allow the ANC to change the constitution. It is widely believed that a coalition of opposition parties stands a good chance of replacing the ANC government in 2024, if not in 2019. Nevertheless, the party carried eight of the nine provinces in 2014, with a majority of 52 percent in Zuma's native KwaZulu-Natal.

The official opposition, the DA, won 22.23 percent of the vote, up from 16.66 percent in 2009. The party gained twenty-two new seats for a total of eighty-nine. The EFF won 6.35 percent of the vote and twenty-five seats in parliament in the 2014 elections, the first it contested.

The consensus remains that race affiliation still played a crucial role in voter decisions in 2014. Nevertheless, no survey has been carried out to gauge the exact racial composition of each party's electorate in 2014. However, the DA experienced an estimated increase of support from black South Africans (from 0.8 percent in 2009 to 6 percent in 2014), according to party leader Helen Zille.[19] On the other hand, according to a credible 2013 survey, a large percentage of young black voters still believe that the DA would bring back apartheid.[20]

South Africans do not believe that ANC electoral dominance is inevitable. They cite the experience of the Congress Party of India, which maintained huge majorities that came to an end about twenty years after Indian independence. They also note that the United Kingdom under Prime Ministers Margaret Thatcher and Tony Blair saw the Tory and Labour governments rule for over a decade, each with consecutive landslide election victories. For democracy to be effective, a strong government and a strong opposition are required. After the 2014 elections, South Africa has had a weakening government and a strengthening opposition.

Can a democratic South Africa make it? The answer appears to be yes. From the perspective of sustainable democratic institutions, the country now has a twenty-plus-year track record. Despite the pervasiveness of racial identities and inequalities, a democratic culture is being created. But President Zuma and parts of the ANC are challenging the principle of the accountability of the executive to the law. The outcome is in doubt and accounts for the qualification of the yes.

Executive leadership is crucial to maintain and promote these institutions. South Africa has had four presidents since 1994. Nelson Mandela left office voluntarily after only one term. Thabo Mbeki left office when the ANC concluded that he had become a political liability. He left the presidency when he concluded that he could not continue in office if he was no longer the ANC leader. This position is consistent with the principles of proportional representation. The deputy president, Kgalema Motlanthe, served as president until the elections of 2009, when Jacob Zuma, at the lead of the ANC list, was elected president. Zuma remains under a political cloud because of unresolved corruption charges and ignoring the courts. It is possible that he may be removed from office before his term is up.

Hence, since 1994, the chief of state has been subject to the constitution and the political process. But, in 2015, the principle of presidential accountability to the law is being challenged, notably by President Zuma and the ANC majority in the National Assembly. Zuma is stonewalling the National Assembly over public spending on his private house, and he refused to hand over Sudanese president Omar al-Bashir to the International Criminal Court as required by South African law and a high court order. As of June 2015, the opposition parties in the National Assembly, much of the media, and civil society were seeking to hold the Zuma administration somehow accountable for the incident with al-Bashir, perhaps by a judicial ruling that he was in contempt of court. It remains to be seen if they are successful. If they are, that will provide additional grounds for optimism about South Africa's future.

But if not, failure might be a sign that South Africa is sliding away from the democratic institutions in place since 1994.

8

THE BILATERAL RELATIONSHIP BETWEEN THE UNITED STATES AND SOUTH AFRICA

At the time of the transition to nonracial democracy and Nelson Mandela's inauguration as president, American interest in the well-being of the new South Africa was intense. Within the Clinton administration (1993–2001), it looked like a special relationship was in the offing.

The United States and South Africa shared democratic commonalities and the historical experience of white supremacy and its consequences. That would seem to be a good foundation for a special diplomatic relationship. At the time of the 1994 transition, many in the Clinton administration, including Vice President Al Gore and Secretary of Commerce Ron Brown; members of the Congressional Black Caucus; American civil rights leaders such as Andrew Young and Jesse Jackson; enthusiastic editorial writers; and a few private-sector business leaders anticipated that future bilateral ties between the two multiracial democracies would be close, exceptional, and mutually beneficial. President William J. Clinton and Vice President Al Gore both identified with the American South (Arkansas and Tennessee, respectively), and both had been involved in the civil rights movement, had observed racism firsthand, and supported the principles of the anti-apartheid movement. Vice President Gore, his wife Tipper, and First Lady Hillary Clinton attended Nelson Mandela's inauguration as South Africa's president, and their support for the new nonracial dispensation was highly visible.[1]

Almost a generation later, the official relationship is correct, even cordial, but hardly special. It often resembles that between Washington and other African states that are smaller and less influential. Moreover, the likelihood is remote of a close partnership anytime soon. Ties between the United States and South Africa could be closer, but only if each side develops more realistic expectations about the other.

FAILURE TO BUILD A SPECIAL RELATIONSHIP

What happened, especially in light of the mutual enthusiasm of the Clinton and Mandela administrations at the time of the transition? One answer is that the relative absence of shared diplomatic goals and common security concerns has mitigated against a close partnership. At a deeper level, history, and often the distorted memory of that history, has been a brake. South Africa and the United States were allies during World War I, World War II, and the Cold War. South African statesman Jan Smuts was active at the Paris Peace Conference that ended World War I, later served in Prime Minister Winston Churchill's war cabinet during World War II, and was made a field marshal in the British army in 1941.[2] At that time, the governments of South Africa, the United States, and the United Kingdom saw their interests as congruent: the defeat of Nazi Germany and imperial Japan. But those now in power in Pretoria regard the South African governments that participated in those struggles as at best "colonial" and fundamentally racist. Hence, they view these wartime alliances with ambiguity if not distaste. Field Marshal Smuts is not a hero for the ANC. For former freedom fighters, there is little history of a commonality of interest between South Africa and the United States.[3]

UNREALISTIC EXPECTATIONS

In the euphoric atmosphere of the 1994 transition to nonracial democracy, expectations within the Clinton and Mandela administrations were mutually unrealistic, setting the stage for eventual disappointment. In 1994, most Americans viewed South Africa as potentially the continent's beacon of democracy and the rule of law. Especially within the

African American community there was the hope that the South African example might kick-start the seemingly stalled civil rights movement in the United States. For them, South Africa's ending of apartheid also represented an American victory over the racism common to the two countries.

In the aftermath of the transition, many Americans anticipated that South Africa would lead the continent in the direction of Western values, be an engine of growth for the African continent, and act as a force in the developing world for democracy and human rights. Their assumption was that South Africa would be as natural an ally as Australia. The new African government would somehow retain or assume a "Western" calling and identity.

Those expectations have been dashed. Instead, from the perspective of Americans interested in Africa, South Africa's government has compromised on democracy and the rule of law outside its boundaries to pursue the chimera of leadership of the Global South without much vision, the necessary resources, or the domestic popular support that such an effort requires. Successive South African governments have declined to support human rights in places such as Burma and Zimbabwe. The *New York Times* and *Washington Post* were bewildered as to why South Africa in 2009, 2011, and 2014 declined to welcome the Dalai Lama, an icon of religious freedom, clearly because of the objections of the Beijing government. (The Zuma government's denial that it was influenced by Chinese objections also had little credibility among the South African public.) In June 2015, the Zuma administration flouted its own judiciary and its own laws by facilitating the departure of Sudanese president Omar al-Bashir, under indictment by the International Criminal Court for war crimes, before he could be arrested.

On the other hand, many, perhaps most, South Africans concerned with international relations still see the United States as tepid in its support for post-apartheid democracy, as awash with "unilateralism," and unwilling to subordinate its national interests to international organizations, especially the United Nations and the African Union. Many South Africans on the left from all ethnic groups instinctively see the United States as still fundamentally racist in its domestic and foreign policies. This perception owes much to the South African replay of U.S. media coverage of instances of violent racism in the United States, such as the 2014–2015 police killings of black men in Ferguson, Missouri;

Staten Island; Baltimore; and Cincinnati and the killings by a white supremacist of congregants in a Charleston, South Carolina, church. In the latter case, the perpetrator had photographed himself wearing the flags of the former racist Rhodesia and apartheid South Africa.

MEMORY

Feeding these suspicions is the memory of successive Washington administrations cooperating closely with the apartheid regime on issues of mutual concern, notwithstanding the American imposition of sanctions against Pretoria that came only late in the struggle. During the bloody civil war in Angola, the apartheid government and Washington supported the same side, while the other (in fact, the winning side) was allied with the ANC, then in exile. That side also included the Cubans, then closely allied to the Soviet Union, a financial backer of the ANC.

U.S. sanctions against apartheid were pushed through by public opinion and Congress. President Reagan vetoed the Comprehensive Anti-Apartheid Act on the basis of Cold War concerns and, in a rare move, was overridden by Congress. Subsequently, however, President Reagan concluded that support of the apartheid regime was contrary to American interests and values. He was the first president to appoint an African American, Edward Perkins, as U.S. ambassador to South Africa. But it is the Reagan veto that is firmly implanted in South African memory.

In 1994, Mandela and many others in the liberation movement anticipated that the United States would provide very large amounts of development assistance and that American private investors would flock to South Africa. The expectation was that development assistance and private investment would be of sufficient magnitude to transform the South African economy and address the pervasive poverty of the black majority.

Driving Mandela's and Mbeki's subsequent coolness toward Washington was that American levels of official development assistance and private investment were far lower than South Africans had expected. The former reflected Washington's inevitable fiscal constraints. As for U.S. private investment, administrations have little impact on private American decisions. For many American businesspeople, there was uncertainty as to whether the new government would respect property rights, concerns based in part on liberation movement rhetoric. South Africa's very high crime statistics also discouraged visits by potential American investors.

GORE-MBEKI COMMISSION

In the optimistic days of Mandela's inauguration, Deputy President Thabo Mbeki and Vice President Al Gore envisaged a mechanism for promoting close U.S.–South African relations. The resulting Gore-Mbeki Commission was established as a means to resolve bilateral issues in the aftermath of a dialogue that had been stunted except for Cold War issues during the apartheid era. It was also predicated on an ongoing, even personal, relationship between the highest leadership of the two countries.[4]

Both Vice President Gore and Deputy President Mbeki had anticipated a special relationship between the two democracies. But, even as early as the first year of President Mandela's administration, the bloom went off the rose. If South Africans were disappointed in levels of American economic and development assistance, Washington disliked the Mandela administration's ongoing warm ties with Fidel Castro and Muammar Gadhafi, both of whom Mandela favored, at least in part because they had financially supported the ANC during the anti-apartheid struggle.

Subsequently and over time, Mugabe's wholesale violation of the rule of law in Zimbabwe also inhibited American investment in South Africa. As South African journalist and historian Allister Sparks has observed, too many American and other businesspeople from outside Africa failed to make the distinction between the two southern African states, and, among the more sophisticated, there was also fear of the possible demonstration effect of Mugabe on the left wing of the ANC.[5]

These realities dampened expansion of trade relations between the United States and South Africa. In recent years, the United States and South Africa have signed a series of bilateral trade agreements, including most recently an amendment to the Trade and Investment Framework Agreement (TIFA), aimed at deepening trade and investment between the two countries. Nevertheless, South Africa is still only the thirty-ninth-largest goods-trading partner of the United States, with USD 21 billion in total goods and services traded in 2012. The total U.S. goods and services trade deficit with South Africa was USD 300 million in 2012, with a goods trade favoring South Africa (USD 1.2 billion deficit in 2012) and a services trade balance favoring the United States (USD 770 million surplus in 2012). The United States exports machinery and vehicles as well as agricultural products (dairy, wheat, and planting seeds). It imports platinum and diamonds, cars, iron, and steel from South Africa. U.S. foreign direct investment (FDI) in South Africa experienced a decrease in 2012. (Its total value was USD 5.5 billion in 2012, a 5.6 percent decrease from 2011.[6]) Hence, economic ties were too weak to drive a special relationship. The geographical distance between the two countries, the small size of the South African market, and the country's narrow range of exports to the United States constrained the growth of a strong economic relationship.

Finally, for Americans, the Mandela administration's inattention to HIV/AIDS and Mbeki's blatantly unscientific approach to the crisis during the first years of his administration were largely incomprehensible—and deplorable. From the perspective of American popular opinion, that reality reduced the attraction of a special bilateral relationship should one even have been possible.

The Gore-Mbeki Commission morphed by intermediate stages into the U.S.–South Africa Strategic Dialogue and associated instruments. Absent the Gore-Mbeki personal partnership, it has never lived up to the expectation that it would be the vehicle for a special relationship between the two countries, though the mechanisms have been useful on many essentially technical issues.

HOW FOREIGN POLICY IS MADE

Foreign policy making in the United States and South Africa is very different. In the United States, there are multiple drivers of foreign policy. The president and the executive branch have primary responsibility. Traditionally, the lead role has been assigned to the Department of State. Most of the time, the U.S. secretary of state is one of the nation's most prominent political personalities. Nevertheless, the making of foreign policy is multifaceted, including the Congress and the media as well as the executive. The results may be sloppy, contradictory, incoherent, and frequently insensitive.

In addition to State, departments and agencies ranging from Treasury, Defense, and Commerce to the Centers for Disease Control and the Agency for International Development among others play important roles depending on the issue at hand. The National Security Council, part of the White House, is responsible for coordination among departments and agencies, but it also on occasion makes policy on matters large and small. Congress has a strong role through its power of the purse and its responsibility to confirm diplomatic appointments and to approve or disapprove treaties. Members of Congress regularly make use of hearings to try to shape the U.S. approach to foreign policy issues.

Outside of government, there are myriad groups and interests that seek to influence U.S. foreign policy, ranging from the business community and organized labor to nongovernmental organizations (often human rights advocates), think tanks, and the media. Civil society in all its varieties and contradictions is very strong in the United States and can be highly influential on particular foreign policy issues. It was an alliance between civil society and Congress that forced President Ronald Reagan to accept the Comprehensive Anti-Apartheid Act.

Historically, the U.S. foreign policy myth has been that it is "bipartisan." During times of crisis—the Pearl Harbor attack of 1941 or the 2001 Twin Towers al-Qaeda attack—foreign policy becomes genuinely bipartisan, but that approach then quickly dissipates. At present, foreign events and an administration's response to them are regularly exploited for partisan advantage. A notable example has been the Republican Party's use of the 2012 jihadist attack on an American diplomatic establishment in Benghazi, Libya, and the killing of the American ambassador to attack the Obama administration on a variety of issues. Earlier, Democrats exploited the unpopular wars in Afghanistan and Iraq to attack the George W. Bush administration on unrelated domestic and foreign policy issues.

In part because it is a world power, foreign affairs are a matter of intense interest in the United States among a broad range of elites that on occasion can engage the mass of the population to oppose a president's policy. The antiwar movement during the era of the Vietnam War is a case in point. Indeed, events far from American shores frequently transform or refocus a presidency. Lyndon Johnson had Vietnam. George H. W. Bush had the first Gulf War. George W. Bush had the al-Qaeda attacks of September 11, 2001, on New York and Washington, D.C., and the subsequent wars in Iraq and Afghanistan. The trajectory of Barack Obama's presidency was influenced by multiple conflicts in the Middle East.

Foreign policy is made very differently in South Africa. From the post–Boer War settlement of 1911 until the present, foreign relations—and foreign policy—have largely been the purview of the executive. Unlike in the United States, the national legislature has played a minimal role in South Africa's foreign affairs. Even though South Africa's economy was dominated by large corporations, both under apartheid and subsequently, a business lobby has been largely absent or ineffective. Business spokesmen complain vocally that the Mandela, Mbeki, and Zuma administrations conducted foreign policy without reference to the country's real economic interests.[7]

South African civil society is strong, and it played a major role in the destruction of apartheid and the establishment of nonracial democracy. It has successfully rallied public opinion in defense of the country's liberal and constitutional arrangements. But its coordination on foreign policy issues is underdeveloped. Hence, while civil society (including the churches) opposed the Zuma government's multiple denials of a visa to the Dalai Lama at the behest of the Beijing government, it was unable to force the administration to reverse itself. It remains to be seen whether civil society and the judiciary will be able to hold the Zuma government accountable for its 2015 welcome of Sudanese president Omar al-Bashir.

The bottom line is that South African administrations do not have to take into account public opinion in the realm of foreign affairs except under rare circumstances. Nor is the executive beholden to other branches of government. All chief executives, of course, prefer an arrangement in which there is limited input in foreign policy making by outsiders.

No doubt the reasons for public disengagement are deep and complex. But surely South Africa's internal divisions and the focus on domestic issues monopolize public attention and absorb the energy that might otherwise be devoted to foreign affairs. That could change in the future. All South Africans can vote, and parliamentary politics are vigorous. The media is free. The instruments are there for wider public engagement in foreign policy. Though it has not yet happened, public indignation over the Zuma government's exclusion of the Dalai Lama and its welcome of al-Bashir may be a harbinger of change.

WASHINGTON'S SEARCH FOR AN AFRICAN DIPLOMATIC PARTNER

Despite the different ways foreign policy is made and the outcome of the Gore-Mbeki Commission, the commonalities and shared historical experience of the United States and South Africa over the long term could provide the foundation for closer relations in the future.

From a Washington perspective, South Africa is now the only African country with the economic and political clout to partner with the United States on many strategic African issues. In the past, Nigeria played that role. But Abuja is currently facing multiple domestic crises, and that capital is no longer as diplomatically active as it was under former president Olusegun Obasanjo. In its own strategic interests, Washington should strengthen its diplomatic ties with Pretoria. But American outreach, should it come, will require a positive South African response.

For the Zuma government, the Obama administration's 2013 approach to the Libya crisis was characteristic of American unwillingness to take into account African sensitivities. The Zuma government and most others in sub-Saharan Africa regard Libya as part of Africa, and the African Union (AU) as the relevant and appropriate regional security organization. The U.S. Department of State and NATO regard Libya as part of the Middle East and coordinated their intervention with the Arab League, not the AU. Libya is a clear example of Washington and Pretoria talking past each other because of different assumptions.

From Washington's perspective, South Africa's stance during the 2012 Libya crisis overlooked the urgency of the bloodbath unleashed by Gadhafi against his own people. And, given that urgency, there was impatience with the view that the AU should somehow trump the Arab League.[8]

On the other hand, despite numerous differences, there has been something of an ambiguous convergence between Washington and Pretoria over Iran, even if neither particularly acknowledges it. The United States is deeply concerned that Iran is in the process of acquiring a nuclear weapons capability. The U.S. response has been to lead in the establishment of UN-mandated sanctions against Iran. These sanctions inhibited Iranian oil exports. That, in turn, directly impacts South Africa, which has long sourced a major portion of its oil from Iran and has built refineries with the specific capacity to refine Iranian oil. It remains to be seen what the impact on South African domestic nuclear policy will be now that the international community has lifted its sanctions against Iran.

South Africa often appears skeptical about U.S. concerns. Nevertheless, South Africa followed the UN Security Council's authorized sanctions regime, a manifestation of its general policy of support for international organizations. That required Pretoria to find new sources for imported oil and gas, resulting in rising fuel prices that have affected the economy to its detriment. Broadly speaking, the United States and South Africa have been on the same side with respect to Iran. Yet the paradox is that the Iranian nuclear issue feeds a domestic South African perception that it has somehow been bullied by the United States. It is unfortunate from the perspective of the larger bilateral relationship that South Africa is not a more significant partner in the Obama administration's Power Africa initiative, which assists African efforts to increase power generation.[9]

Oil sanctions against Iran heightened South Africa's sense of vulnerability about meeting its future energy needs at the same time that they are growing rapidly. It is an ANC goal to bring electricity to townships and informal settlements. That makes expansion of South Africa's nuclear power industry especially attractive to the Zuma government. Further, with relatively large uranium deposits and with experience and experts in nuclear matters, South Africa is well positioned to move forward. There is South African domestic opposition to the expansion of nuclear power, however. The anti–nuclear power arguments are largely the same as in the United States. Especially within the opposition Democratic Alliance (DA), the argument is that the development of solar and wind power would be less expensive and far less dangerous. Nevertheless, by 2015, the government was moving forward on the nuclear option.[10]

NUCLEAR ISSUES

The bilateral relationship between the United States and South Africa on nuclear energy issues is as ambiguous as its other dimensions. South Africa supports the right of any country to develop a nuclear power sector, including the production of highly enriched uranium (HEU).[11] This is the common view within the nonaligned movement. South Africans observe that Canada, Belgium, and the Netherlands, as well as itself, continue to use HEU in producing medical isotopes. The United States, however, is reluctant to endorse HEU when countries like Iran and North Korea appear aggressively to be pursuing nuclear arms capability. How can it be guaranteed that a stockpile of HEU, such as South Africa has and wants to expand, will not fall into the hands of rogue states or international terrorists?

Bilateral dialogue on nuclear and other issues takes place against a backdrop of disappointment on both sides of the relationship. For many South Africans, U.S. concern over the production of HEU is misplaced, given the enormous size of the American nuclear arsenal. American credibility on Iran's intentions suffers from the experience of Iraq, where a cause of the war was to eliminate Saddam Hussein's supposed weapons of mass destruction program. Yet the only such weapons found were those dating from the Iraq-Iran War.[12] From the American perspective, however, a 2007 breach of security at South Africa's Pelindaba nuclear facility highlights the risks that expanded HEU could be diverted to weapons use by rogue, non–South African elements.

From the perspective of the formal conduct of international relations, a significant difference between the United States and South Africa is that the former is a world power, while the latter is at best a regional power, a power in the Global South. From an American perspective, South African foreign policy is often parochial in outlook, while South Africans see Washington as too ready to resort to force, as indifferent to world opinion, and as reluctant to make use of multilateral organizations that it does not dominate as it pursues its worldwide interests.

There has been an expansion of the American military presence in Africa, symbolized by the establishment of a U.S. Africa Command (AFRICOM). (Africa was previously under the U.S. European Command.) The stated focus of the new command is to facilitate humanitarian relief and to help build the capacity of African states to meet their security needs. It was directly involved in the destruction of the Gadhafi government in Libya but also in the 2014 international relief effort for victims of Ebola in Guinea, Sierra Leone, and Liberia. The American military presence also reflects the emergence of jihadist terrorism in the Horn of Africa and the Sahel. Many Americans are haunted by the ghost of Osama Bin Laden and fear that the so-called Islamic State has penetrated the Sahel. Unique among U.S. military commands, AFRICOM's leadership has a civilian component drawn from the Department of State, USAID, and domestic agencies. Unlike the other U.S. military regional commands, the deputy is usually a civilian, an ambassador. There is now a large and expanding U.S. military base in Djibouti, Camp Lemonier. There are also more than a dozen U.S. drone facilities, mostly in the Horn and West Africa, devoted to intelligence gathering.

South African political opinion is viscerally opposed to AFRICOM and to an expanding U.S. military presence in Africa. The upper reaches of the government will not engage with AFRICOM; as of late December 2014, the minister of defense had not met with any visiting senior AFRICOM official. Moreover, as important as specific opposition to AFRICOM and general suspicion of U.S. alleged "unilateralism" are to Pretoria's U.S. policy, many South Africans fundamentally question the American commitment to post-apartheid South Africa.

U.S. security preoccupations and its visa policy have long haunted the bilateral relationship. Nelson Mandela remained on a U.S. terrorist "watch list" until only seven years before he died and long after he had left office as chief of state. As late as 2014, other liberation leaders now in senior positions in South African politics and business remained on such lookout lists, apparently the result of U.S. bureaucratic inertia. U.S. watch lists, and the inability to purge them in a timely way, contributed to a jaundiced view of the United States, especially among many in the ANC leadership. [13]

SOUTH AFRICA IN AFRICA

With the coming of democracy, blacks now dominate the South African government, and, as Zuma's first presidential inauguration illustrated, they have little interest in perpetuating the Western character imposed by whites. For the black majority, South Africa is an African country naturally tied to the Global South, an identity expressed through participation in the AU and the consultative group BRICS (Brazil, Russia, India, China, and South Africa). China has also become South Africa's largest bilateral trading partner.[14]

With respect to the rule of law, South Africa has been scrupulous at home, at least until the 2015 al-Bashir episode. But, earlier, Mandela, Mbeki, and Zuma looked the other way as Zimbabwe systematically ran roughshod over it in pursuit of Robert Mugabe's vision of justice and personal enrichment for himself and his cronies. The Mandela, Mbeki, and Zuma administrations were silent as Mugabe dismantled Zimbabwe's independent judiciary, in effect abolished the rule of law by seizing private property without compensation in the name of "land reform," and made widespread use of thugs (often masquerading as "war veterans") to intimidate and ultimately destroy any political opposition. For a time, Mugabe even made war on the Anglican Church, Zimbabwe's largest, which has close ties with South African Anglicans, including Archbishop Tutu. Mbeki, particularly, claimed that he was pursuing "quiet diplomacy" to rein in Mugabe, an approach that manifestly failed.

Zuma initially took a sterner line on Mugabe than Mandela and Mbeki had. Unrest in Zimbabwe had led to migrant flows into South Africa that in turn generated outbursts of xenophobia that deeply embarrassed the South African government. In the aftermath of Zimbabwe's bloody elections of 2008, Zuma, working through the Southern African Development Community, brokered an arrangement in which Mugabe shared power with the leading opposition party, the Movement for Democratic Change, led by Morgan Tsvangirai. But in 2013, Zuma, too, accepted Mugabe's rigged elections and even fired his special envoy to Zimbabwe at Mugabe's insistence.

In 2010–2011, the Zuma administration bitterly opposed NATO's decision not to work with the AU during the Libyan intervention. Though South Africa had voted for UN Security Council resolution 1973 authorizing "all necessary measures" to protect Libyan civilians, the Zuma administration concluded that NATO far exceeded its mandate when it destroyed the Gadhafi government. The Libya episode led to a cooling of official relations between Washington and Pretoria that persisted as late as 2015. The subsequent imploding of Libya with a vicious civil war reenforces the South African view that its approach would have been the better choice.

The Zuma administration shows ambivalent signs of ambition to lead sub-Saharan Africa, if not necessarily the commitment to do so. In 2012, the Zuma administration's chief foreign policy goal appeared to be to secure the election of Nkosazana Dlamini-Zuma as chairperson of the AU Commission, in effect the chief executive of the AU. A medical doctor by training, she is a former minister of health, former minister of foreign affairs, and a former wife of Jacob Zuma. Her election was contested by a candidate from francophone Africa, and eventual success cost the Zuma administration political capital among francophone countries.[15]

After Dlamini-Zuma's election, the Zuma administration increasingly adhered to the AU's position on international issues. In 2007, the Zuma administration sent a small contingent of the South African Defense Force (SADF) to the Central African Republic (CAR), ostensibly to help the incumbent president build capacity to counter an insurrection. After fourteen South Africans were killed, Zuma withdrew the force in 2013 in the face of rare parliamentary criticism that it had not authorized the intervention.[16] It was unclear whether the Zuma administration had informed the National Assembly of the deployment of South African troops or whether there was an AU fig leaf to cover the operation.

Originally a strong advocate for the International Criminal Court (ICC), the Mbeki government had incorporated its founding statutes into South African law in 2003. But by 2015, the Zuma government had joined the chorus of critics of the ICC as a "neocolonialist" institution that unfairly targets African states. President Zuma also accepted the AU contention that chiefs of state should be immune to the ICC's jurisdiction, including Sudan's al-Bashir. In 2015, the ANC adopted as a party position South Africa's withdrawal from the ICC. The argument was that the court discriminated against Africa, and certain "powers" supported it but refused to accept its jurisdiction, a reference to the United States, which signed the ICC founding treaty but has never ratified it.

The 2015 al-Bashir episode was one of those rare occasions where foreign policy and South African institutions of governance collided.

Zuma's welcome of al-Bashir and his facilitation of the Sudanese president's departure were highly popular with the AU chiefs of state. But those steps broke South African law and opened the administration to charges of contempt of court. They were also domestically unpopular.

South Africa's leadership vocation and capacity is not clear. A 2014 South African Defense Review concluded that the country's military capability was in a "critical state of decline" that would require a decade to overcome.[17] The report cited force imbalance, obsolescence, and an inability to meet defense commitments. The defense budget—USD 3.5 billion—is slightly more than 1 percent of GDP.[18] The Zuma government, like its predecessors, favors domestic priorities over defense.

It is also striking that even though Nkosazana Dlamini-Zuma is the chairperson of the AU Commission, South Africa has played a minor role in the AU's response to the Ebola crisis in West Africa. Unlike other much poorer African countries, South African bilateral assistance to Liberia, Guinea, and Sierra Leone has been very small.

A WAY FORWARD?

There could be a certain confluence between U.S. and South African positions on nuclear energy and nonproliferation issues. Based on a common outlook, Washington and Pretoria working together might have the potential for improving the quality of the broader relationship. A shared perspective could start to build a reservoir of goodwill and understanding now absent that might facilitate progress on bridging differences in other areas. Already under way are relatively low-level, unofficial efforts, dialogues, and exchanges on nuclear issues between the two countries. On nuclear issues, South Africa has unique credibility because it voluntarily gave up its nuclear weapons capability.[19] South Africa is also the home of significant nuclear technology that is devoted to civilian purposes, such as the production of power and for medical purposes, as we have seen. This capacity is unique on the African continent.

Forging a closer bilateral relationship between Washington and Pretoria based on nuclear and nonproliferation issues would not be easy. The differences run deep. South Africa strongly supports nuclear disarmament and is critical of Washington's apparent reluctance to give up nuclear weapons. Pretoria also gives priority to its role as a "bridge builder" between the nuclear weapons states on the one side and the majority of non–nuclear weapons states (NNWS) on the other. Such factors constrain the degree to which Washington and Pretoria can align on specific issues.

There also remains a deep dividing line between South Africa and the United States regarding their divergent approaches to national, regional, and global security. The United States and its NATO and other strategic allies consider nuclear weapons to be fundamental in their defense strategies. In contrast, South Africa holds that the development of new types of nuclear weapons or the rationalization of their use contradicts the spirit of the Non-Proliferation Treaty (NPT) and its review conferences. South Africa fundamentally holds that its national security—and the security of the African region—is guaranteed by a strong nonproliferation regime, not by nuclear weapons. Therefore, a dominant view in Pretoria is that nuclear weapons provide only an illusion of security for those who possess them. While South Africa defends its nonproliferation policy as based on principle, it sees the United States and its allies as approaching nuclear nonproliferation, arms control, and disarmament solely from a national security perspective.

New Delhi and Washington: A Distant Mirror?

With respect to the current, official bilateral relationship between the United States and South Africa, there are some similarities to the often rocky road trod by Washington and New Delhi for almost five decades after India's independence in 1947. Except for a brief interregnum, India has been a democratic state conducted according to the rule of law, as South Africa has become. With China, India and the United States confronted a common rival. Nevertheless, shared democratic values were not enough to overcome New Delhi's anticolonialist fear of great power dominance and its rivalry with American ally Pakistan. New Delhi forged a close relationship with Moscow, lubricated by Soviet assistance in the construction of infrastructure. Washington, in turn, was deeply suspicious of India's close ties with the Soviet Union, and it was unsympathetic to the "socialist" values of the governing Indian National Congress. U.S. Cold War preoccupations and Indian anticolo-

nialism trumped shared democratic values. A closer bilateral relationship has developed only in the last decade, more than a generation after
India's independence, a departure from the political scene of India's
first generation of postcolonial leaders, and after the collapse of the
Soviet Union. But a 2013 diplomatic spat between New Delhi and
Washington over diplomatic privileges and immunities involving an Indian vice consul in New York demonstrated how fragile the new understanding was.

NO SPECIAL RELATIONSHIP

South Africa's foreign policy is controlled by President Jacob Zuma and
other ANC leaders who come disproportionately from those who were
in exile and participated in the armed struggle against apartheid. The
Zuma administration, like those of Mandela and Mbeki, affirms its
identification with the Global South, with the nonaligned, and with
Africa. Zuma and his generation of the ANC leadership remember (and
exaggerate) the U.S. partnership with the apartheid regime. It has little
understanding or regard for the worldwide outlook and responsibilities
of the United States.

For Washington, Africa remains a largely marginal interest, except
when it is the theater for international conflict, such as jihadist terrorism centered in Somalia and the Sahel, or humanitarian catastrophes,
such as the spread of the Ebola virus in West Africa. With respect to
South Africa, American opinion no longer sees the country as pointing
the way toward a democratic and economically developing Africa.

Under these circumstances, the special relationship foreseen by Vice
Presidents Gore and Mbeki between two "nonracial" democracies remains stillborn. The official relationship is likely to remain cordial, but
not special. However, because foreign policy is so much the purview of
the South African executive, a change in the presidency could make a
closer relationship possible. The DA leadership is instinctively pro-
American. Cape Town mayor Patricia de Lille displays several photo-
graphs of former New York mayor Michael Bloomberg in her office.
But, at least until 2019, there will be an ANC-dominated government,
though Jacob Zuma could leave the presidency before then. Of his
possible successors, Cyril Ramaphosa, with his sophistication and inter-

national business links, might see the advantage of a warmer relationship with the United States. The Obama administration and its successor should be sensitive to the opportunities that a change in the South African presidency might present.

For now, with Pretoria's focus on the Global South and hopes for a partnership with the BRICS, areas of cooperation between the United States and South Africa on African issues are likely to be limited. Nevertheless, South Africa's success as a democracy conducted according to the rule of law, on a continent where both are rare, remains in America's interests. The rocky landscape of the bilateral relationship between the United States and South Africa puts a premium on initiatives to strengthen bilateral communications to forestall a lack of mutual understanding, as happened with respect to Libya. That would imply a greater diplomatic effort by the U.S. Department of State, likely involving an expansion of the personnel assigned to the U.S. missions in South Africa and the Africa Bureau in Washington.

Greater U.S. outreach to the "democrats" within South Africa's political parties could pay dividends because those groups share the American commitment to democratic institutions and the rule of law. This shared commitment provides a common vocabulary for consideration of specifically diplomatic and security issues. U.S. outreach to South Africa's democrats would be strengthened by an expansion of programs such as the Fulbright program of academic exchanges and the International Visitor Program, whereby young political leaders come to the United States for a three- or four-week in-depth introduction to aspects of the United States related to their specific interests. There are myriad other exchange programs, some of which are public and private partnerships, that should be encouraged and expanded.

More specifically, the United States should look for opportunities to build on its existing relationship with the SADF. It is the SADF that would be the instrument for South African participation in UN and other peacekeeping operations. But, as its performance in the Central African Republic in 2014 and the 2015 Defense Review both demonstrate, it is inadequate to take on additional tasks.

The International Military Education and Training (IMET) program is the usual mechanism by which the United States provides training to partner militaries. The program's funding for South Africa has been steadily declining, from $1,058,000 in FY 2009 to a State Department request for $650,000 in 2015. In the short term, the U.S. Departments of State and Defense should explore with the South African Ministry of Defense and the SADF an expansion of the program.

There is already in place a partnership between the New York National Guard and the SADF.[20] South Africa's was the National Guard's first African partnership. The New York National Guard has trained with the SADF since 2003. The program is very small. Nevertheless, it is an example of a small-scale effort that over time contributes to warmer bilateral relations.

The South African Police Service (SAPS) is coming under increasing South African criticism for brutality, as was demonstrated at Marikana in 2012. The United States has a small relationship with SAPS, mostly involving training for narcotics enforcement. It might be possible to expand the relationship. For example, in Nigeria, U.S. contractors (mostly retired District of Columbia police) trained the Nigerian police in patrolling using bicycles in dense urban areas. That training might have applicability in the similarly dense townships of South Africa.

Expansion of exchange programs by and large does not involve the South African government. Nevertheless, growth of a relationship with the military and the police would require official partnership. The hostility of the Zuma administration to AFRICOM could be a barrier. To address this hostility, AFRICOM should consider a strategy of invitations to high-level South African civilian politicians, military leaders, and civil society personalities to visit its headquarters in Stuttgart, Germany, to better understand AFRICOM's mission.

CONCLUSION

Morning in South Africa

The consequences of apartheid still rest heavy on South Africa. The 1994 transition to nonracial democracy was no revolution. It was a deal somewhat reminiscent of the post–Boer War settlement between the British Empire and the Afrikaners. In both cases, there was a transfer of political power, but with guarantees for the economic status quo.

The Afrikaners lost the Boer War but won the peace. Following the 1909–1911 settlement, Afrikaners governed all of the Union of South Africa, including the Cape Province, the more than half of the country that had been under direct British rule after 1806. The political settlement was within the framework of democratic institutions governed by the rule of law, but restricted to white males only. The Afrikaner majority among white males guaranteed that South Africa's government would be Afrikaner. Between 1911 and Nelson Mandela's inauguration as president in 1994, the style of governance became progressively more "Afrikaner" and less British or "Western." But the rule of law guaranteeing property rights ensured that British domination of the mining industry and much of the rest of the modern economy would continue. The Anglo-Boer settlement notably left "native affairs" to the new Afrikaner government, which gradually eliminated the limited political rights of blacks and coloureds under the British and, ultimately, established apartheid.

The 1994 transition was a deal between two roughly equal forces: the liberation movements supported by international opinion and the National Party that controlled the security forces. The essence of the deal was the transfer of political power from Afrikaners and other whites to the former liberation movements, primarily the African National Congress (ANC). The latter, while multiracial, was black dominated. Just as governance of the old Union of South Africa became progressively more Afrikaner, the political style post-1994, and especially since President Mbeki's inauguration in 1999, has become more "African." For example, ANC-dominated local government authorities have substituted wholesale "African" names for those of European or Afrikaner origin, and the Zuma government rhetorically strongly identifies with the "Global South" and BRICS, even if there are few practical consequences. However, white control of the economy—and, in effect, the basis of white privilege—has been largely left in place.

As in 1909–1911, the 1994 settlement reflected a democratic context and the rule of law. The post-1994 constitution and legal institutions went even further in their guarantees of human rights than those that existed in most other democracies. The constitution also established mechanisms that limited the power of the majority, both in parliament and the executive.

The 1994 settlement dismantled the legal basis of apartheid, but not its consequences. The traditional racial hierarchy, with whites at the top and blacks at the bottom, largely remained in place. White capital, accumulated during the long years of white supremacy, was untouched. Most whites continued to benefit from educational and health services far superior to those of the majority of the population. Whites continued to be much richer and to live longer than other South Africans. Only after 1994 were whites joined by a small but growing black elite and middle class. The mass of the population, however, remained poor. A major driver of black poverty continued to be unemployment, which in turn reflected inferior educational and health services and a labor policy that did not encourage the creation of low-wage jobs.

Nevertheless, the 1994 transition strengthened the rule of law while at the same time establishing legal and constitutional institutions by which South Africa could address contemporary and future issues. Within the context of absolute freedom of speech, an independent judiciary, and free and credible elections, South Africa has moved to reform education, health, and land tenure. The legalities have been observed, but progress has been slow.

The post-apartheid government has built houses, improved infrastructure, and established a safety net of allowances for the poorest of the poor. However, perhaps for most South Africans, there has been little change in their personal situation since the end of apartheid. Township dwellers, especially, are losing patience. Some of them are the constituency of Julius Malema and his Economic Freedom Fighters (EFF). This new party would dismantle some constitutional guarantees, especially those related to private property. Often explicitly antiwhite in its rhetoric, it would expropriate without compensation white-owned property, thereby destroying the economy. It also disrupts parliament with demonstrations on the floor. But, with only 6 percent of the vote in 2014, it does not represent a genuine threat to South African democracy conducted according to the rule of law. That said, the profound discontent and alienation of which the EFF is merely a symptom does represent a potential threat to South Africa's constitutional democracy.

Constitutional and legal institutions are crucial to the political health of a democratic South Africa. Hence the alarm felt by civil society at efforts by the Zuma administration to curtail the powers of those institutions, especially those that limit the executive and the security services. There is fear that Zuma and the "Africanists" around him aim for the "big man" style of government associated with Zimbabwe's Robert Mugabe or Uganda's Yoweri Museveni, to cite two from a dishearteningly long list. It is widely believed that some of those initiatives are designed to cover up evidence of official corruption and cronyism. But, in virtually every case, those efforts have been defeated by civil society, the free media, and the opposition parties in parliament against the backdrop of an independent judiciary. Hence, the 1994 settlement is showing resilience, but continued vigilance is required.

Many of South Africa's long-term social and economic trends are favorable, despite the current economic malaise. The birthrate is falling, and the growth of the population is now less than economic growth averaged over the past decade. Unlike other African countries, South Africa's population is now growing only slightly more than 1 percent a year.[1] It is true that the persistent maldistribution of educational and health assets results in a disproportionately small, mostly white, part of society that benefits the most. But, over time, stable population numbers will facilitate more broadly based economic growth if implementation of the National Development Plan leads to the reduction of unemployment through better delivery of health and education services. Increased employment in the townships and in rural areas would drive poverty reduction, which in turn would reduce South Africa's very high levels of inequality.

HIV/AIDS remains a significant driver of South Africa's high mortality rates. However, the Zuma administration is fully engaged in the fight against the disease. South Africa is the only recipient of funds from the U.S. President's Emergency Plan for AIDS Relief (PEPFAR) that is moving toward assumption of complete fiscal responsibility for the program. Partly due to HIV/AIDS, the general health of the population does not approach that of the developed world. Life spans are relatively short across the racial spectrum, though whites live much longer on average than members of other racial groups. However, the government's planned overhaul of the health care system is credible, and its implementation should improve the general health of the population. Its initiatives appear to reflect a broad consensus.

Since 1994, the racial integration of South African education has been an achievement, even if whites continue to benefit disproportionately from high-quality institutions of apartheid and even pre-apartheid foundation. Nevertheless, a much greater percentage of nonwhites now have access to education at all levels, including the most prestigious institutions, even if the quality available to most South Africans remains low.

Too many pedagogical issues remain unresolved. But what is hopeful is that they are vigorously debated, experiments are under way, and there is willingness to spend the necessary tax monies on education. The goals of the National Development Plan focus on expansion of enrollments rather than the transformation of instruction, about which there is little agreement in South Africa or anywhere else. In the view of a credible South African observer, it is likely that the plan's narrower education goals can be met even if the rate of economic growth remains modest.[2] Moreover, the national debate over how to improve the quality of instruction may over time lead to pedagogic reforms that will result in a workforce better prepared for an advanced economy than at present.

South Africa's globalized economy makes it vulnerable to contractions elsewhere. The structure of South Africa's economy, with its high capitalization and too few unskilled jobs, ensures that unemployment will decline only slowly. As in the United States, the dynamic parts of the economy are knowledge and technology based, not labor intensive. Whites and asians, especially those who are English speakers, with access to better education and possessing accumulated capital, are better placed to take advantage of the globalized economy than most blacks and coloureds. The current high levels of black and coloured unemployment reflect poor access to education, too little opportunity to acquire technical skills, and inadequate English-language skills. A result is their continued impoverishment. On the other hand, government allowances have reduced levels of absolute poverty, and a huge housing program has greatly expanded home ownership among the poor, with the possibility of capital accumulation among a part of the population where up to now it has been all but impossible.

While it is sometimes associated with the new "African" style of politics, corruption has long been a feature of South African governance. It has been a brake on the country's economic development, though less so than in Nigeria or Kenya. The Zuma administration has been inept in controlling it, and the president himself is widely regarded as personally benefiting from it, a perception now a major contributor to his political weakness. A growth in public intolerance of corruption is encouraged by a vigorous free press. The emergence of strong opposition parties prepared to ask tough questions in parliament about government contracts and backroom deals will also have a positive influence over time. There is growing public awareness of the close relationship between corruption and poor service delivery in the townships and in rural areas. That translates into residents' growing willingness to fight against it and to hold perpetrators accountable. In the short term, this will likely have the paradoxical consequence of corruption appearing to be more salient and more widespread than it was in the past. Though hard to prove, that presumption is likely false. Corruption under apartheid, which we now know was common, was largely invisible at the time because of the authoritarian style of governance, shackles on the press, and civil society's focus on the struggle against apartheid rather than on other governance issues.

Corruption affects the police and the security services, though to a lesser extent than in other African countries. More generally, however, the security services can still play an unhealthy role in national life, as their presumed sponsorship of the "secrecy bill" demonstrated. But the concerted opposition to such proposed legislation, not least within the ANC, led to its significant modification and illustrates the limits to security service influence.

The danger that South Africa could become a one-party state dominated by the ANC is receding as internal fissures within the party reduce its monolithic character and opposition parties strengthen. Voting remains largely along racial lines. However, the Democratic Alliance (DA) on the center-right and the gradual emergence of opposition parties on the left, with the ANC in the middle, could accelerate the emergence of issue-based, rather than race-based, voting patterns.

The darkest cloud in South Africa's morning sky is the quality of its political leaders at the top, especially within the ANC. President Zuma has been disappointing.[3] Nevertheless, the ANC government does remain a broad church with an important democratic element as well as a Marxist-Leninist faction in decline and a growing traditionalist African one. Any of the factions of the ANC could produce the next president. Within the party, there is genuine competition for senior positions, and the party election outcomes are difficult for outsiders to predict. Therefore, the party may throw up a dark horse presidential candidate who is relatively unknown. Deputy President Cyril Ramaphosa's further ascent to the presidency is not guaranteed, and though acquitted by a parliamentary investigation, he remains under a political cloud from his involvement with the Marikana mine violence.

Already Ramaphosa faces two women as potential rivals, Baleka Mbete and Nkosazana Dlamini-Zuma. The former is the speaker of the National Assembly and the chairperson of the ANC. She served as deputy president in 2008–2009 under President Motlanthe during the interregnum between Mbeki's departure and Zuma's election. A Zulu, she has strong support in KwaZulu-Natal. The latter was minister of health and subsequently foreign minister. As minister of health, she compromised herself by following Mbeki's antiscientific line on HIV/AIDS. As foreign minister, she declined to confront Mugabe. She is now chairman of the African Union Commission. A medical doctor and

Zuma's ex-wife, she likely would protect Zuma's children and other family interests. She, too, is a Zulu.

There are many other potential contenders for the presidency. One is Kgalema Motlanthe, former president and former deputy president. Based in Johannesburg, he is popular among the ANC rank and file. Another is Blade Nzimande, the minister of education and general secretary of the South African Communist Party. He has opposed the domination of Afrikaans as a language of instruction and has pushed for faster racial integration of Afrikaner universities. Though a communist, he has opposed nationalization of enterprises as being counterproductive to the interests of the working class.

Of all these candidates, Cyril Ramaphosa is the best known within the party rank and file and abroad. In addition to being deputy president, Zuma has appointed him the chairman of the National Planning Commission and thereby responsible for the implementation of the National Development Plan. His background is the trade union movement and the United Democratic Front (UDF), and he was not part of the ANC in exile. With Roelf Meyer, he was one of the two lead negotiators in 1993–1994 of the transition settlement. It is widely said that he was Mandela's first choice to be his deputy president and eventual successor. But Mbeki had greater support in the part of the party that had been in exile, to which Madiba deferred. Further, Ramaphosa did not fight for the position. It remains to be seen whether he will fight for the presidency in 2019, or whether he will again step aside. His political base is in Gauteng Province (Johannesburg). There are signs that Zuma has turned against him as his star has risen and the president's has waned.[4]

Of these prominent candidates to succeed Zuma, the youngest is Blade Nzimande, who was born in 1958. All the rest are in their seventh decade: Motlanthe, Baleka Mbete, Dlamini-Zuma, and Ramaphosa. Along with Ramaphosa, they are far better formally educated than Zuma. Motlanthe graduated from Orlando High School, Soweto, and received a grant to attend St. Christopher's College in Swaziland, which the apartheid government blocked. Ramaphosa studied law at the University of South Africa and the University of the North. Baleka Mbete has a teacher's certificate and a postgraduate certificate from the University of Cape Town. Dlamini-Zuma has an MD from the University of Bristol (UK) and an undergraduate degree in zoology and botany. Nzi-

mande has a PhD in philosophy from the University of Natal. Ramaphosa and Nzimande did not go into exile during the apartheid struggle.
Baleka Mbete was in exile in a number of African countries, Dlamini-
Zuma in the United Kingdom. Motlanthe was imprisoned for ten years
on Robben Island.

Of these potential ANC heads of state, none represents a genera-
tional change. Perhaps of even greater concern, the ANC does not
seem to be moving toward grooming a new generation for leadership,
and in a multiracial country, the diversity of the party's leadership is
declining. There is the risk that the ANC will increasingly be perceived
as the Zulu party.

As a group, ANC party leaders are not particularly elderly compared
with other African elites. But they have all been involved with governance for at least twenty years and often appear to have run out of ideas
and energy. They are increasingly defensive about criticism, which
makes them sympathetic to the blandishments of the security services
and impatient with the media. Many South Africans find their vision
clouded, and the wealth some have accumulated raises questions about
their commitment to genuine change, which likely would be at their
expense as well as that of the white minority.

The ANC's future appeal to township and rural dwellers, the core of
its constituency, is likely to continue to be based on identity politics and
memories of Nelson Mandela. But, with the alternative of Julius Malema's Economic Freedom Fighters or a foreseen left-wing labor party, it
is unclear how long those who have been left behind will continue their
support of the ANC.

Within the opposition DA, Helen Zille and Patricia de Lille dominate the party. Helen Zille believes a strong black DA candidate could
become president, if not in 2019 then in 2024. Accordingly, she sponsored Mmusi Maimane, a strong campaigner and now the head of the
party. In the 2016 local government elections, the DA is targeting for
victory Johannesburg and Port Elizabeth. Such a goal is now credible.

Patricia de Lille and Helen Zille are the same age, both born in
1951, and are about the same age as the leaders of the ANC. Helen
Zille graduated from the University of Witwatersrand, while Patricia de
Lille graduated only from high school, a reflection of the limited educational opportunities for coloureds of her generation. Maimane, born in
1980, has master's degrees from the University of Witwatersrand and

the University of Wales. Lindiwe Mazibuko, whom Zille has also groomed for leadership, has a master's degree from the University of Cape Town and in May 2015 completed an MPA at Harvard. She is expected to return to South Africa by 2016.

The DA, with its emphasis on the sanctity of the constitution, the rule of law, efficiency of government, and hostility to corruption associated with patronage, is well placed to expand its support among the parts of the emerging black middle class not dependent on ANC patronage. Zille is premier of the Western Cape, de Lille the mayor of Cape Town. Both entities are commonly regarded as the best governed in South Africa, and their success is a powerful point of attraction. Should the metalworkers' union launch a genuine left-wing political party with a comprehensive and politically realistic program of social and economic reform, it could take significant electoral support away from the ANC but probably not the DA. A strong left-wing party might provide the opportunity for the DA to form a government, most likely in coalition with a rump of the ANC.

South Africa is already a model for other states for a transition to democracy. A South Africa that is diplomatically active in Africa has the potential for promoting stability and fostering "African solutions for African problems," in Thabo Mbeki's words. But, to be sustained, that will require South Africa to embrace an African leadership vocation that goes beyond the Zuma government's support for veterans of liberation movements, its adoption of a superficial "African" style, and its visceral oversensitivity to real or imagined "neocolonialism." Moreover, there is not yet a new dawn in the bilateral relationship between Pretoria and Washington, nor is there likely to be until the current generation of the ANC's leadership passes from the scene.

Some veterans of the liberation movements, remembering the U.S. partnership with the apartheid government, will always be profoundly suspicious of American motives—and of the persistence of American racism as portrayed in the American media: police killings of unarmed black men in Ferguson, Missouri; Staten Island; Baltimore; and Cincinnati strike close to home for many township dwellers. The 2015 church killings in Charleston, South Carolina, resonate with black South African churchgoers, a very large percentage of the population. Further, perceptions of Western countries for many ANC operatives are colored by "the enemy within," continued white privilege in South Africa that at least some liberation veterans also identify with the United States. The fact that South Africa and the United States are multiracial democracies conducted according to the rule of law is insufficient to overcome different readings of the past and differences of focus at present.

In some ways, Nelson Mandela's death in December 2013 marked the close of the apartheid era and the anti-apartheid struggle. The Cold War, the context for Washington's relations with Pretoria during much of the apartheid era, has been over for almost a generation. As the anti-apartheid leadership slowly passes from the scene, there may be new opportunities for Pretoria and Washington to explore areas of cooperation, such as nuclear nonproliferation. Washington should be sensitive to new possibilities and openly welcome a strategic partnership with Pretoria on issues of mutual concern that might become possible for the first time since the days of Gore and Mbeki.

Developing closer ties with "nonracial" and democratic South Africa is in America's long-term interests. Yet Washington is little prepared to pursue a new relationship with South Africa. Building a partnership will require resources and skill, most of which are diplomatic. However, American diplomatic capacity worldwide has been underfunded since the end of the Cold War, and neither Africa nor South Africa is a particular priority. In U.S. academia, there has been an African "recessional," with universities failing to replace retiring faculty, many of whom were strong supporters of the anti-apartheid struggle. American business in general remains timid about Africa, except where quick profits usually involving primary commodities are possible. These realities may inhibit a transformation of the official relationship even if and when other factors favorably align.

Is South Africa's glass half empty or half full? Economic and social change is occurring at a snail's pace. If the legal basis of apartheid is gone, its social and economic consequences remain. However, South Africa's post-1994 achievements are significant. The government is now implementing sound health policies. Efforts have been made at education reform. There is a broad consensus in favor of land reform and black economic empowerment, even if there is disagreement about how to implement programs to achieve these goals.

Above all, South Africa's democratic institutions are continuing to mature. Since 1994, there has been a consistent pattern of credible elections. Proportional representation has ensured that a range of political voices are heard, despite the ANC's overwhelming domination of electoral politics. Freedom of speech is absolute, and there has been no infringement on the guarantees of human rights enshrined in the constitution. The rule of law holds sway, despite challenges to it. The judiciary has remained independent. Civil society is strong. On balance, even with clouds, it is morning in South Africa.

NOTES

INTRODUCTION

1. For a major study of the U.S. response to apartheid, see Robert Massie, *Loosing the Bonds: The United States and South Africa in the Apartheid Years* (New York: Nan A. Talese/Doubleday, 1997).

2. BRICS is a consultative group of emerging economies initially made up of Brazil, Russia, India, and China. The group invited South Africa to join in 2010.

3. The tag refers to South Africa's multiracial character and was popularized by Archbishop Desmond Tutu.

4. A court decision in 2008 reclassified the Chinese who were South African citizens prior to 1994 and their descendants as "black" for them to gain access to Black Economic Empowerment. It is estimated that up to three hundred thousand Chinese have settled in South Africa since 1994. It is also estimated that South African citizens of Chinese descent who arrived before 1994 and their descendants number only twelve thousand. See Sky Canaves, "In South Africa, Chinese Is the New Black," China Realtime, *Wall Street Journal*, accessed September 29, 2015, http://blogs.wsj.com/chinarealtime/ 2008/06/19/in-south-africa-chinese-is-the-new-black.

5. Richard Downie and Sahil Angelo, *Counting the Cost of South Africa's Health Burden* (Washington, DC: Center for Strategic and International Studies, 2015), 5.

6. On civil society generally, see Thomas Carothers and William Barndt, "Civil Society," *Foreign Policy* 117 (1999): 18–29; and Robert Putnam, *Bowling Alone: The Collapse and Revival of American Community* (New York:

Simon and Schuster, 2000), based on his 1995 *Journal of Democracy* article of the same title.

7. Under apartheid, black political activity, including voting, was to take place only in the "independent" and "self-governing" homelands. Blacks could also vote for certain local councils, widely hated for collaborating with the apartheid government. Once apartheid was fully achieved, which it never was, no blacks would have had South African citizenship.

8. South Africa has three capitals. Pretoria is the administrative center, the parliament meets in Cape Town, and the Supreme Court is based in Bloemfontein. Accordingly, the U.S. embassy's leadership moved from Pretoria to Cape Town when parliament was in session.

1. THE ARGUMENT

1. For a detailed and thoughtful exposition of this perspective, see Robert Rotberg, ed., "Strengthening Governance in South Africa: Building on Mandela's Legacy," *Annals of the American Academy of Policy and Social Science* 652 (2014): 70–238.

2. "Madiba" was Mandela's clan name and was widely used as a term of affectionate address.

3. See chapter 4 for a discussion of wealth and poverty. Broadly speaking, the white wealth differential reflects capital accumulated over the generations, higher incomes, access to much better education opportunities, and better health.

4. Thabo Mbeki, *Africa: The Time Has Come* (Cape Town: Tafelberg, 1998), quoted in David Everatt, "The Politics of Poverty," *Bangladeshi e-Journal of Sociology* 2, no. 1 (2005): 1–15.

5. Marna Kearney and Ayodele Odusola, "Assessing Development Strategies to Achieve the MDGs in the Republic of South Africa" (United Nations Department for Social and Economic Affairs, 2011), 9.

6. "South Africa," World Bank, accessed October 14, 2015, http://www.worldbank.org/en/country/southafrica.

7. Simon Allison, "'Black Economic Empowerment Has Failed': Piketty on South African Inequality," *Guardian*, October 6, 2015, http://theguardian.com/world/2015/oct/06/piketty-south-africa-inequality-nelson-mandela-lecture.

8. "2014 National and Provincial Elections Results," Electoral Commission of South Africa, accessed October 15, 2015, http://www.elections.org.za/resultsNPE2014.

9. James L. Gibson, "Land Redistribution/Restitution in South Africa: A Model of Multiple Values, as the Past Meets the Present," *British Journal of Political Science* 40, no. 1 (2010): 155.

10. This has been a ubiquitous theme in my conversations with black civil servants and professionals. Max du Preez describes much the same in his *A Rumor of Spring: South Africa after 20 Years of Democracy* (Cape Town: Zebra Press, 2013), 39–41.

11. Judith February lays out the indictment in "South Africa: A Year of Passing the Buck," Institute for Security Studies, *ISS Daily*, December 3, 2014, accessed October 15, 2015, http://www.issafrica.org/iss-today/a-year-of-passing-the-buck.

12. Iris Wielders, "Perceptions and Realities of Corruption in South Africa" (Afrobarometer Briefing Paper No. 110, 2013); Steven Gordon et al., "Business Unusual: Perceptions of Corruption in South Africa," *Human Sciences Research Council Review* 10, no. 2 (June 2012).

13. "Corruption Perceptions Index, 2014," Transparency International, accessed October 15, 2015, https://www.transparency.org/country/#ZAF.

14. Since 1994, the rand (ZAR) has fallen from 3.55 for USD 1 to 16.42 for USD 1 in January 2016.

15. Mary Tomlinson, "South Africa's Housing Conundrum," *Liberty: The Policy Bulletin of the South African Institute of Race Relations*, no. 4, issue 20 (2015).

16. The 2015 Ibrahim Index of African Governance, http://www.moibrahimfoundation.org/iiag/data-portal.

17. The removal of Mbeki is analyzed and described in detail in Frank Chikane, *Eight Days in September: The Removal of Thabo Mbeki* (Johannesburg: Picador Africa, 2012).

18. For details on health statistics, see chapter 5.

19. National Development Commission, *National Development Plan: Vision for 2030*, November 11, 2011.

20. Gibson, "Land Redistribution," 149.

21. *The Economist*, "Democracy Index 2012: Democracy at a Standstill," The Economist Intelligence Unit, 2012, http://www.eiu.com/Handlers/WhitepaperHandler.ashx?fi=Democracy-Index-2012.pdf&mode=wp&campaignid=DemocracyIndex12.

22. J. P. Landman, *The Long View* (Auckland: Jacana Media, 2013), 53–55.

23. Citizen Surveys, "Summary of Results: Afrobarometer Round 5 Survey in South Africa," Afrobarometer, 2011, accessed October 15, 2015, http://afrobarometer.org/sites/default/files/media-briefing/south-africa/saf_r5_presentation1.pdf.

24. BEE and BBBEE make use of racial categories as defined under apartheid.

25. The Truth and Reconciliation Commission provided amnesty for those who confessed their crimes.

26. Pierre de Vos, interviewed by Fazila Farouk, August 29, 2014, transcript, South African Civil Society Information Service, Johannesburg.

27. The name comes from the fact that the headquarters of the World Bank (WB) and the International Monetary Fund (IMF) are in Washington, D.C.

28. "South Africa GDP Annual Growth Rate," Trading Economics, accessed October 15, 2015, http://www.tradingeconomics.com/south-africa/gdp-growth-annual.

29. Whether unemployment actually increased is moot because black unemployment was undercounted under apartheid, especially in the "independent" and "self-governing" homelands.

30. "National Development Plan 2030," South African Government, accessed October 15, 2015, http://www.gov.za/issues/national-development-plan-2030.

31. Du Preez, *A Rumor of Spring*, 43.

2. THE HISTORICAL TRAJECTORY

1. The ANC usually received about two-thirds of the votes cast in national elections. In 2014, its share fell to about 61 percent. Its supporters include some coloureds and even some asians and whites. But blacks are the ANC's largest support group. If blacks are 80 percent of the population and most vote ANC, why does the ANC not have approximately 80 percent of the seats in parliament? A partial answer may be that blacks vote in smaller percentages than other racial groups, in part because many live in rural areas, and while more blacks vote for the ANC than any other party, blacks also vote for other parties.

2. Dale T. McKinley, "The Real Story of South Africa's National Elections," South African Civil Society Information Service, accessed October 14, 2015, http://www.sacsis.org.za/site/article/2001.

3. I am grateful to Merle Lipton for this point.

4. According to the South African census of 2012, white households had an average income six times greater than that of black households. There is a large literature on the disparity between black and white incomes and wealth, and also on inequality within races. Among blacks, post-apartheid, there is a growing middle class and a few oligarchs; blacks are overwhelmingly poor, but not all are. With the end of apartheid's job guarantees, there are now poor whites.

But most whites have higher incomes and greater net worth than most blacks. For a scholarly, exhaustively documented study, see Carlos Gradin, "Race, Poverty, and Deprivation in South Africa," *Journal of African Economics* 22, no. 2 (2011): 187–238. Also helpful is Drew Desilver, "Chart of the Week: How South Africa Changed, and Didn't, over Mandela's Lifetime," Pew Research Center, http://www.pewresearch.org/fact-tank/2013/12/06/chart-of-the-week-how-south-africa-changed-and-didnt-over-mandelas-lifetime. According to the 2011 South African census, white South Africans' share of total GDP has declined since apartheid ended for many reasons, most notably demographic changes. That is, whites are a smaller percentage of the total population.

5. Federal Reserve System, *Survey of Consumer Finances 2013* (Washington, DC, 2013).

6. Alistair Sparks shows the Dutch insistence on separateness from the very earliest settlement in *The Mind of South Africa* (New York: Knopf, 1990).

7. The literature on South Africa's history is very large. Helpful for nonspecialists are Sparks, *The Mind of South Africa*; Frank Welsh, *A History of South Africa* (London: HarperCollins, 1998); and T. R. H. Davenport, *South Africa: A Modern History*, 4th ed. (London: Macmillan, 1992). For more details, see Monica Wilson and Leonard Thompson, eds., *The Oxford History of South Africa*, 2 vols. (Oxford: Oxford University Press, 1969 and 1971).

8. *Bantu* is actually the Xhosa-Zulu term for "people." It is derived from the word *Ubuntu*, which means "man." In reality, if not in mapmaker legend, the Portuguese encountered Bantu-speaking people in the Cape of Good Hope in 1488. Noel Mostert, *Frontiers: The Epic of South Africa's Creation and the Tragedy of the Xhosa People* (London: Knopf, 1992), 40–41.

9. Welsh, *A History of South Africa*, 15.

10. Ibid., 16.

11. *Proceedings of the 23rd International Conference on Computational Linguistics* (Beijing: Chinese Information Processing Society, 2010), 1020–28, http://www.aclweb.org/anthology/C10-1115.

12. For a history of the conflict between the Zulus and the British Empire, see Donald R. Morris, *The Washing of the Spears: The Rise and Fall of the Zulu Nation* (New York: Simon and Schuster, 1965).

13. Daniel Scott Smith, "The Demographic History of Colonial New England," *Journal of Economic History* 32, no.1 (1972): 165–83.

14. Statistics Canada, 2014, http://www.statcan.gc.ca.

15. Robert Montgomery Martin, "Southern Africa: Comprising the Cape of Good Hope, Mauritius, Seychelles, &c.," in *The British Colonial Library: In 12 Volumes*, vol. 3 (Mortimer, 1836), 112.

16. Sparks, *The Mind of South Africa*, 43.

17. Christianity may have penetrated more deeply in South Africa than anywhere else on the continent. Albertina Sisulu indicates that this is a reason why the 1994 transition became possible. Her implication: ultimately, it was white Christians talking to black Christians. For Albertina Sisulu's comment, see Herman J. Cohen, *The Mind of the African Strongman: Conversations with Dictators, Statesmen, and Father Figures* (Washington, DC: New Academia Publishing, 2015), 174.

18. For example, there was an important Scottish community that retained for long a separate identity. See John M. Mackenzie and Nigel R. Dalziel, *The Scots in South Africa: Ethnicity, Identity, Gender and Race, 1772–1914* (Manchester: Manchester University Press, 2007).

19. "SA Jewish History," South African Jewish Board of Deputies, accessed October 14, 2015, http://www.jewishsa.co.za/about-sajbd/sa-jewish-history.

20. H. Giliomee and B. Mbenga, *New History of South Africa* (Cape Town: Tafelberg, 2007); Volker Wedekind, "Rearranging the Furniture? Shifting Discourses on Skills Development and Apprenticeship in South Africa," in *Apprenticeship in a Globalised World: Premises, Promises and Pitfalls*, ed. S. Akoojee et al. (Berlin: Munster Lit, 2013).

21. David Elits and David Richardson, "Assessing the Slave Trade," Trans-Atlantic Slave Trade Database, accessed December 15, 2015, http://www.slavevoyages.org/assessment/estimates.

22. As late as 1994 the author witnessed a fistfight in Cape Town between a coloured and a black over the former's insistence that he was "European."

23. For example, they could not establish businesses in the white central business districts of South Africa's cities. But they could establish and operate strip malls in some suburban areas.

24. Afrikaans developed out of several Dutch dialects. Most of the vocabulary is Dutch, but its morphology and grammar is more regular. Dutch and Afrikaans are mutually intelligible. Even as late as the nineteenth century, Afrikaans was regarded as less "refined" than Dutch.

25. See especially Mostert, *Frontiers*.

26. The euphonious-sounding "Johannesburg" can be translated from Afrikaans to English as "Jacktown," perhaps a better reflection of its origins as a mining camp.

27. "South Africa: White Domination and Black Resistance (1881–1948)," Electoral Institute for Sustainable Democracy in Africa (EISA), Johannesburg, February 1, 2011.

28. There is an extensive literature of the parallels between the post–Civil War American South and post–Boer War South Africa. See, inter alia, George M. Fredrickson, *Racism: A Short History* (Princeton, NJ: Princeton University Press, 2002); Anthony W. Marx, *Making Race and Nation: A Comparison of*

South Africa, the United States, and Brazil (Cambridge: Cambridge University Press, 1998); and Robert Massie, *Loosing the Bonds: The United States and South Africa in the Apartheid Years* (New York: Nan A. Talese/Doubleday, 1997).

29. Fredrickson includes Nazi Germany with South Africa and the American South as the three areas where white supremacy was most institutionally developed. However, Nazi Germany looked toward the Holocaust and the destruction of Jews, whom he sees as roughly analogous to blacks in South Africa and the American South. By contrast, the purpose of apartheid and American segregation was never to destroy the black population but rather to preserve it and manage it as a cheap source of labor. That makes Nazi Germany different.

30. David Welsh, "Urbanization and the Solidarity of Afrikaner Nationalism," *Journal of Modern African Studies* 7, no. 2 (1969): 265–76.

31. Welsh, *History of South Africa*, 401.

32. Ibid., 414.

33. "Negro," now regarded as pejorative in the United States, was the usual term used to self-identify by black people until the 1960s.

34. There were pro-Nazi elements within the National Party, largely marginalized by the more mainstream leadership. On the elections of 1948, see Stephen Ellis, *External Mission: The ANC in Exile, 1960–1990* (London: Hurst, 2012), 3–4.

35. Straight was "white"; curly denoted "black" or "coloured."

36. Eugene D. Genovese, *A Consuming Fire: The Fall of the Confederacy in the Mind of the White Christian South* (Athens: University of Georgia Press, 2008), 97.

37. Estimates of lynching in the United States range from 3,446 blacks (plus 1,297 whites, often Mexicans or Chinese in the West) between 1882 and 1968 to almost 4,000 blacks in the Southern states from 1877 to 1950. See "Lynchings: By State and Race, 1882–1968," University of Missouri–Kansas City School of Law, accessed July 26, 2010, http://law2.umkc.edu/faculty/projects/ftrials/shipp/lynchingsstate.html; "Lynching in America: Confronting the Legacy of Racial Terror" (Equal Justice Initiative, Montgomery, Alabama, 2015), 4–5. "Lynching in America" documents 3,959 lynchings of black people in twelve southern states between 1877 and 1950.

38. "South Africa Overcoming Apartheid and Building Democracy: Forced Removals," Michigan State University, accessed October 14, 2015, http://overcomingapartheid.msu.edu/multimedia.php?id=65-259-6.

39. For a thorough review of apartheid history, see David Welsh, *The Rise and Fall of Apartheid from Racial Domination to Majority Rule* (Johannesburg: Jonathan Ball, 2010).

40. Some apartheid fanatics urged that the indian population be "repatriated" to South Asia.

41. Apartheid South Africa established ten homelands, four of which were granted "independence." They were Transkei, Bophuthatswana, Venda, and Ciskei. There were no coloured or indian homelands.

42. Native American residents of reservations are full American citizens (since 1924) as well as having allegiance to a specific tribe. They pay most taxes, though they are exempt from federal and state tax on incomes from tribal lands.

43. In general in the southern states it was participation in the Spanish American War that marked reintegration into the Union. Racial segregation legally endured until 1954 and de facto until now in various aspects of American life.

44. The beginning of the armed struggle is usually dated from the launch of Umkhonto we Sizwe (MK) in 1961.

45. For a comprehensive history of the United Democratic Front (UDF), see Jeremy Seekings, *The UDF: A History of the United Democratic Front in South Africa, 1983–1991* (Cape Town: David Philip, 2000).

46. On the role of the South African Communist Party (SACP) in the armed struggle, see Ellis, *External Mission*, 1–40.

47. This argument was advanced by a senior Struggle operative in 2015 during a private conversation that took place in Washington, D.C.

48. The liberation struggle was a broader movement, not confined to any particular dates, and was not analogous in racial concerns to the armed struggle. Most races were represented in the liberation struggle.

49. Statement issued by the SACP, December 6, 2013, quoted in Alex Mashilo, "Nelson Mandela Was a Member of Our CC at the Time of His Arrest," Politicsweb, December 6, 2013, http://www.politicsweb.co.za/politicsweb/view/politicsweb/en/page71654?oid=473454&sn=Detail&pid=71616. For a discussion of the likelihood of Mandela's membership in the SACP, see Ellis, *External Mission*, 20–23. That debate has ended with the ANC's official obituary that listed Mandela as a communist and a member of the Central Committee.

50. See Stephen Ellis, "The Genesis of the ANC's Armed Struggle in South Africa, 1948–1961," *Journal of Southern African Studies* 37, no. 4 (2011): 657–76. Ellis makes a convincing case that Mandela launched the "armed struggle" following consultations with Mao.

51. Merle Lipton, "Is South Africa's Constitutional Democracy Being Consolidated or Eroded?," *South African Journal of International Affairs* 21, no. 1 (2014): 1–26.

52. In part because South Africa's Jewish community was urban and more liberal than most whites on racial matters, anti-Semitism developed, especially among Afrikaners, during the 1930s, often with the identification of "Jewish" with "communist."

53. For a helpful discussion of the debate, see Philip Levy, "Sanctions on South Africa: What Did They Do?" (Center Discussion Paper No. 796, Economic Growth Center, Department of Economics, Yale University, February 1999).

54. Gary Hufbauer, Jeffrey Schott, and Kimberly Ann Elliott, *Economic Sanctions Reconsidered: History and Current Policy*, 2nd ed. (Washington, DC: Institute for International Economics, 1990), cited by Levy, "Sanctions on South Africa," 7.

55. For a full discussion of the role of the American mission, see Daniel Whitman, *Outsmarting Apartheid* (Albany: State University of New York Press, 2015).

56. Welsh, *A History of South Africa*, 490–91.

57. The popular spontaneity of some township protests may be seen as South Africa's "Arab Spring," almost a generation earlier than Cairo's Tahrir Square.

58. Princeton N. Lyman was the U.S. ambassador to South Africa from 1992 to 1995, the period of the transition. He chronicles the U.S. role in *Partner to History: The U.S. Role in South Africa's Transition to Democracy* (Washington, DC: United States Institute of Peace Press, 2002).

59. Herman J. Cohen comment in "Nelson Mandela and Capitalism," *Africa in Transition* (CFR blog), December 10, 2013, http://blogs.cfr.org/campbell/2013/12/10/nelson-mandela-and-capitalism. Cohen was assistant secretary of state for Africa, 1989–1993.

60. South Africa was a major beneficiary of the President's Emergency Plan for AIDS Relief (PEPFAR). It emphasized the building of South African medical capacity.

61. In April 2014, Nigeria claimed to have surpassed South Africa in GDP. However, on a per capita basis, South Africa's GDP was more than double that of Nigeria. See World Bank Data, "GDP per Capita (current US$)," *World Bank Data by Country*, 2013, http://data.worldbank.org/indicator/NY.GDP.PCAP.CD.

3. TWO INAUGURATIONS AND A FUNERAL

1. Many in the liberation movements saw much of the violence as fomented by right-wing whites, but the evidence is inconclusive.

2. William Beinart, *Twentieth Century South Africa* (Oxford: Oxford University Press, 2001), 277.

3. Padraig O'Malley, "The Heart of Hope—South Africa's Transition from Apartheid to Democracy," in *The Nelson Mandela Center of Memory* (chapter 7), https://www.nelsonmandela.org/omalley/index.php/site/q/03lv00000.htm. The 1994 murder of whites included the American social worker Amy Biehl in Cape Town and eleven white victims of a church bombing, also in Cape Town, in 1993. An additional fifty were wounded. See "St James Church Massacre," *South African History Online*, accessed June 30, 2015, http://www.sahistory.org.za/dated-event/st-james-church-massacre.

4. Nelson Mandela, "Statement of the President of the African National Congress, Nelson Mandela, at His Inauguration as President of the Democratic Republic of South Africa" (speech, Union Buildings, Pretoria, May 10, 1994), http://www.africa.upenn.edu/Articles_Gen/Inaugural_Speech_17984.html.

5. Desmond Tutu, "Funeral Oration for Chris Hani, Leader of the South African Communist Party," 1993, quoted in Philippe Joseph Salazar, *An African Athens: Rhetoric and the Shaping of Democracy in South Africa* (Mahwah, NJ: Erlbaum, 2002).

6. Guccio Gucci was a Florentine designer of high-end leather goods, especially shoes. Emilio Pucci was a well-known Italian high-end fashion designer. Some South Africans referred to an elaborately dressed woman as "Gucci'd and Pucci'd" in the last decade of the twentieth century.

7. Mary Robinson, "Nelson Mandela Annual Lecture," transcript, Nelson Mandela Centre of Memory Digital Archive, August 5, 2012, https://www.nelsonmandela.org/news/entry/transcript-of-mary-robinsons-nelson-mandela-annual-lecture.

8. Quoted in Ernest Ogbozor, *Love and Forgiveness in Governance: Exemplars: Desmond Tutu* (The Beyond Intractability Project and the Conflict Information Consortium, Boulder, Colorado, 2013), http://www.beyondintractability.org/lfg/exemplars/dtutu.

9. Some were dismantled even before the transition was complete. The Comprehensive Anti-Apartheid Act lapsed in 1989, its conditions having been met by the national government.

10. The episode was captured in the 2009 Hollywood film *Invictus*, directed by Clint Eastwood, with Morgan Freeman as Mandela and Matt Damon as Francois Pienaar. Subsequently, Mandela became a godfather of Pienaar's son.

11. Gunnar Theissen, *Between Acknowledgement and Ignorance: How White South Africa Has Dealt with the Apartheid Past* (Johannesburg: University of Witwatersrand Center for the Study of Violence and Reconciliation, 1997).

12. Under apartheid, only whites were subject to military conscription.

13. The deputy minister of agriculture is Dr. Pieter Mulder, the leader of the Freedom Front Plus, an Afrikaner political party.

14. Zwelinzima Vavi, the now-suspended secretary general of the Congress of South African Trade Unions (COSATU), and the third member of the governing Triple Alliance, is not a Zulu. He is a Xhosa from the Northern Cape.

15. South Africa Institute of Race Relations, *South Africa Survey 2014/2015* (Johannesburg, 2014), 13.

16. "White Flight from South Africa: Between Staying and Going," *The Economist*, September 25, 2008.

17. See chapter 4.

18. Robinson, "Nelson Mandela Annual Lecture."

19. "When the Clouds Cried," *Africa Confidential* 54 (December 13, 2013): 25, http://www.africa-confidential.com/article/id/5149/When_the_clouds_cried.

20. The stadium is named for the First National Bank, the result of a 1989 naming deal before the end of apartheid. At the time, few commented on the irony that the funeral of Mandela, once a left-wing hero, took place in a stadium named for a bank.

21. "When the Clouds Cried."

22. Anthony Sampson, *Mandela: The Authorized Biography* (London: HarperCollins, 2000), 543.

23. Anthony Sampson, in *Mandela: The Authorized Biography*, writes that Mandela's marriage to his first wife, Evelyn Mase, ended in part because of his philandering.

24. Nadine Gordimer, "Postscript: Nelson Mandela," *New Yorker*, December 16, 2013, 24.

25. Married to Samora Machel, head of state in Mozambique, and to Nelson Mandela, she is one of the very few to have served as first lady of two separate states.

26. BBC World, "Interview with Thabo Mbeki," *BBC World's Hard Talk, South Africa Special*, December 10, 2013, quoted in John Allen, "South Africa Boos & Cheers Leaders as It Celebrates Mandela," *All Africa Analysis*, December 10, 2013, http://allafrica.com/stories/201312101752.html.

4. THE BENCHMARK

1. Colin Coleman, "Two Decades of Freedom: A 20-Year Review of South Africa," Goldman Sachs International (Johannesburg, 2014), accessed October

30, 2015, http://www.goldmansachs.com/our-thinking/archive/colin-coleman-south-africa-page.html.

2. While economic growth has not been high enough to eliminate poverty, nevertheless it has averaged roughly 3 percent a year over two decades.

3. Social grants: Africa Check, "Factsheet: Social Grants in South Africa—Separating Myth from Reality," Africa Check, 2015, https://africacheck.org/factsheets/separating-myth-from-reality-a-guide-to-social-grants-in-south-africa; South Africa Gross National Income, 1993–2013, Trading Economics, 2015, http://www.tradingeconomics.com/south-africa/gross-national-product.

4. Kate Lefko-Everett, *SA Reconciliation Barometer Survey: 2012 Report* 10, no. 3 (2012): 14.

5. Quoted in Alec Russell, *After Mandela: The Battle for the Soul of South Africa* (London: Hutchinson, 2009), 4.

6. South Africa Institute of Race Relations, *South Africa Survey 2014/2015* (Johannesburg, 2014), 321.

7. Quoted in Russell, *After Mandela*, 15.

8. Cardell K. Jacobson, Acheampong Yaw Amoateng, and Tim B. Heaton, "Inter-racial Marriages in South Africa," *Journal of Comparative Family Studies* 35, no. 3 (2004): 443–58; Human Sciences Research Council, "Child Youth and Family Development" (Department of the Human Sciences Research Council report commissioned by the South African Department of Social Development).

9. The U.S. and South African statistics are of similar magnitude, but they are not exact equivalents in terms of what they are measuring. The South African figures are age limited, while those for the United States are for all marriages.

10. *SA Reconciliation Barometer Survey: 2012 Report*, 43.

11. Karen E. Ferree, "Explaining South Africa's Racial Census," *Journal of Politics* 68, no. 4 (2006): 803.

12. *SA Reconciliation Barometer Survey: 2012 Report*, 7.

13. For a thorough discussion of African statistics, see Morten Jerven, *Poor Numbers: How We Are Misled by African Development Statistics and What to Do about It* (Ithaca, NY: Cornell University Press, 2013). He includes extensive reference to South African statistics and concludes that they are the best in Africa.

14. *South Africa Survey 2014/2015*.

15. *South Africa Survey 2014/2015*, 7. The values are midyear estimates. The World Bank provides a population statistic of 39.12 million.

16. *The World Factbook* (Washington, DC: Central Intelligence Agency, 2013).

17. The white population was always small; at its highest, the number of whites in Zimbabwe was 270,000 in 1970, out of a total population of five million. ZimStats, *National Report: Census 2012* (Harare, 2012).

18. Namibia was governed by South Africa from 1920 to 1990 and was part of its political economy, including apartheid.

19. South Africa's population is from "Population," Statistics South Africa, 2015, http://www.statssa.gov.za. Demographics for Namibia, Kenya, Nigeria, Ethiopia, and Congo are from *The World Factbook*, 2013. The populations for Mauritius and Seychelles are from "Data: Population," World Bank, accessed January 17, 2013, http://data.worldbank.org/indicator/SP.POP.TOTL.

20. The United States is 81.6 percent urban; the UK, 82.6 percent. All figures are from *The World Fact Book* (Washington, DC: Central Intelligence Agency, 2015), accessed January 4, 2016, UK, https://www.cia.gov/library/publications/the-world-factbook/fields/2212.html#uk; US, https://www.cia.gov/library/publications/the-world-factbook/fields/2212.html#us.

21. *South Africa Survey 2014/2015*, 17.

22. Ibid., 17.

23. Ibid., 26–30. The survey data compared the data from sixteen economic regions in 2000 and 2013.

24. The governor of the Western Cape, Helen Zille, is white, the only one among the eight provincial governors.

25. The 2014 population figures are midterm estimates by the South African Institute of Race Relations.

26. *South Africa Survey 2014/2015*, 5.

27. Rita M. Byrnes, ed., *South Africa: A Country Study* (Washington, DC: Government Printing Office, 1996), http://countrystudies.us/south-africa/44.htm.

28. Ibid., 5. The values documented are midyear estimates.

29. *South Africa Survey 2014/2015*, 26–30. East Rand is now called Ekurhuleni; Durban is called eThekwini; Pretoria is called Tswana. The renaming has been carried out by local government authorities. The name changes reverse Mandela's policy of leaving geographic place-names unchanged.

30. Ibid., 11.

31. Jonathan Crush and Vincent Williams, "Labour Migration Trends and Policies in South Africa" (Policy Brief No. 23, Southern African Migration Project, 2010), 11, http://www.queensu.ca/samp/sampresources/samppublications.

32. MPI Data Hub, "International Migrants by Country of Destination, 1960–2013," Migration Policy, accessed October 20, 2014, http://www.migrationpolicy.org/programs/data-hub/charts/international-migrants-country-destination-1960-2013?width=1000&height=850&iframe=true.

33. *South Africa Survey 2014/2015*, 78.

34. Statistics South Africa, "Discussion Document D035.4: Documented Immigration in South Africa 2011" (Pretoria, 2013), 35–37.

35. Immigration South Africa, "Home Affairs Facing Large-Scale Court Action," *Immigration South Africa Blog*, June 6, 2014, http://www. immigrationsouthafrica.org/blog/home-affairs-facing-large-scale-court-action.

36. The white and asian birthrate is slightly below reproduction level, comparable to that of Europe. The coloured birthrate is greater than the reproduction level, but coloureds suffer from a greater disease burden than whites and asians. The black birthrate is higher, but it is falling rapidly.

37. "South African National HIV Prevalence, Incidence, and Behaviour Survey, 2012," Human Sciences Resource Council (Cape Town, 2014), 25.

38. South Africa Institute of Race Relations, *South Africa Survey 2013* (Johannesburg, 2013), 3. For figures on Canada, Australia, New Zealand, and Mozambique, see "Census Undercount and Strategies," Version 6, *Statistics South Africa*, 2011, 8.

39. *South Africa Survey 2013*, 59.

40. *South Africa Survey 2014/2015*, 8–9.

41. South African Institute of Race Relations, *South Africa Survey 2009/2010*, Demographics (Johannesburg, 2010), 47–48.

42. *South Africa Survey 2014/2015*, 50. World Bank, "Life Expectancy at Birth, Total (Years)" (Washington, DC, 2014), http://data.worldbank.org/indicator/SP.DYN.LE00.IN; United Nations Development Programme, "Life Expectancy at Birth (Years), South Africa" (Human Development Reports, 2013), http://hdr.undp.org/en/69206. Note, however, that the South Africa Medical Research Center states that the average life expectancy in 2012 was 61.3, a figure substantially higher than the World Bank's and UNDP's. See South Africa Medical Research Council, "Rapid Mortality Surveillance Report 2013," Burden of Disease Research Unit (Cape Town, 2013), http://www.mrc.ac.za/Media/2015/1press2015.htm.

43. *South Africa Survey 2014/2015*, 49.

44. Ibid., 574–75.

45. Ibid., 18.

46. See Khadija Patel, "SA Crime Statistics: Sunny with a Chance of Murder," *Daily Maverick*, September 19, 2013, http://www.dailymaverick.co.za/article/2013-09-20-sa-crime-statistics-sunny-with-a-chance-of-murder/#. VZGytPlVhBc.

47. *South Africa Survey 2014/2015*, 705.

48. Pusch Commey, "Pistorius, Race, Crime and Gun Culture," *New African* 543 (2014): 9; *South Africa Survey 2014/2015*, 755.

49. Brian A. Reeves, "Census of State and Local Law Enforcement Agencies," Bureau of Justice Statistics, 2008, http://www.bjs.gov/index.cfm?ty=pbdetail&iid=2216.

50. "Kill and Be Killed: Where Policing Is a Dangerous Job and a Danger to the Community," Middle East and Africa, *The Economist*, August 27, 2011, http://www.economist.com/node/21526932.

51. South African Institute of Race Relations and Centre for Risk Analysis, *FastFacts* 10, no. 278 (2014).

52. Ibid., 11.

53. Russell, *After Mandela*, 45.

54. *South Africa Survey 2014/2015*, 298. In 2013, the exchange rate ranged from 9 to 10 rand to the U.S. dollar.

55. Ibid., 302. At the time this book was written, the exchange rate was approximately 1 USD for 16 rand.

56. "South Africa Economic Update: Fiscal Policy and Redistribution in an Unequal Society," World Bank (Washington, DC, 2014).

57. The eleven other middle-income countries were Armenia, Bolivia, Brazil, Costa Rica, El Salvador, Ethiopia, Guatemala, Indonesia, Mexico, Peru, and Uruguay.

58. Household consumption is a measure of how much a household at a specific income level spends. The rich spend more, the poor less.

59. Elodie Morival, *Top Incomes and Racial Inequality in South Africa: Evidence from Tax Statistics and Household Surveys 1993–2008* (master's thesis, Paris School of Economics—Master Analyse et politique economique, 2011), 40. The thesis was supervised by Thomas Piketty.

60. Tami Luby, "Worsening Wealth Inequality by Race," CNNMoney, June 21, 2012, http://money.cnn.com/2012/06/21/news/economy/wealth-gap-race.

61. Stephen Robinson, "Bring Me My Machine Gun: That's the Chilling Cry of the '100 per cent Zulu Boy' Who Will be Elected South Africa's President This Week," *Daily Mail Debate*, April 23, 2009, http://www.dailymail.co.uk/debate/article-1172414/Bring-machine-gun-Thats-chilling-100-cent-Zulu-boy-elected-South-Africas-President-week.html; Allison Barrie, "The 'Bring Me My Machine Gun' Campaign," FoxNews, January 10, 2008, http://www.foxnews.com/story/2008/01/10/bring-me-my-machine-gun-campaign; "Jacob Zuma Sings the Cabinet Will Shoot the Boer at ANC Celebrations RSA," YouTube video posted January 11, 2013, by South Africa—the REAL Issues, https://www.youtube.com/watch?v=4NVkRmBTB7k.

62. The polling data cited here are from "Coming to Terms with History" (South Africa Reconciliation Barometer Survey Report, Cape Town, 2012), 37.

5. POVERTY, EDUCATION, AND HEALTH

1. Estimates of the percentage of whites living in poverty range from 2 percent to 10 percent. The wide range reflects various factors, including different definitions of what constitutes living in poverty.

2. Katherine S. Newman and Ariane De Lannoy describe coping mechanisms in *After Freedom: The Rise of the Post-Apartheid Generation in Democratic South Africa* (Boston: Beacon Press, 2014).

3. United Nations International Children's Emergency Fund (UNICEF), *South Africa Statistics*, 2013, http://www.unicef.org/infobycountry/southafrica_statistics.html.

4. Leonie S. Joubert and Eric Miller, *The Hungry Season: Feeding Southern Africa's Cities* (Johannesburg: Picador Africa, 2012).

5. In South Africa, as elsewhere, rape is woefully underreported to the authorities. This figure is no more than a credible estimate. R. Jewkes and N. Abrahams, "The Epidemiology of Rape and Sexual Coercion in South Africa," *Social Science & Medicine* 55, no. 7 (2002): 1231–44.

6. R. Jewkes, Y. Sikweyiya, R. Morrell, and K. Dunkle, "Understanding Men's Health and Use of Violence: Interface of Rape and HIV in South Africa" (Medical Research Council Technical Report, Pretoria, 2008); "Sexual Violence and HIV/AIDS: Executive Report on the 2002 National Survey," CIETafrica (South Africa, 2004).

7. Office of Internal Oversight Services, Inspection and Evaluation Division, *Evaluation of the Enforcement and Remedial Assistance Efforts for Sexual Exploitation and Abuse by the United Nations and Related Personnel in Peacekeeping Operations*, May 15, 2015, 13. There were nine credible allegations of sexual exploitation and abuses by South African peacekeepers in selected peacekeeping operations between 2010 and 2013. There were eight for Uruguay and seven for Nigeria. For all other countries providing peacekeepers, there were one or two.

8. Robyn Dixon, "Year of Terrible Headlines Sees South Africa's Homicide Rate Leap Again," *Los Angeles Times*, September 29, 2015.

9. The number of those who pay income tax, company tax, and inheritance tax is small, less than three million. See Claire Bisseker, "Taxpayers—How Many Are They, Again?" *Financial Mail*, March 11, 2013, http://www.financialmail.co.za/economy/2013/03/11/taxpayers---how-many-are-there-again.

10. Ed Stoddard, "Africa Investment—South Africa's Social Grant Helps Children Grow, but Is It Sustainable?," *Reuters Industries*, August 1, 2014, http://www.reuters.com/article/2014/08/01/safrica-children-idUSL6N0Q66YH20140801.

11. South Africa Institute of Race Relations, *South Africa Survey 2014/2015* (Johannesburg, 2014), 171.

12. Ibid., 173.

13. South African Revenue Service, "Corporate Income Tax," SARS.gov.za, accessed October 28, 2015, http://www.sars.gov.za/TaxTypes/CIT/Pages/default.aspx.

14. South African Revenue Service, "Tax and Inheritance," SARS.gov.za, accessed October 28, 2015, http://www.sars.gov.za/ClientSegments/Individuals/Tax-Stages/Pages/Tax-and-Inheritance.aspx.

15. *South Africa Survey, 2014/2015*, 172.

16. Company tax is similar to, but not identical to, U.S. corporate tax. VAT is a sales tax. South Africa's VAT operates in ways similar to that of the United Kingdom. On South Africa's taxes, see Paul Joubert, "How Many Taxpayers Are There Really (2013)?" Politicsweb Solidarity Research Institute, February 25, 2013, http://www.politicsweb.co.za/politicsweb/view/politicsweb/en/page71619?oid=360155&sn=Detail&pid=71619. See also Bisseker, "Taxpayers—How Many Are They, Again?"

17. Joubert, "How Many Taxpayers."

18. J. P. Landman, *The Long View: Getting beyond the Drama of South Africa's Headlines* (Johannesburg: Picador Africa, 2013), 39.

19. John Kane Berman, "Give the Poor Back Their Right to Work: A 10-Point Plan for Jobs," *@Liberty* 19, no. 3 (June 24, 2015). Berman cites Statistics South Africa for the unemployment statistic.

20. *South Africa Survey 2014/2015*, "Employment" (Johannesburg, 2014), 258.

21. On South Africa's informal economy, see David Neves and Andries du Toit, "Understanding Self-Employment at the Margins of the South African Economy: Findings from a Pilot Study on Qualitative Approaches to Self-Employment," Institute for Poverty, Land and Agrarian Studies (Cape Town, 2007). See also David Neves and Andries du Toit, "Money and Sociality in South Africa's Informal Economy," *Africa* 82, no. 1 (2012): 131–49.

22. *South Africa Survey 2014/2015*, 262.

23. Landman, *The Long View*, 43–57; World Bank, "South African Data," accessed October 24, 2014, http://data.worldbank.org/country/south-africa.

24. See chapter 4.

25. South African Press Association (SAPA), "Jansen Is Wrong about English as a Primary Tuition Language, Says EFF Plus," *Mail & Guardian*, last modified October 2, 2013, http://mg.co.za/article/2013-10-02-jansen-speech-on-language-in-education-was-distorted.

26. "South African Languages: Tongues under Threat," *The Economist* (print edition), 2011.

27. South Africa National Treasury, "Budget 2013 People's Guide," accessed March 7, 2014, http://www.treasury.gov.za/documents/national%20budget/2014/guides/2014%20People's%20Guide%20English.pdf.

28. National Planning Commission, *Diagnostic Overview* (South Africa, 2011), 14.

29. Alec Russell, *After Mandela: The Battle for the Soul of South Africa* (London: Hutchinson, 2009), 99–101.

30. *South Africa Survey 2014/2015*, 448. Section 3 of the South African Schools Act (1996) made it mandatory for children aged seven to fifteen to attend school.

31. It ranks the University of Cape Town at 126 out of 500, between the Tokyo Institute of Technology (125) and Dartmouth College (127); the University of Witwatersrand is grouped at between 226 and 250, with, among others, Simon Fraser University and Tulane University; it groups Stellenbosch University at between 301 and 350, along with Drexel University and Bangor University (UK). "The World University Rankings 2013–2014," *Times Higher Education Magazine*, 2014, https://www.timeshighereducation.co.uk/world-university-rankings/2014/world-ranking#.

32. Moeletsi Mbeki, the brother of Thabo Mbeki, has been an advocate for a network of Anglican Church schools to serve township residents.

33. Congress of South African Trade Unions (COSATU), "Address by Zwlinzima Vavi General Secretary of COSATU to the SADTU Regional Biennial General Meeting," last modified August 9, 2013, http://www.cosatu.org.za/show.php?ID=7629%20-%20sthash.hGppT6xF.dpuf.

34. Centre for Development and Entreprise, *Mathematics Outcomes in South African Schools* (Johannesburg, 2013).

35. COSATU, "Address by Zwlinzima Vavi."

36. "South Africa to Build 43 Hospitals," February 19, 2014, http://www.southafrica.info/about/health/1639680.htm.

37. Stellenbosch University Hospital in 2015 announced the world's first successful penis transplant.

38. National Planning Commission, *Our Future—Make It Work: National Development Plan*, November 11, 2011, 331, http://www.poa.gov.za/news/Documents/NPC%20National%20Development%20Plan%20Vision%202020 30%20-lo-res.pdf.

39. Ibid., 340.

40. Department of Labour South Africa, "The Shortage of Medical Doctors in South Africa," Research Consortium, March 2008, 10, http://www.labour.gov.za/DOL/downloads/documents/research-documents/Medical%20Doctors _DoL_Report.pdf.

41. National Planning Commission, *National Development Plan*, November 11, 2011, 301.

42. Department of Health, *National Health Insurance in South Africa* (Policy [Green] Paper, Pretoria, 2011). For an overview, see "National Health Insurance: The First 18 Months," *South African Medical Journal* 103, no. 3 (2013).

43. Ibid.

44. *South Africa Survey 2014/2015*, 574.

45. "HIV/AIDS in South Africa: Just Cap It," *The Economist*, March 10, 2012.

46. AVERT, "South Africa HIV & AIDS Statistics" (West Sussex, 2012), http://www.avert.org/hiv-aids-south-africa.htm.

47. South African Government News Agency, "SA Makes Inroads in Tackling HIV/AIDS," February 18, 2014, http://www.sanews.gov.za/south-africa/sa-makes-inroads-tackling-hivaids.

48. Ibid.

49. Statistics South Africa, "Mortality and Causes of Death in South Africa, 2013: Findings from Death Notification," December 2, 2014.

50. SouthAfrica.info, "SA's Mortality Rate at Its Lowest in Over a Decade," December 3, 2014, http://www.southafrica.info/about/health/mortality-report-031214.htm#.VH8u98mtaF8.

51. Tshilidzi Tuwani, "South Africa Attempts to Set New HIV Testing World Record," Health-e, December 1, 2014.

52. Rebecca Davis, "Death Stats SA: It's Disease, Not Crime, Killing Us Softly," *Daily Maverick*, December 3, 2014, http://www.dailymaverick.co.za/article/2014-12-03-death-stats-sa-its-disease-not-crime-killing-us-softly/#.VH8nw8mtaF8.

53. South African Institute of Race Relations, "Press Release: South Africa: New HIV Infections Halve from Almost 2000 to Fewer Than 1000 a Day," February 10, 2014, http://irr.org.za/reports-and-publications/media-releases.

54. Ibid.

55. South African Government News Agency, "SA Makes Inroads in Tackling HIV/Aids," February 18, 2014, http://www.sanews.gov.za/south-africa/sa-makes-inroads-tackling-hivaids.

56. Circumstances around female circumcision by contrast probably facilitate the transmission of HIV. See UNFPA Frequently Asked Questions: http://www.unfpa.org/resources/female-genital-mutilation-fgm-frequently-asked-questions#linkages_fgm_hiv.

57. Ibid.

58. South African Institute of Race Relations, "Press Release: South Africa."

59. U.S. Diplomatic Mission to South Africa, "10 Years of PEPFAR: The Power of Partnership," 2013, https://za.usembassy.gov/our-relationship/pepfar/overview.

60. These figures are from the World Bank. Note, however, that South African sources are positing a much greater improvement, with an average life expectancy of sixty years. See David Smith, "AIDS Drugs Increase South African Life Expectancy by Five Years," *Guardian*, December 3, 2012, http://www.theguardian.com/world/2012/dec/03/aids-drugs-south-african-life.

61. National Planning Commission, *National Development Plan*, November 11, 2011, 268, http://allafrica.com/download/resource/main/main/idatcs/00041101:c9bd950570730f3cabe7f67cdaf618a2.pdf.

62. *South Africa Survey 2014/2015*, 438.

63. In 2010, the life expectancy of whites was 72.5; for blacks, it was 55.8. In the United States, life expectancy was 79 (2011); in Nigeria, it was 52. See South Africa Institute of Race Relations, *South Africa Survey 2013* (Johannesburg, 2013), 57–64.

6. LAND

1. Africa Research Institute, "Waiting for the Green Revolution: Land Reform in South Africa," Briefing Note 1301, May 2013.

2. For a full discussion of the land question, especially its emotional dimensions, see Bernadette Atuahene, *We Want What's Ours: Learning from South Africa's Land Restitution Program* (Oxford: Oxford University Press, 2014).

3. For a layman's introduction to the complexity of land in the former "independent" or "self-governing" homelands, see Aninka Claassens, "Haste over Land Rights Bill Not Just in Aid of Buying Votes," *Business Day* (SA), April 4, 2014. My thanks to Merle Lipton for calling my attention to this.

4. Africa Research Institute, "Waiting for the Green Revolution."

5. South Africa Institute of Race Relations, *South Africa Survey 2013* (Johannesburg, 2013), 297.

6. Ibid., 297. This number is aggregated by subtracting government-owned land (14 percent), black-owned land (18 percent, see note 7 below), and land owned by corporations from the total of land.

7. Yolandi Groenewald, "Who Owns What Land in South Africa?," *Mail & Guardian*, January 23, 2009.

8. *South Africa Survey 2013*, 297.

9. For Zimbabwe's figures, see Food and Agriculture Organization, "WTO Agreement on Agriculture: The Implementation Experience—Developing

Country Case Studies," 2003, http://www.fao.org/docrep/005/y4632e/
y4632e0y.htm. For South African figures, see "South African Agriculture,"
southafrica.info, accessed October 28, 2015, http://www.southafrica.info/
business/economy/sectors/agricultural-sector.htm#.VjEaOrerS71.

10. Africa Research Institute, "Waiting for the Green Revolution."

11. In fact, Slovo's position on land was nuanced. For example, in 1986 he
also said, "The redistribution of the land is the absolute imperative in our
conditions, the fundamental national demand." See Cheryl Walker, "The Limits to Land Reform: Rethinking the 'Land Question,'" *Journal of Southern
African Studies* 31, no. 4 (2005): 811.

12. This point is developed at length by James L. Gibson, "Land Redistribu-
tion/Restitution in South Africa," *British Journal of Political Science* 40, no. 1
(2010): 135–69. See also Atuahene, *We Want What's Ours.*

13. Integrated Regional Information Networks, "South Africa: Land Reform Programme Unsustainable," IRIN Johannesburg, September 2, 2009.

14. Gugile Nkwinti, "Building Vibrant, Equitable and Sustainable Rural
Communities," speech in Parliament, Pretoria, February 2013.

15. Atuahene, *We Want What's Ours*, 97.

16. Ibid., 74, 81, 162.

17. Rural Development and Land Reform Minister Gugile Nkwinti 2013
statement to parliament as reported by IRIN News in *Why South Africa's
Land Reform Agenda Is Stuck*, accessed October 28, 2015, http://www.
irinnews.org/printreport.aspx?reportid=98572.

18. Atuahene, *We Want What's Ours*, 172–74.

19. Ibid., 100.

20. "Willing Buyer, Willing Seller Principal [*sic*] to Go: Zuma," South Africa
Press Association, February 14, 2013, http://www.iol.co.za/news/politics/
willing-buyer-willing-seller-principal-to-go-zuma-1.1470624#.VZLojvlVhBc.

21. Edward Lahiff and Guo Li, "Land Redistribution in South Africa—A
Critical Review," World Bank (2012), 18.

22. Author's private conversations with various KwaZulu-Natal landowners,
2013–2015.

23. Democratic Alliance, "Land Reform and the Willing Buyer, Willing
Seller Principle," http://da.wwc.co.za/documents.htm?action=view-
document&document=488.

24. Piotr Cieplak, "Shunting Hectares: Land Reform in South Africa," Africa Research Institute, 2013.

25. Ben Cousins, "Land Redistribution: Part of a Wider Agrarian Strategy,"
Umhlaba Wethu 15, PLAAS, University of the Western Cape, September
2012, http://www.africaresearchinstitute.org/publications/briefing-notes/
waiting-for-the-green-revolution-land-reform-in-south-africa.

26. Joseph Ochieno, "18 Years of Progress but . . . ," *New African*, February 2013.

27. Africa Research Institute, "Waiting for the Green Revolution."

28. South African Government News Agency, "South Africa: Agriculture Sector Grows Employment by 65,000," March 4, 2014, http://www.sanews.gov.za/south-africa/agriculture-sector-grows-employment-65-000.

29. Institute for Poverty, Land and Agrarian Studies (PLAAS "Fact Check 4,"), University of the Western Cape (Cape Town, 2013), http://www.plaas.org.za/sites/default/files/publications-pdf/No4%20Fact%20check%20web.pdf.

30. Africa Research Institute, "Waiting for the Green Revolution."

31. Thembela Kepe, "Review of Land, Power & Custom: Controversies Generated by South Africa's Communal Land Rights Act," *International Journal of the Commons* 3, no. 1 (2009).

32. Mthatha is the new name of Umtata, the former capital of the "independent homeland" of Transkei. The Uniting Reformed Church resulted from a 1994 merger of black, white, and coloured Dutch Reformed churches that had emerged during the colonial and apartheid eras.

33. Iol News, "Dozens Invade Church Land Near Mthatha," November 1, 2011, http://www.iol.co.za/news/south-africa/eastern-cape/dozens-invade-church-land-near-mthatha-1.1169490#.VD7IhPnF_zg.

34. South Africa Press Association, "Group Invades 'Forefathers Land'—Report," November 1, 2011.

35. Gibson, "Land Redistribution," 149.

36. Africa Research Institute, "Waiting for the Green Revolution."

37. Gugile Nkwinti, "Building Vibrant, equitable and Sustainable Rural Communities," speech in parliament, February 2013.

38. Africa Research Institute, "Waiting for the Green Revolution."

39. For a thoughtful presentation of the argument for ending "willing buyer, willing seller," breaking up some of the large commercial farms, and encouraging small-scale agriculture, see Edward Lahiff's PBS interview, "Q&A: Land Reform in South Africa," July 6, 2010, http://www.pbs.org/pov/promisedland/land-reform-in-south-africa.

40. *Business Report*, September 2, 2009, http://www.busrep.co.za.

7. GOVERNANCE

1. He also gives to numerous other causes. In October 2013, he donated USD 1 million to Guinea to help fight Ebola. See "Ebola Crisis: South African Tycoon Motsepe Donates $1m," BBC World, October 29, 2014, http://www.bbc.com/news/world-africa-29814998.

2. Bruce Gorton, "The Five Richest Black South Africans and Their Politics," *Times Live*, October 12, 2014, http://www.timesline.co.za//politics/2014/10/02. Personal links can be close. Ramaphosa is married to Motsepe's sister.

3. Adam Harris, "The End of Race-Based Politics in South Africa," *Washington Post*, January 29, 2014, http://www.washingtonpost.com/blogs/monkeycage/wp/2014/01/29/the-end-of-race-based-politics-in-south-africa.

4. Roy Robins, "South Africa's Never-Ending Party," *Foreign Policy*, modified May 13, 2014, http://foreignpolicy.com/2014/05/13/south-africas-neverending-party.

5. ANC Press Statement, "The Passing of Cde Nelson Rolihlahla Mandela," December 5, 2013, http://www.anc.org.za/show.php?id=10658.

6. Alan Cowell, "South African Union Breaks from A.N.C. as Alliance Frays Further," *New York Times*, October 27, 2014, http://www.nytimes.com/2014/10/28/world/africa/union-breaks-from-anc-as-south-africa-alliance-fraysfurther.html.

7. Ministers heading these two departments were often thought to be members of the South African Communist Party. However, only the minister of trade and industry, Rob Davies, openly acknowledges he is a member. Blade Nzimande and Ebrahim Patel are widely thought to be party members, but they do not openly acknowledge it.

8. This comment is based on numerous conversations with white businesspersons in the 2012–2015 time frame.

9. "South Africa Fool's Gold," *The Economist*, April 27, 2013, http://www.economist.com/node/21576655/print.

10. Private conversation with a U.S. businessman.

11. The government has claimed that the Dalai Lama's visa applications did not meet bureaucratic requirements. Nobody is fooled, and the Zuma administration's ineptness generated contempt, especially from former ANC stalwarts.

12. BRICS members Russia and China are far from being democracies and have compromised reputations with respect to human rights.

13. Malan's concerns are not new; some of the stories in *The Lion Sleeps Tonight* are more than a decade old.

14. Lindiwe Mazibuko comes from a Western-educated, prosperous family. Her black critics call her a "coconut," black on the outside but white on the inside.

15. They are the Public Protector; the South Africa Human Rights Commission; the Cultural, Religious and Linguistic Commission; the Commission on Gender Equality; the Auditor General; the Independent Electoral Commission; and the Independent Authority to Regulate Broadcasting.

16. The international financial community regarded Manuel as one of the strongest and most accomplished members of the South African government.

He was born in 1956 in Cape Town and under apartheid was classified as a coloured. Active in the United Democratic Front struggle against apartheid, he was regularly arrested, detained, and then released, only to be rearrested from 1986 to 1990. In 1992 he was made the director of the ANC Department of Economic Planning. Mandela made him minister of trade and industry in 1994; in 1996 he became finance minister, a post he retained until 2009. Zuma appointed him minister in the presidency for the National Planning Commission in 2009, a post he retained until 2014 when he retired from political life.

17. *National Development Plan: Vision for 2030*, November 11, 2011.

18. David Smith, "South Africans Vote in First Election for 'Born Free' Generation," *Guardian*, May 8, 2014, accessed October 28, 2015, http://www.theguardian.com/world/2014/may/07/south-africans-first-election-born-free-born-after-apartheid.

19. Harris, "The End of Race-Based Politics."

20. "Sample Survey of Young Blacks Believe DA Would Bring Back Apartheid," *Mail & Guardian*, April 23, 2013, http://mg.co.za/article/2013-04-23-study-shows-most-surveyed-young-blacks-believe-da-would-bring-back-apartheid.

8. THE BILATERAL RELATIONSHIP BETWEEN THE UNITED STATES AND SOUTH AFRICA

1. American involvement in the anti-apartheid movement is thoroughly documented in Robert Massie, *Loosing the Bonds: The United States and South Africa in the Apartheid Years* (New York: Nan A. Talese/Doubleday, 1997).

2. *The Royal Gazette*, May 23, 1941, https://www.thegazette.co.uk/London/issue/35172/supplement/3004.

3. The irony is that South Africa's participation in the two world wars was opposed by many of the architects of apartheid, who, however, did support involvement with the West in the Cold War.

4. For more information on the Gore-Mbeki Commission, see Martha Bridgeman, "The US-South Africa Binational Commission," *South African Journal of International Affairs* 8, no. 1 (2001): 89–95, http://www.tandfonline.com/doi/pdf/10.1080/10220460109545343.

5. Allister Sparks, *Beyond the Miracle: Inside the New South Africa* (Chicago: University of Chicago Press, 2003).

6. Office of the United States Trade Representative, "South Africa Profile," accessed December 17, 2014, http://www.ustr.gov/countries-regions/africa/southern-africa/south-africa.

7. John Siko's *Inside South Africa's Foreign Policy: Diplomacy in South Africa from Smuts to Mbeki*, International Library of African Studies (New York: I. B. Tauris, 2014) is a thorough examination of how the country's foreign policy is made. I am grateful to Mr. Siko for making an advance copy available to me.

8. James Blitz, "Pressure on South Africa to Recognize Libya NTC," *Financial Times*, August 25, 2011, http://www.ft.com/intl/cms/s/0/b18f8c0e-cf13-11e0-86c5-00144feabdc0.html.

9. Power Africa is an Obama administration initiative to leverage private capital to develop African generating capacity in selected countries. It seeks to leverage private capital for investment in Africa.

10. Judith February, "Why SA's Nuclear Plan Is Everyone's Business," Institute for Security Studies, September 30, 2015, accessed October 28, 2015, https://www.issafrica.org/iss-today/why-sas-nuclear-plan-is-everyones-business.

11. "Civilian HEU: South Africa," Nuclear Threat Initiative, January 8, 2014, accessed October 28, 2015, http://www.nti.org/analysis/articles/civilian-heu-south-africa.

12. C. J. Chivers, "The Secret Casualties of Iraq's Abandoned Chemical Weapons," *New York Times*, October 14, 2014, http://www.nytimes.com/interactive/2014/10/14/world/middleeast/us-casualties-of-iraq-chemical-weapons.html.

13. South Africa's relations with Morocco also remain cool because of the latter's close ties with the apartheid state, while the Polisario liberation movement in the Sahara had close relations with the ANC in exile.

14. SouthAfrica.info, "China Is Now SA's Top Trade Partner," September 29, 2009, based on statistics from the Department of Trade and Industry.

15. Dimpho Motsamai, "South Africa's Vision for the AUC Chairperson—the Road to Malawi," Institute for Security Studies, March 29, 2012.

16. The evidence is ambiguous as to whether the government informed parliament of its impending intervention in the CAR. Broadly speaking, the ANC said that it had, while the opposition parties said that it had not.

17. Jakkie Cilliers, "The 2014 South African Defence Review: Rebuilding after Years of Abuse, Neglect, and Decay, Policy Brief 56," Institute for Security Studies, June 2014, accessed October 28, 2015, https://www.issafrica.org/uploads/PolBrief56.pdf.

18. Helmoed Romer, "South African Defence Budget Down in Real Terms," Jane's, March 8, 2015, accessed October 28, 2015, http://www.janes.com/article/49795/south-african-defence-budget-down-in-real-terms.

19. It is the only country to give up willingly a nuclear weapons capability after developing its own weapons program. Other states, notably Germany, Japan, and Italy, clearly have the capability to become nuclear weapons states

but have declined to do so. The United States, Russia, the United Kingdom, France, and China are the only members of the Treaty on the Non-Proliferation of Nuclear Weapons. However, India, Pakistan, and North Korea have declared their possession of nuclear weapons. Israel is believed to have nuclear weapons as well. Iran may be seeking to acquire that capability.

20. "New York and the Republic of South Africa State Partnership Program," New York Division of Military and Naval Affairs, accessed October 28, 2015, https://dmna.ny.gov/spp.

CONCLUSION

1. World Bank, "Data: Population Growth (Annual %)," South Africa, 2014, http://data.worldbank.org/indicator/SP.POP.GROW.

2. Jakkie Cilliers and Hanna Camp, "Highway or Byway? The National Development Plan 2030" (African Futures Paper No. 6, Institute for Security Studies, 2013).

3. For example, see "South Africa: The Succession Has Begun," *Africa Confidential* 55 no. 24 (2014): 8.

4. Ibid.

INDEX

ABOUT THE AUTHOR

John Campbell is the Ralph Bunche senior fellow for Africa policy studies at the Council on Foreign Relations (CFR) in New York. Rowman & Littlefield published his book *Nigeria: Dancing on the Brink*; the second edition was published in June 2013. He writes the blog *Africa in Transition* and edits the Nigeria Security Tracker.

From 1975 to 2007, Ambassador Campbell served as a U.S. Department of State Foreign Service Officer. He served twice in Nigeria, as political counselor from 1988 to 1990 and as ambassador from 2004 to 2007. Ambassador Campbell's additional overseas postings include Lyon, Paris, Geneva, and Pretoria during South Africa's transition to nonracial democracy. He also served as deputy assistant secretary for human resources, dean of the Foreign Service Institute's School of Language Studies, and director of the Office of UN Political Affairs.

From 2007 to 2008, he was a visiting professor of international relations at the University of Wisconsin–Madison. He was also a Department of State midcareer fellow at the Woodrow Wilson School, Princeton University. Prior to his career in the Foreign Service, he taught British and French history at Mary Baldwin College in Staunton, Virginia.

Ambassador Campbell received a BA and MA from the University of Virginia and a PhD in seventeenth-century English history from the University of Wisconsin–Madison.